John Sandford is the co-author, with his wife Paula, of *The Transformation of the Inner Man*, a classic in the field of inner healing, and *Healing the Wounded Spirit*. Together the Sandfords founded Elijah House, a counselling and teaching centre in Idaho.

Their son Mark Sandford has worked as a counsellor in Florida and is now a staff member of Elijah House.

# Delivered or Healed?

## John and Mark Sandford

Marshall Pickering
*An Imprint of* HarperCollins*Publishers*

Marshall Pickering is an Imprint of
HarperCollins*Religious*
Part of HarperCollins*Publishers*
77–85 Fulham Palace Road,
Hammersmith, London W6 8JB

First published in the United States of America in 1992
by Chosen Books, a division of Baker Book House,
under the title Deliverance and Inner Healing
Published in Great Britain in 1993 by Marshall Pickering
1 3 5 7 9 10 8 6 4 2

A catalogue record for this book
is available from the British Library

ISBN 0 551 02838 6

Printed in Great Britain by
HarperCollinsManufacturing Glasgow

Substantial portions of chapters 14 and 15 have been taken from *Healing the
Wounded Spirit* by John and Paula Sandford. Published by Victory House, Inc.,
P.O. Box 700238, Tulsa, OK 74170, USA. Used with permission.

Unless otherwise noted Scripture quotations from John Sandford's chapters are
from the New American Standard Bible, copyright © The Lockman Foundation
1960, 1962, 1963, 1968, 1971, 1972, 1973, 1975, 1977.

Unless otherwise noted Scripture quotations from Mark Sandford's chapters are
from the Holy Bible, New International Version, copyright © 1973, 1978, 1984
International Bible Society. Used by permission of Zondervan Bible Publishers.

Scripture quotations identified RSV are taken from the Revised Standard Version of
the Bible, copyright © 1946, 1952, 1971 and 1973 by the National Council of the
Churches of Christ, USA, and used by permission.

Scripture quotations identified KJV are from the King James Version of the Bible.

Names have been changed throughout the book to protect privacy

To our wives,
**Paula** and **Maureen**,
who have stood by us on difficult days,
comforted us in sorrow,
strengthened us for labor,
prayed alongside us,
and celebrated our joys and triumphs.

# Contents

## SECTION 3: The Relationship of Occultism, Spiritualism and Cults to Demons, Deliverance and Inner Healing

# Preface

This book grew in the telling. Originally Mark and I intended solely to reconcile and unite the two fields of deliverance and inner healing. That effort has become the first section, entitled "The Relationship Between Deliverance and Inner Healing." Then our editor asked me to write a chapter on "Delivering Places." That grew into a second chapter, entitled "Delivering Animals and Objects."

Those essays catapulted the concept of the book beyond the mere knitting of the two fields. I found myself thinking of a more comprehensive manual for deliverance and inner healing. Thus, Sections 2 and 3 evolved, "Deliverance and Healing from Types and Functions of Demons" and "The Relationship of Occultism, Spiritualism and Cults to Demons, Deliverance and Inner Healing."

We have tried to be biblically sound, theologically orthodox, exacting in scholarship and as circumspect as we know how to be, while producing something eminently readable by lay people!

In a few places Mark and I have duplicated teachings because we believe the material is so important as to warrant two witnesses saying the same things from different points of view. Besides, the book is written so that each chapter can stand by itself or be used for teaching or magazine articles; so in some instances similar material has been inserted into several chapters.

Our hope and aim for the entire book is twofold: *to bring understanding and reconciliation between the disciplines of deliverance and inner healing; and to equip the Body for the ministry of deliverance and healing to which the Lord calls us in these days.* The world is fractured into disheveled enclaves of harassed, hurting people. Mankind has turned more and more from God in fulfillment of the prophecy that in the last days men's love will grow cold and that there will be a general falling away from the faith. Families have shattered and their dysfunctional ways have produced broken people in numbers beyond count!

But God is pouring out His Spirit on all flesh, as prophesied in Joel 2:28-29. Note that Joel did not say God's Spirit will be poured out on Christians only, but on all flesh. This creates hunger in those who do not know God for the things of the Spirit. Not knowing the right way, the multitudes seek to satisfy that hunger however they can. Thus, devotees of occultism, Satanism and New Age thinking are multiplying everywhere. The Body of Christ must be prepared to deliver and heal the resultant deluded and wounded masses.

The greatest age of healing evangelism is on us. The need has never been greater. The call of the Lord is incisive and imperative:

> Vindicate the weak and fatherless;
> Do justice to the afflicted and destitute.
> Rescue the weak and needy;
> Deliver them out of the hand of the wicked.
>
> Psalm 82:3–4

# Acknowledgments

Mark and I would be remiss if our first thanks did not go to our wives, who have put up with our long hours in research and writing—and consequent absentmindedness and inability to pay attention to what they have been saying in family matters from day to day.

We acknowledge and appreciate the many Christians who have gone before in the rediscovery of both deliverance and inner healing. Some have authored books and pamphlets we have used in research and writing. All have blundered and stumbled along the path, as we have. But through them, wisdom has come down to us, and we hope that more refinement and purer wisdom and knowledge will result when our readers put to the test what we (and others) are saying.

God is purifying His Church, and that has been one of our major goals, too, in writing this book. We give thanks in advance to those who will modify and improve what we say here, and we acknowledge with joy the growing wisdom in the Body of Christ.

Our special thanks to Tony Lincoln, my son-in-law (Mark's brother-in-law), who has labored faithfully and intensely to make readable our complex and sometimes jumbled thinking. And our thanks to Jane Campbell and Ann McMath at Chosen Books for their patience and encouragement as we have struggled to complete the writing and editing before printing and publishing "windows" passed us by.

The research and writing have seemed (no, they *were*) at times veritable warfare with horrendous powers of darkness that did not want this book written. Our thanks to the many intercessors who have stood in the gap for us that we might have clear heads and hearts to write.

We are grateful beyond measure for the sure guidance and teachings of the Word of God. And more grateful yet for the patient love of our Lord Jesus Christ, to whom we owe everything we are and ever hope to be.

John Sandford

# The Relationship Between Deliverance and Inner Healing

# 1

## Deliverance and Inner Healing: Both-And, Not Either-Or

Deliverance or inner healing—which is right? Is either one valid? Controversy has raged for years about both ways of ministering. Some look at deliverance as superstitious foolishness; others think it does more harm than good. Some think inner healing is at best nothing but pop psychology and thus out of place in the Church, at worst unscriptural and damaging.

Both are recently rediscovered skills. Deliverance is as old as the Bible. We find it again and again throughout the New Testament. (See Appendix 1 for a complete list of Scripture references.)

A good case can be made that Jesus was ministering inner healing when He spoke to the woman at the well, who then went into the city proclaiming, "Come, see a man who told me all the things that I have done" (John 4:29). Jesus may have been healing her entire life. Those who practice inner healing are convinced it is not only scriptural but a main theme in God's Word. (See Appendices 2 through 6.)

So how did we arrive at such a state of mutual distrust between the deliverance and inner healing camps? Perhaps a brief historical overview might help.

## Reliance on Rationalism

Starting with the Age of Enlightenment in the eighteenth century, heralded by men like Voltaire and Rousseau, men and women began to rely more on intellectualism and rationalism than trust in God by faith. This was reinforced by the Industrial Revolution in the early nineteenth century, and especially after about 1870 with the dawn of scientific technology.

To the Western mind, belief in the absolutes of the Bible was gradually abandoned. Waiting on God for one's destiny, and the consequent life of prayer and piety, were left in the dust. The watchword became *progress*, which was to be accomplished through man's rationality and ingenuity. Surely science and common sense would soon clear away all the cobwebs of ignorance and superstition that had plagued mankind for millennia. "Utopia" lay just over the horizon.

Hardly anyone believes that anymore. Technology, along with its advances, has unleashed and empowered man's inhumanity to man. Two world wars and numerous military operations, the threat of nuclear holocaust and of worldwide ecological devastation, along with the ever-present problems of famine, poverty and racism, have shattered the naïve platitudes of previous generations. No wonder it was reported recently that fully half of American adolescents have seriously considered suicide!

## Dealing with the Demonic

Since the advent of the Age of Enlightenment, however, and the onslaught of scientific technology on the Bible and thus on faith, many began to question the existence of demons, even of Satan and hell. Those were just the superstitious projections of a less enlightened age. Who needed them today? Science and logic would soon dispel whatever mysteries remained unsolved.

Psychiatrists began to name and treat through medication and therapy what earlier generations thought were demons. Modern mankind heaved a collective sigh of relief: The "dark ages" were truly over. The shadowy world of the demonic had been banished by the light of superior reasoning. Whatever had not yet been discovered scientifically and resolved rationally soon would be.

Today, some naïve idealists and the "you-can-be-successful-by-the-power-within-you" gurus of the New Age still cling to forlorn hope in humanity's supposed goodness and rationality, unwilling to admit the possibility of demonic forces, despite mounting evidence to the contrary. A few wild-eyed exorcists who see demons everywhere and in everyone have unfortunately buttressed the case of such idealists for hiding behind denial and "rationality." Movies like *The Exorcist* and its ilk have not helped. People want to flee such terrifying possibilities to the "safer" world of the psychoanalyst's couch.

But despite our all-out efforts to rationalize evil away, the bestiality of mankind—seen in rape, incest, battered wives, abused children and the rising crime rate, to say nothing of brutal guerrilla wars and insane terrorist killings—has opened the door to thoughts about unseen spiritual realities.

Thus, many Christians who believe in the gifts of the Holy Spirit for today have had little difficulty "re-believing" what the Bible has always said was real. Especially now, as Satanism becomes increasingly brazen and overt, even the secular world has begun to admit (however grudgingly) the possibility of demonic beings.

So the main problem is no longer doubt that such things exist. Rather, it is that only in the latter half of the twentieth century has the Body of Christ, using the gifts of the Spirit (the *charismata*) begun to practice deliverance on a large scale. Consequently, the field is relatively new, subject to the stumblings and bumblings that accompany the coming of age of any endeavor.

Deliverance has never been absent from any era in the Church's history, but in most previous generations it was looked on with such fear or disdain that it was often relegated to the weird or occult fringes of the Church. Witness the extreme caution of the Roman Catholic and Episcopal Churches in this regard today, partly from wise restraint in an area open to abuses, but how much from fear of the field of deliverance itself?

The medical field, for its part, has made its mistakes and continues to do so as it has matured into a respected office for healing. But doctors bled George Washington to death trying to alleviate a simple cold, and immersed both Tchaikovsky and his mother to their deaths in boiling water, trying to shock disease out of them.

Given our natural fear of the unknown and the supernatural, we have met errors made in the field of deliverance with less than the forbearance and charity we grant to practitioners in other fields.

Put thus on the defensive, deliverance practitioners have sometimes claimed too much for what they can do, and have often looked with a jaundiced eye on those in inner healing. Although inner healers usually try to dissociate themselves from psychology, those in deliverance do not often know this. And while psychologists have sometimes considered deliverance ministers naïve "witch-hunters," deliverance ministers have accused the psychological field, in turn, of having occult origins. They have characterized inner healing as ineffective, off-balance and blind to demonic realities. A few have gone so far as to call inner healing satanic because of its alleged connections to the "demonic" field of psychology.

## What Exactly Is Inner Healing?

Like deliverance, inner healing is a rediscovery of an ancient ministry. *Inner healing* is actually a misnomer. It was first called the "healing of memories," which was even more incorrect. What it truly is and should be called is "prayer and counsel for sanctification and transformation."

It is not merely a way to restore hurting people, though it does that. It is a ministry within the Body of Christ to enable believers to come to more effective and continual death on the cross, and resurrection into the fullness of life in Christ. Inner healing is a tool the Lord uses to mature His people. "Speaking the truth in love, we are to grow up in all aspects into Him, who is the head, even Christ" (Ephesians 4:15).

Inner healing is actually the application of the crucified and resurrected life of Jesus Christ and His blood to those parts of my heart and yours that did not fully "get the message" when we first received Jesus as Savior. Paul wrote, "Take care, brethren, lest there should be in any one of you an evil, unbelieving heart, in falling away from the living God" (Hebrews 3:12). Because some areas deep in our hearts have not believed and accepted the good news of our death and rebirth in Him, the fullness of His work has not yet happened for us. We are new creatures in Christ, but some of our old nature continues to act in its ugly old ways, as though we had not yet received the Lord.

Inner healing, then, is evangelism to the unbelieving hearts of believers. (We will explore this in much detail in chapter 3.)

Paul refused to regard any Christian from merely a human point of view. To him, every born-again believer has been recreated: "Therefore if any man is in Christ, he is a new creature; the old things passed away; behold, new things have come" (2 Corinthians 5:17). But he also called us to work out that salvation "with fear and trembling" (Philippians 2:12). It is a "both-and" message. Positionally we have been made perfect, but we have to take hold of that salvation and make it effective in every area of our life.

Inner healing is a tool of prayer and counseling to make salvation fully effective in all dimensions of our life and character.

When Abraham came through Canaan, God gave him the land. From that time on, therefore, positionally the Jews owned Palestine. But then the Lord told him that he and his people would have to go down to "a land that is not theirs," Egypt, and be slaves there for four hundred years (Genesis 15:13–16). Then they had to cross the Jordan, kill the giants and conquer the fenced and walled cities to possess what they already owned!

In like manner, when we receive Jesus as Lord and Savior, positionally we possess the perfection of our souls. But we must yet cross our own inner Jordans, kill our own giants and conquer the fenced and walled areas of our own stony hearts to possess what we already own. Inner healing is a discipline of prayer and counsel to accomplish that task.

Inner healing practitioners look at character, therefore, to discover what practices in the old nature did not die when we first received Jesus as Lord and Savior.

## Conflicts Between the Two Disciplines

There exist at least two areas of conflict between inner healing and deliverance.

First, looking at character structures has seemed to many deliverance ministers too close to psychology, and thus possibly hooked into the deceits of the occult.

Second, inner healing ministers maintain that practices of the "old man" in our character serve as houses for demonic inhabitation. They have often been grieved, therefore, when some deliverance ministries cast out demons as though they alone were the cause of trouble, and failed to dismantle their dwelling places on the cross of Christ. The result: Outcast demons have wandered around in waterless places and then come back, bringing seven others worse than themselves (Matthew 12:43–45).

All too often Paula and I have had to "mop up" after immature deliverance ministries—just as deliverance people have had to mop up after certain inner healers' efforts, casting away demonic presences they failed to see or deal with.

Inner healing has thus been besmirched and become unnecessarily controversial. Part of the problem: Some spiritually immature believers have entered the field who were not sufficiently grounded in Scripture. Some entered into false uses of imagination (also called visualization), occult practices or overdependence on secular psychological techniques. And some have not— but have nonetheless been accused of it.

Let me personalize this. Paula and I have always warned against the false use of imagination. Throughout the first seven chapters of *The Transformation of the Inner Man* we sounded a clarion trumpet about the limits and deceits of psychology and urged inner healers to stand purely upon the Word of God. Nevertheless, we have been labeled (actually, libeled) as teachers of psychology. We have warned continually against the New Age movement, only to be rejected by many who think we ourselves are part of it.

The same treatment, in varying degrees, has happened to nearly every person involved in inner healing.

The underlying reason for such libelous opposition, I believe, is neither the immaturity of the field nor the errors of its practitioners. Rather, it is the fear of Christians to admit there is a sinful nature within each of us that must be recognized and put to death after we receive Jesus as Lord and Savior. Any excuse will do in order to avoid looking at sin and putting it to death. To be sure, the mistakes of some in the field have provided ample ammunition. But some believers have concentrated on the errors of the few to the exclusion of the valid contributions of more mature practitioners. And to date, these companion fields have not for the most part respected or understood one another's contributions to the Body of Christ.

Let me speak personally once again. Paula and I have been involved in deliverance ministry since 1958 and the beginning of the charismatic renewal. I suppose we have done as many deliverances as anyone in the Body of Christ, except perhaps Derek Prince or Bill Zubritzky. Furthermore, we have been among the foremost pioneers in the rediscovery of prayer and counseling for sanctification and transformation. *The Transformation of the Inner Man* is used by many Christian colleges as a basic textbook for counsel and prayer.

Our son Mark grew up surrounded by such ministry. As a child of five, he was molested by a gang of teenage boys. The incident was so traumatic he suppressed all memory of it. Then, as an adult, while he was counseling others, the Lord began to recall to him what had happened. (This is reported in Paula's book *Healing Victims of Sexual Abuse*.) Subsequently Mark underwent much counseling in which he was set progressively free from many demons and residual character structures.

Thus, he understands the relationship of deliverance ministry and inner healing from the best of all perspectives—as a postgraduate of the Holy Spirit's "School of Hard Knocks." He has become a very effective counselor and teacher on our staff at Elijah House.

Mark and I feel uniquely qualified and called to attempt to reconcile these two fields. We believe deliverance and inner healing need each other. Both are incomplete and inadequate by themselves.

We will try to show how these two currently contending fields can and should work together to accomplish more of the fullness of deliverance and sanctification and transformation in the Body of Christ.

So read on. But come with an unbiased mind. We wouldn't want to have to deliver you from a demon of doubt and skepticism just so you can read and understand this book! But we will if we have to. . . .

# 2

## A Sensible View
## of Deliverance

Soon after the Holy Spirit fell on a few devout but unsuspecting souls in 1906 on Azusa Street in Los Angeles, a great wave of God's power swept across the United States, then the world. From that move of the Holy Spirit were born the Assemblies of God, the International Church of the Foursquare Gospel, the Church of God (Cleveland, Tennessee), Elim Bible Institute and many others incorporating *Pentecostal* into their title.

Almost immediately, deliverance ministry began to happen among these fledgling groups and denominations.

The Holy Spirit did not fall on the older mainline denominations until almost a decade after World War II. In the late 1950s a few Episcopalians, Methodists, Presbyterians, Lutherans and Congregationalists (my denomination at the time) began to rediscover the power of the Holy Spirit. Successive waves of anointing over the next ten years brought increasing numbers of mainline Protestants into fullness of life in the Holy Spirit, then smatterings of Roman Catholics.

In the 1970s, multitudes of Protestants and even more Roman Catholics came to experience the fullness of the Spirit. Most of these remained within their respective denominations, though some came into the Assemblies and other "firstborn" churches looking for spiritual food, hungry to learn more about the Holy Spirit. But these new charismatics (from *charismata*) possessed long-held traditions of rationalism and intellectualism. Most had not yet shaken free from the trappings of the Age of Enlightenment.

They were reluctant to venture into the emotionally charged field of deliverance, for example, reluctant even to admit the possibility of demonic oppression. To them it smelled of superstition, which their education and rationalism could not accept.

Their older cousins, some of whom had been touched by the Holy Spirit in the Latter Rain revival of the late 1940s, came for the most part from blue-collar backgrounds. Fewer social and cultural inhibitions blocked their way. Their country music was more openly emotional than the classics or even the swing music enjoyed by the upper middle classes of the '40s and '50s. Feelings were natural ground to them, and they were unhampered by the intellectual strictures of a white-collar orientation. And, although they made mistakes and suffered excesses, they had grown naturally into an understanding of deliverance.

(There were, of course, many white collars among the earlier Pentecostals, and perhaps more blue collars among the old-line churches. We are speaking in generalities, which do not fit every situation. Let the reader look into his or her own heritage and consequent ways of thinking, and see whether this analysis is helpful.)

White-collar mainline Christians put up nearly a decade of resistance to the ministry of deliverance. Rationalism and intellectualism had given them a sense of control over their lives, a freedom from superstition and fear of the unknown and an accompanying unconscious pride and one-upmanship over the less educated. Now to have to admit what those less educated had long known about—that there could be entities whose mental powers could be superhuman and could actually overcome them—was something they did not want to allow into the hitherto "clean" realm of rationality.

Worse, to face the possibility that demonic beings could be inside of them, even controlling their thinking, was horrifying.

Finally, in the late '70s and early '80s, charismatics could deny the reality of the demonic no longer. But they began to see demons everywhere, in everyone and everything. Capitulation had blown away both their common sense and their balance. Rationality and intellectualism had proven blockades to the discovery of reality, rather than its watchdogs. Apparently they could no longer rely on reason to protect them.

The college-educated had been trained to study and analyze issues until they could be classified and thus dealt with. But this demonic reality defied rational explanation. It refused to fit into a nice, neat box. A massive army of evil spiritual entities dedicated to unreasoning, mindless destruction and carnage threatened to upset the entire charismatic world view. Life was supposed to be positive and safe. Their watchword had been *progress*. Now it seemed chaos had become the order of the day!

Along with the disruption caused by admitting the reality of the demonic came the more upsetting realization of the idolatry of the rational mind and its control over the Christian life. Without knowing it, charismatics had adopted a basically Gnostic approach to faith. Only if something could be explained rationally was it to be believed. All spiritual things had to be reducible to understanding or they were not to be regarded as real. One engaged the rational mind to handle the issues of life, especially the traumatic.

This is not the way of faith, of course, for the children of God are to walk by the Spirit (Romans 8:14). Issues are to be handled by prayer, not intellectualization. But old habits die hard. Consequently, most charismatics in the late '70s and early '80s were still walking more by the dictates of long-practiced ways of thinking than by the new way of prayer and restful dependence on the Holy Spirit. We had not yet come to comprehend Habakkuk 2:4 experientially: "As for the proud one, his soul is not right within him; but the righteous will live by his faith."

I believe God used the influx of demonic demonstrations and deliverance ministry to force us to see how much we were ruled by our logical systems and unconscious biases, rather than the Holy Spirit. Even today when I encounter a Christian who refuses to admit the reality of demons or the validity of some deliverance ministries, I recognize a believer whose security is less in our Lord Jesus Christ than it is in his own cherished, even idolized thought world. Admitting the possibility of evil beyond the scope of one's own logic threatens to undo one's center of self-control, which is not the Holy Spirit but the tyranny of one's own mind.

For a while, then, a sector of the Church lurched into foolishness. Vomit buckets appeared in prayer and counseling rooms. People were going to have to "upchuck" their demons, be convulsed and roll on the floor. (To be sure, people do sometimes vomit and become convulsed as demons leave, but when doing that became the spiritual "fashion," it became ridiculous and degrading.)

Many seemed to think, moreover, that demons are deaf and that the only way to deliver people was to shout at the top of one's lungs. For a while every attitude and thought were treated as demonic, as though demons were omnipresent and all-powerful. Christians began to look over their shoulders continually, lest something demonic slip up on them unawares.

At last—it was only a few years but it seemed interminably longer!—the Church came back to balance. Today, for the most part, we examine other possibilities before leaping to the conclusion that demons are the primary cause for whatever problem we encounter. Most Spirit-empowered Christians wait for careful discernment before acting and are willing to check their personal perceptions against the discernments of others. We have matured into doing deliverances in carefully thought-out ways, such as by teams working together rather than by "lone rangers." We recognize the need to follow up. We have learned how to perform deliverances without expecting wild signs and actions, while maintaining our poise if demonstrations do occur.

Most importantly, some in the Body of Christ have learned how to combine deliverance and inner healing.

I do observe a great lack of knowledge and wisdom, however, among many in the field. Therefore, this book. Though I am regarded by many as an expert in deliverance, it seems to me we are all novices. (At least I know I am still learning more every day!) Nevertheless, after 33 years of experience, and in order to share some of what I have learned, let me review who and what demons are, and then explore four levels of demonization, whether of unbelievers or of believers.

## Demons as Fallen Angels

The Church generally agrees that demons are the fallen angels who rebelled against the Lord during the insurrection of Lucifer:

> And another sign appeared in heaven: and behold, a great red dragon having seven heads and ten horns, and on his heads were seven diadems. And his tail swept away a third of the stars of heaven, and threw them to the earth.
>
> Revelation 12:3–4a

Thus, a third of God's angels became the servants of Satan—the fallen angels we call demons.

Noel and Phyllis Gibson in their book *Evicting Demonic Squatters and Breaking Bondages* address what demons are and whence they came:[1]

> It is very evident from the New Testament that demons must have originally been in the presence of God, and were fully aware of spiritual realities:
>
> (1) Demons are stated to be angels who sinned and did not retain their original state (1 Peter 3:19; 2 Peter 2:4; Jude 6).
>
> (2) Demons, like Satan, are evil, wicked and unclean—a reversal of their former glory (Ephesians 6:12; Mark 7:25; 9:25).
>
> (3) Demons show an intimate knowledge of the deity, authority, and power of Jesus Christ (Mark 1:24; 3:11; 5:7; Luke 4:41; Acts 19:15).
>
> (4) Demons fear their judgment and confinement in the Abyss (Luke 8:28, 31).
>
> (5) Demons showed that Jesus Christ had total authority over them on earth, by obeying every command he gave (Matthew 8:31–32; Mark 1:25–26).
>
> (6) Demons still fear and obey the name of Jesus when it is used in faith (Mark 16:17; Acts 8:5–7; 16:18). In this way they submit to the authority of the one who conquered them. This confirms the

timelessness of spiritual beings and the "power of attorney" that believers have on behalf of Jesus Christ. (See appendix 3.)

Derek Prince, Bill Zubritzky and every other writer whose works on demonic powers I have read agree that demons are the fallen angels that have become Satan's hierarchy and that attack mankind.

Within that third of the angels, and mimicking God's structure of angels and archangels, are hierarchies. Ephesians 6:12 calls these "the principalities . . . powers . . . world rulers of this present darkness . . . spiritual hosts of wickedness in the heavenly places" (RSV). Satan, copying the way of the Lord, has apparently appointed principalities to rule over regions.

In the Old Testament, Daniel set himself to pray for his people but had to persevere in fasting and prayer for three weeks before the angel of the Lord arrived. When at last he came, he said, "The prince of the kingdom of Persia was withstanding me for twenty-one days; then behold, Michael, one of the chief princes, came to help me, for I had been left there with the kings of Persia" (Daniel 10:13).

Because there was only one king of Persia at the time, and because the angel spoke of "the kings of Persia," he could not have been speaking of an earthly king. Besides, what earthly power could have withstood an angel of the Lord? No, it seems clear to me (and to many) that he had been assisted by the archangel Michael in resisting principalities.

## Infestation

I do not believe that a Holy Spirit–controlled Christian can be fully possessed. But I have ministered to hundreds of Christians, some of them long-time stalwart warriors in the Lord, who yet remained demonized in one degree or another.

The first level I call *infestation*. In this case, demons are not usually within the person but gathered all about him. Infestation happens to unbelievers and to carnal and spiritual Christians alike, though less harmfully the more a believer's old nature is crucified with Christ.

Infestation means that demons gain temporary control in certain limited areas of our life, because our sinful nature gives them access through unredeemed aspects of our character.

If a man thinks of himself as fair and just, for example, but has been unwilling to crucify his racial prejudices, then whenever a situation arises calling for unbiased actions or thoughts, he finds himself propelled into doing what Christ would disapprove.

He may deny a job to a person of color, for instance, who is eminently well qualified, and rationalize choosing a less qualified white person, unaware that his choice has not been rational at all, but rather controlled demonically. Demonic infestation has linked with his as-yet-uncrucified old nature and temporarily overcome his new walk in Christ. It is not that the demon violated his free will, but that it overpowered his Christlike intentions by working on his hidden motives, like one wave converging with another.

Or a man who has not faced the roots of his jealousy over his wife may make a fool of himself over an issue that, in some other area, he would have handled easily. Demons had access to take hold through that unredeemed area in his nature.

In some cases of infestation, there is little or no need for deliverance. Repentance and inner healing remove the ground of demonic access. But if a practice in the old nature has been long indulged or has deep and powerful roots in childhood, deliverance may be required. That deeply entrenched practice may act as a house for demonic forces.

In such a case, a demon has found an area of the Christian's character that stands as an open door. It is too painful for the demon to enter the depths of that Christian's personal spirit, where the Holy Spirit and the occasional flow of the blood of Christ can afflict it and thrust it out. But it works continually within the Christian's character to enlarge its area of control, plunging its victim into emotions, thoughts and actions until he has developed what psychologists would call an obsession. (See the third level of demonization, "Obsession.")

When the person comes to repentance and receives forgiveness, and the roots are dealt with through inner healing, the demon's carefully constructed theatre of operations is demolished, and it must leave.

### Blocking Spirits

Often, when infestation has progressed to obsession, a blocking spirit is also involved and can easily be discerned. You know the person is not stupid, but he just cannot comprehend a simple concept. Or he cannot put two facts together and come up with the conclusion a child could reach. Or he comprehends what you have been explaining to him, but five minutes later he has lost it and you have to explain it all over again. You may have to remove the blocking spirit before you can "plunder his house."

Blocking spirits can also be discerned in that if you are ministering, you may unaccountably have trouble keeping track of your own thoughts. You knew a moment ago what you wanted to ask next, but now you cannot think of it. Or you lose your train of thought in the middle of a sentence. Or although you have been trained to remember what people tell you, you cannot recall what your counselee just said. You might start to pray for the person, and you cannot remember what you had discussed and decided to pray about.

Sometimes as I start to pray, I am embarrassed momentarily (until I struggle clear again) because I cannot even remember the person's name, though he or she might have been a close friend for years!

Incidentally, anyone who has done much public speaking or teaching has most likely experienced what a blocking spirit does. These same things can happen in the middle of the most anointed teaching—a demon clobbers your mind and causes you to lose track for a moment.

In counseling interviews, the spirit attached to the person can get to you because you must empathize and identify with your counselee. What blocks *him*, therefore, now has access to block *you*. But that is a blessing to a trained counselor since it confirms what you may already have been suspecting. Now you know it is indeed something you must defeat in the Lord's power.

We remove blocking spirits simply by binding them, commanding them to be still and casting them away. If we have spo-

ken with the person about his being blocked, we may say a
prayer for deliverance aloud with him. But if we have only discerned its presence and it does not seem wise to mention it—
sometimes speaking of it may allow that demon to make the person argue about whether it is blocking you, and so it has indeed
blocked you!—we bind and cast away silently. I have found this
very effective, and necessary in many counseling situations.

### Familiar Spirits

A familiar spirit is Satan's "angel" assigned to a family to use
unredeemed areas in its history and whatever demons are available to "steal, and kill, and destroy" family members (John 10:10).
It is usually a familiar spirit within the family that employs the
blocking spirit and the demons in hopes of frustrating the counselor (or whoever is ministering) and thus destroying the person.
(Familiars are discussed more fully in later chapters.)

Whoever ministers may therefore also have to pray about the
person's generational sin patterns in order to ensure that the
familiar and its blocking spirits do not regain their hold. (See our
teaching on "Generational Sin," chapter 13 in *Healing the
Wounded Spirit.*)

In short, whatever sins and sin natures have not come to the
cross within the family history can serve as points of access and
control for demonic forces. Succeeding generations, therefore,
find themselves being pushed to act in ways they normally would
not.

We pray, placing the cross between the person and his or her
ancestry, claiming that all the destructive patterns of his or her
family history are stopped and destroyed upon the cross of
Christ. We bind the familiar over the family, cast it away and call
for the Lord to send His strong angels to watch over and deliver
the family from harm (Psalm 91:11–12; 34:7).

It is not always necessary to cast away a blocking spirit or
cast away the familiar of the family or pray about the family history. These actions become necessary only in ascending order. If
our friend is unable to repent of the aspects of his nature that
allow the infestation, we suspect that his own stubborn nature
may have found aid through a blocking demon.

If binding and casting away a blocking spirit do not immediately open the mind and heart, or closure and ignorance keep returning, we suspect that the familiar of the family may be energizing the blocking spirit to resist or to return. If we seem unsuccessful casting and keeping the familiar away, we know we must investigate and pray about the family history, for that is what gives the familiar and its demons control over the person.

It is unwise as a matter of course to tackle all these at the same time. The person may be unready to release more than that particular structure in the mind and heart that gives access. To deal with all the possible blocking spirits, familiars and family structures (just in case they might be there) may violate the process of long-term healing that the Lord knows is necessary for the restoration of the person's soul.

Like soldiers in an army, we must capture only those hills of the soul our Commander orders at the moment. And if we find an infestation stubbornly resisting transformation and release, we are *not* to proceed automatically into all the successive steps we have outlined here.

It is here that understanding the relationship between deliverance and inner healing is crucial. We may not be able to stop the inroads of infestation simply by the inner healing of the character structures that give the demons access. A blocking spirit may be preventing. But it may stymie us through some other unhealed area of the heart and mind, which we may have to call to repentance before we can cast it away. And that area, in turn, may have its roots in some unredeemed factor in the family history, for thus a familiar employs demons and the blocking spirit to maintain control of the victim. We may have to cast away the familiar before we can successfully plunder the family history so as to bring the pertinent practices in the family (and the person) to death on the cross.

The prudent, therefore, tackle the simple problems first. If deliverance and healing do not result, the wise servant will ask the Lord, "Do I go to stage two? What is the next step in this battle?" If first prayers have accomplished healing, let well enough alone. If they seem unsuccessful, we are not impelled to plunge ahead. We wait for the Lord to clarify His plan. He will reveal whether another deliverance or an inner healing must be done next—or nothing more at all. He alone knows whether the person is ripe or prepared in heart to receive more at this time.

Those who minister inner healing and deliverance must learn to be humble and patient, waiting on the Lord. Every life is in His hands. He is the Good Shepherd who knows us all by name. He will instruct His listening servants to cast away demons or to heal the inner heart whenever each step is appropriate.

Paula and I and our Elijah House team have had to clean up after countless servants in both inner healing and deliverance who thought that the discernment of something was a call to act, employing the full arsenal of everything they knew to do. They often caused more harm than would have resulted from doing nothing.

## Inhabitation

I call the second level of demonization *inhabitation*. Inhabitation means that a spirit has entered a person but has been corraled and is unable to affect much of the person's emotions and thoughts. The person's strength of character, aided by the Holy Spirit, has been able to resist the urgings of the demon, and has shut it down.

An appropriate simile might be to think of the demon as a tubercular infection. The white cells of the body's defense mechanism have nearly encysted it and it cannot do much damage. Nevertheless there it is, living inside the person. At some point it may surface and have to be cast out.

That was my case. Even as a child, I "knew" in levels below conscious thought that there was a high calling on my life. In the spring of my senior year in high school, the Lord spoke clearly to me and told me I was to be a minister. That fall, after I preached my first sermon, my mother sat me down to tell me of a call that had come to her in a powerful spiritual dream eight months before I was born, that I would become a pioneering prophet for the Lord.

This only confirmed to me what I had always known, and I plunged into a frantic search to find out what I was supposed to do.

Two questions drove me. Where was the power that had been evident in the early Church? And why did so few seem able to live the lifestyle Jesus did? I saw no one living to the full His kindness, His love and sacrifical life for others.

Having been raised in a liberal church, I did not search in the Bible and within the Church. Instead I studied every kind of mysticism—Hindu, Buddhist, American Indian, *ad nauseam*. I tried out Rosicrucianism, read the works of theosophists such as Madame Blavatsky, pored over writings about reincarnation by Edgar Cayce, Gina Cerminara and others. (I now know reincarnation is a most anti-Christian concept, denying as it does the central issue of resurrection into eternal life.) I even attended one "scientific" seance (hosted in a local Methodist church, of all places!).

Along the way I became inhabited by a demon. I possessed enough moral character and strength of spirit to fight that thing down and encase it so that it had very little access to my thoughts or emotions. But there it was, living inside of me.

Within a week after I received the baptism of the Holy Spirit, the demon surfaced and had to be cast out. The Holy Spirit could not tolerate that unclean thing so close to His domicile and so forced it out of hiding where it would be cast away.

From this experience I learned a number of things from the inside out. I know that a Spirit-controlled Christian can indeed have a demonic presence inside him for a while. (Notice I did not say that a Spirit-controlled Christian can be possessed. That thing could not *possess* me, which indicates domination and control. But it could exist within me.) I know, too, that the moment the Holy Spirit is given permission to rule within us, the battle is on. He will not rest until His enemy is cast from His temple.

Let me clarify what I mean by *inside* and *outside*. Paul speaks of three levels within us:

> For I delight in the law of God, *in my inmost self*, but I see *in my members* another law at war with the law *of my mind* and making me captive to the law of sin which dwells in my members.
>
> Romans 7:22, RSV, italics mine

My understanding is that, by *inmost self*, Paul meant his spirit. *In my members*, to me, refers to the dwelling place of practices in the old nature, of which Paul speaks in Colossians 3:5-10, saying that these must be put to death. *In my mind* in this case means Paul's conscious mind, which had been made captive to the unredeemed drives within his members.

I do not believe that any demon can lodge in the inmost self, where the Holy Spirit dwells in a Christian. But it can inhabit practices in the members and influence the mind.

It might be helpful to think of the Holy Spirit as a bonfire that burns within our spirit. Paul was writing to Spirit-filled Christians when he said, "Beloved, let us cleanse ourselves from all defilement of flesh and *spirit* . . ." (2 Corinthians 7:1). And James 4:5 warns us, "Do ye think that the scripture saith in vain, *The spirit that dwelleth in us lusteth to envy*?" (KJV, italics mine in both). Thus, it is clear scripturally that we can and do sin even in our renewed spirit. But the sinful structures that remain therein can be viewed as logs, which the Holy Spirit is working to burn up.

Whoever comes too close to a fire gets burned. In the same way, though a demon can inhabit any one of our unruly members, invited by the sinful structures that remain in our members, it cannot enter our inmost self for fear of being destroyed by fire. Therefore, the further outward in our nature a demon can latch on, the more comfortably it can maintain its place, just as there is less danger of being singed the farther one stands from a blaze.

The Holy Spirit wants to baptize us more and more fully with the fire of the Lord until all our dross has been consumed and nothing demonic remains within our nature.

An infesting demon is not usually within the unruly members; it is outside the person, reaching in wherever the members have been seen by the demons and can be manipulated. Picture it as though each sinful practice offers strings to a demon by which it can operate the person like a puppet. All the while the infesting demon is, as it were, offstage, like a puppeteer.

Inhabitation, by contrast, means that although a demon cannot dwell within the inmost self, it can dwell in the members. In my case, the practice of occult searches served as the "member" the demon could inhabit. When I turned from the occult to the

Lord, His presence and my repentance made the house of the unclean spirit unlivable and it had to surface. If my upbringing had not instilled in me strong moral controls, I could not have kept the demon encased and ineffective in my life.

I know by my own experience, then, and through delivering many others, that Christians can truly be inhabited in their members. I have often been called on to finish the deliverance the Holy Spirit began the moment He was invited to rule in a person's heart.

The essential thing to comprehend about inhabitation is that the demon does dwell within the members, but is dormant. This can continue only within unbelievers and nominal Christians. By *nominal* I mean one who may even have been a long-time church member but does not yet know what it is to be born anew.

If an inhabited unbeliever begins to sin grossly, however, or if a nominal or charismatic Christian begins to leave the Lord or commit flagrant sins, that demon can then burst out of its cell and try to assume control of the person. Likewise, if the person (as in my case) begins to become more alive and active in the Spirit, the inhabiting spirit is forced up and out.

The difference between the two is control. The demon did not want to become active and known within the person. It wanted to remain safely hidden. But if the Holy Spirit is given full sway, the demon is forced to surface. If the person enters into manifest sinfulness, on the other hand, the demon thinks it is safe to come out and try to take over. This is no longer a case of a puppeteer pulling strings from offstage. Now it is more like a hand puppet. The demon operates within the members and manipulates the person whenever the opportunity presents itself.

Inhabiting spirits forced to surface are relatively easy to cast away. They are already on their way out. We only complete the work the Holy Spirit has begun. We do so by perceiving them, knowing it is their departure we are witnessing. We may have to issue firm commands, but the demons will ultimately have to obey.

## Obsession

If an inhabiting demon has come out of hiding to assume control of the person, then we have moved to the next level of demonization, which I call *obsession*. Here the unclean one has managed to install itself securely in some area of the person's character structure ("members"). Whatever the person feels or thinks, or however he or she acts within that given area, the demon is able largely to govern. In this way the host person is obsessed and unable to maintain righteous intentions. A man may set himself to be virtuous, but when triggered in that area, he has little or no ability to control himself. The demon is in charge.

There are two kinds of obsession. Within unbelievers and nominal Christians, a demon can live even within the inmost self and energize the psychological obsession. At times the person manages to act in his own rightful mind; at other times the demon is in control.

But Holy Spirit–filled Christians can become obsessed in another way. Demonic forces may be able to enlarge an infestation, as I indicated earlier, until it becomes obsessive. In this case the demon does not reside within the inmost self, but delights in toying with a powerful set of negative or sinful emotions, hidden motives and attitudes in the members. Again, the person is able at times to maintain his or her walk in Christ, but at other times he or she is under the control of the obsessing spirit.

One can see that the closer a Christian walks to the Lord, the more upset the infesting and obsessing demons become, until finally, discomfited, they cannot retain their hold and are rejected.

Clever demons do not want to overplay their hand. They want to involve the person in sins, but not too much, lest he or she become too disgusted and struggle to get free. Even a nominal Christian might garner prayer help to overcome the demon's control, and might even get saved and filled with the Holy Spirit.

Here is a paradox little understood. Often when an inhabited person falls more and more into grossly obvious sins, it is because the demon knows its end is near. Its hiding place has become, for one reason or another, untenable, so it wants to do as much damage as possible before being cast out. We see this in Scripture. The Bible says we should rejoice because "the devil has come down to you, having great wrath, knowing that he has only a short time" (Revelation 12:12).

Mark will discuss in a later chapter (in the story about "Steve") how demons have a way of burrowing into other dimensions of our old nature, so that they do not always remain confined to one area of our life. As I said before, so long as an inhabiting demon has not been able to expand its sphere of influence and has remained encysted, it is relatively simple to cast it out. In my case, I simply renounced the occult and was forgiven, and my friends cast the demon away. But if an inhabiting demon has wormed its way into aspects of our character structure in which it can assert more and more control, the demon has now become an obsession and is difficult to unseat.

Here again, as with infestation, it is important to understand the relationship between inner healing and deliverance. If one discerns only the presence of an obsessive demon and casts it away, its house within the person remains intact. Then the Scripture is fulfilled that says that

> when the unclean spirit goes out of a man, it passes through waterless places, seeking rest, and does not find it. Then it says, "I will return to my house from which I came"; and when it comes, it finds it unoccupied, swept, and put in order. Then it goes, and takes along with it seven other spirits more wicked than itself, and they go in and live there; and the last state of that man becomes worse than the first.
>
> Matthew 12:43–45; see also Luke 11:24–26

Deliverance people must learn to practice inner healing. It is necessary, in cases of obsessing demons, to discover what factors in the person's life helped to construct their houses. When those root causes are forgiven and the character structures put to death on the cross, the house of the demon is dismantled and it finds nothing to return to.

Can inner healing and deliverance be done for nominal Christians and for unbelievers? Absolutely. No one our Lord Jesus healed or delivered was, technically speaking, a Christian! There weren't any. But they were turned toward Him, toward belief.

Often when people come to us for ministry and we discover they are not born again, we inform them that our sole method is prayer to the Lord Jesus Christ. We will not demand that they believe as we do, but they need to know that He is our power; the prayers will work because of our faith. We tell them they can go to a secular counselor if they want, but in us they have come to Christian counselors who operate by faith. And we give them opportunity to leave.

To date, no one in my ministry has ever opted to leave, and very few from our staff at Elijah House. Almost always, before their counseling sessions are completed, they have become Holy Spirit-filled believers.

I have found, strangely, that the Lord often works more demonstrably, quickly and powerfully among "the heathen" than among believers! Perhaps He views it as an opportunity to evangelize. Sometimes I think it is because unbelievers do not have so much to unlearn, "thus invalidating the word of God by your tradition which you have handed down" (Mark 7:13). We all have learned many ways of thinking that we believe are Christian but that in fact may actually block the operation of true faith.

## Possession

The fourth and final degree of demonization is *possession*. Possession means that the inhabiting demon is in full control and the original personality entirely suppressed. It is the demon that thinks, feels, speaks and acts through the person.

Full possession is rare in "Christianized" countries. Perhaps even unbelievers are protected by the Christian atmosphere in countries where the Lord can still find His ten faithful in each city. But Paula and I have been in countries in the Far East where we have seen many cases of nearly total possession.

In Singapore, waiting in line at a taxi stand, I kept hearing a cat meowing loudly. Then I spotted a man trying to earn tips by opening taxi doors. His movements portrayed feline grace, and every minute or so he would meow. He was nearly possessed by a demon that acted like a cat. (If he had been fully possessed, he would not have been able to work at opening doors.)

At a retreat near Tainan, on Taiwan, Paula and I saw a boy fully possessed by a dumb spirit. At the same retreat was an almost completely possessed woman who interrupted the meetings continually by inane and sometimes blasphemous remarks.

I am grieved when I hear of deliverance ministries that try to free possessed people in one session, usually with many demonstrations of superhuman demonic power and hours and hours of shouting at the unclean spirits. That torments the unfortunate victims and seldom accomplishes a full and lasting deliverance. A first session can be dramatic as the power of the ruling demon(s) is broken. But after that, many sessions are needed to expose root causes carefully, then cast away successive layers of demonic control.

We have received some who were dedicated to Satan from within the womb and used for horrible, ritualistic sexual abuse and satanic rites in black masses. These required long, tender sessions, as our Lord would dismantle Satan's creations within them gently piece by piece. I shudder to think what damage would have been done to these hurting souls had they fallen into the hands of some of the immature deliverance people of whom we have heard.

Likewise, I doubt that those who immerse themselves in inner healing and know little or nothing about deliverance would have been effective with these escapees from satanic cults. The Church is long overdue in taking hold of the necessary combination of inner healing and deliverance.

## Unwise and Harmful Practices in Deliverance Ministry

As the Church has grown into accepting and using deliverance, we have also developed some practices that I believe are unscriptural and probably more harmful than helpful.

### Calling Attitudes and Emotions Demons

The first of these practices is that of calling every emotion, attitude or motive within the flesh a demon. Please hear a word of correction, dear Body of Christ. *Such things as anger, lust, greed, hate, fear, envy and jealousy are not demons; they are flesh. And flesh is not to be cast out; it is to be put to death on the cross by repentance.*

A demon may mold itself to an emotional habit within us (as Mark will discuss in later chapters), but the emotion or attitude itself is not demonic. To try to cast out an emotion or attitude is like trying to cut out part of a person's character. That is not the way of Christ, who would transform everything in us to glory by His blood and cross and resurrection life. Our sin nature is not to be cast away; it is to be transformed into the likeness of Christ.

We believe that when unwise deliverance ministries have attempted to cast away such things as fear or hate, and some healing and change have resulted, it is actually because the naming of the sinful attitude or emotion enabled repentance. The repentance accomplished the healing, whether the thing addressed was solely flesh or whether it also had a demon wrapped around it.

Repentance is the most powerful tool we have in spiritual warfare. It removes the ground of Satan's attack. Naming something for what it is energizes deliverance and inner healing because repentance is the key that unleashes God's freeing power. Without repentance, nothing lasting can ever be accomplished.

What are we to do? Find out what has caused the person to entertain and express whatever fruit of the flesh we encounter. Forgive the sins of motives, attitudes and emotions, and crucify the roots and structures within the character. Then, if we discern the continuing presence of a demon, cast it away. Or do it the other way around: first bind and cast away the demon, but then do not fail to do inner healing to destroy the demon's house.

Whether inner healing or deliverance is done first depends on the Lord's guidance in each particular session. If the Lord is not insisting on one or the other, it may not matter which comes first, so long as both are completed.

If an unclean spirit has specialized in expanding some attitude or negative emotion within someone—for example, hatred—then that spirit can be called a demon of hatred. But let us not be deluded into thinking that is all there was to the hateful condition. It is not wrong to call a demon a spirit of hate or fear or whatever, but let us remember that demons must always have houses of flesh to live in.

Deliverance should never be entered into, therefore, without also dealing with the character structures that gave the unclean spirits access and control.

## Commanding Demons to Name Themselves

A second practice I believe is unscriptural and unwise is the current habit of commanding demons to name themselves. Nowhere in Scripture do we see Jesus do this. In fact, Jesus commanded the demons to be still (Mark 1:25, 34; Luke 4:35). (Mark and I will explain about the Gadarene demoniac later; we do not believe Jesus was commanding the demons to name themselves when He spoke to the man.)

Let's use a little common sense. Do we suppose that Jesus, the Lord of the universe, the Good Shepherd who knows all His sheep by name, needed information from the devil in order to defeat him? Did He not know the name of every demon that ever existed? Furthermore, what makes us think that the devil, the father of all lies, will tell us the truth whenever we command? *More importantly, why should we consult demons for truth when we can ask the Holy Spirit?* Why not ask the Holy Spirit for the name of whatever is troubling a person, since Jesus promised that His Spirit (not the devil!) will tell us whatever we need to know (John 14:26).

I believe that commanding a demon to name itself grants it permission to act through the vocal cords of the person; thus, we may actually be expanding its theatre of control rather than reducing it! Why should we run the risk of further endangering the one we are attempting to heal, especially when the Author of our faith, our model in all things, commanded demons to be still, and will Himself tell us the truth?

In the case of the Gadarene demoniac, we may misread what Scripture actually says, and thus misunderstand what happened. I quote here Luke's version, although this story can also be found in Matthew 8:28–34 and Mark 5:1–17.

> And they sailed to the country of the Gerasenes, which is opposite Galilee. [Gerasenes lived within the larger territory of Gad; thus, the possessed man was called a Gadarene.]
>
> And when He had come out onto the land, He was met by a certain man from the city who was possessed with demons; and who had not put on any clothing for a long time, and was not living in a house, but in the tombs.

And seeing Jesus, he cried out and fell before Him, and said in a loud voice, "What do I have to do with You, Jesus, Son of the Most High God? I beg You, do not torment me."

For He had been commanding the unclean spirit to come out of the man. For it had seized him many times; and he was bound with chains and shackles and kept under guard; and yet he would burst his fetters and be driven by the demon into the desert.

And Jesus asked him, "What is your name?" And he said, "Legion"; for many demons had entered him.

And they were entreating Him not to command them to depart into the abyss.

Now there was a herd of many swine feeding there on the mountain; and the demons entreated Him to permit them to enter the swine. And He gave them permission.

And the demons came out from the man and entered the swine; and the herd rushed down the steep bank into the lake, and were drowned.

Luke 8:26–33

The singular and plural nouns and pronouns in this passage may seem confusing. "He had been commanding the unclean spirit [singular] to come out." "For it [singular again] had seized him many times." "He would burst his fetters and be driven by the demon [singular] into the desert." But in the next verse the demon (singular) answered, "'Legion'; for many demons [plural] had entered him."

Was the man possessed by one or many? The answer is both. One ruling demon possesses a person, but it invites others who are under its dominion within the man—even as Jesus said in Matthew 12:45, which we quoted earlier, that the demon "goes, and takes along with it seven other spirits more wicked than itself." Though the others may be worse, the one who has dominion over the man rules whatever other spirits it invites to help it. Thus, the man is possessed by one, but many demons inhabit.

Whom was Jesus asking, "What is your name?" I believe He was asking the man himself, not the ruling demon. He already knows the name of every demon everywhere. He knew the man's name as well.

Then why did He ask? Because He had been commanding the demons to come out.

Let me draw a comparison. A psychiatrist may ask a mentally ill person, "Who are you today?" or, "Where are you today?" If the person replies, "I'm Sam Smith and I'm in the state mental institution," and this is truly the case, the psychiatrist knows his patient is on his way to recovery. Stating who and where he is also helps the patient maintain his hold on reality. But if the person says, "I'm on the island of Elba and I'm Napoleon Bonaparte," the psychiatrist knows his bones are still apart! (Pardon the pun.)

During the deliverance of a fully possessed person, similarly, one test is to ask the person his name. Jesus was most likely ascertaining the degree of deliverance His commands had already accomplished. (Recall that in Mark 8:23–25 He asked the blind man for whom He had prayed what he could now see. And when he revealed that he saw men like trees walking, Jesus prayed again until the man was fully healed.)

So Jesus asked the Gadarene man his name. But it was not the Gadarene who responded. The Scripture says simply, "*He* said, 'Legion.'" Which he? Not the man but the ruling spirit.

This response confirmed what the Lord already knew—that the man was still a long way from being free. The Lord had spoken to the man, but the demon was still in control of his vocal cords.

Also, please note: *Legion* is not a name but a description of how many. A Roman legion comprised three to six thousand soldiers. The ruling demon was boasting that there were thousands of demons within the man, perhaps hoping to discourage Jesus from taking action.

Demons seek to enter people for many reasons, probably foremost because they seek to destroy God's temple. But another reason is that it is a delight to be encased in flesh. Remember that Jesus said that when a demon goes out of a man, it wanders about "seeking rest" (Matthew 12:43). Even a pig's flesh was preferable to being disembodied! For whatever reasons obscure to us that Jesus allowed the demons to enter the swine, He also knew it wouldn't work for them. The pigs rushed to the sea and drowned, and the demons were again bereft of living flesh to inhabit.

If my interpretation of this event is at all accurate, then Jesus was not commanding the demon to name itself, but speaking to the man for his own good. When the ruling demon answered, Jesus persisted in the deliverance until the man was not only free but "sitting down at the feet of Jesus, clothed and in his right mind" (Luke 8:35).

Mark and I believe that this issue and the story of the Gadarene demoniac are important enough that he will address them later from his own unique perspective.

### Demonic Demonstrations and Suggestibility

A third example of unwise, unscriptural practices in deliverance ministry is shouting by the minister or demonstrations by the one being delivered. Though shouting is necessary sometimes and demonstrations do happen, we need to be aware that there is great potential for suggestibility in the recipients of deliverance. I have often seen people being convulsed and trying to vomit when I sensed there was need for neither. My perception was that they were being overly influenced by subconscious and/or conscious suggestions from those doing the ministry.

Deliverance ministers may want desperately to know whether a ministry is real, or if in fact they are being effective. Ministers can feel trapped into needing a sign from their clients, just to feel assured about their own effectiveness. They can therefore broadcast unconscious messages that seduce people into strange behaviors.

Early on in the deliverance ministry, I caught myself at this and repented, asking the Lord to so purify me that no suggestibility defile either the other or myself. I recommend heartily that all who sense the call into deliverance ministry undergo careful prayers of bringing such needs for assurance to death on the cross.

### Reviling Satan in Deliverance Sessions

Yet another unwise practice is when Christians fall into the habit of reviling the devil when doing deliverances: "You old filthy slewfoot, you liar, you destroyer, I hate you with a perfect passion. You get out of _____."

We do not win victories against Satan by becoming like him. The hallmark of God's Kingdom is courtesy. Satan's kingdom is characterized by discourtesy and reviling.

Nor is authority enhanced by shouting and reviling. "But Michael the archangel, when he disputed with the devil and argued about the body of Moses, did not dare pronounce against him a railing judgment, but said, 'The Lord rebuke you'" (Jude 9). Are we greater than the archangel Michael to rail blithely against the devil?

Whatever we do should sanctify the nature of Jesus. Never did He revile anyone. Neither should we.

### Lone Rangers in Ministry

Deliverances should never be done by lone rangers. The Lord sent them out two by two for good reasons (Ecclesiastes 4:9–12): for protection, for confirmation in discernment, for balance, for increased power, for rescue and healing if the deliverer himself becomes wounded, for checks upon one another, for corrections in perception and discernment, for increased wisdom in action, and others.

One alone can act, if called upon to do so, but it is best, whenever possible, to do deliverances as teams.

### Disallowing Women in Deliverance Ministry

Some have said that women should never be allowed to do deliverances. This injunction does not come from Scripture. Mark 16:17 says, "And these signs will accompany those who have believed: in My name they will cast out demons. . . ." We are enjoined, moreover, not to add to or subtract from God's Word (Revelation 22:18–19). And Jesus did *not* say, "Only men who have believed will cast out demons."

When I was delivered of the demon about which I testified earlier, it was Alice Fogg, the rector's wife, who took the lead in delivering me. Some of the finest deliverance ministers I have known have been women. But they should observe the same cautions as anyone, acting only under the authority of the Church and in concert with other brothers and sisters.

## *Other Foolish Notions*

One couple wouldn't do a deliverance unless it was inside a church building—specifically, the sanctuary. While some places may offer a better atmosphere for deliverance, requirements like that are silly. I don't think any of the deliverances our Lord performed were recorded as having been done in the Temple.

Some have thought deliverance requires certain paraphernalia, like crosses to hold in the hand, flasks of anointing oil, etc. I have used some of these and found them helpful, but they are not required. Jesus had none of these and needed nothing more than His own authority. We have that same authority (Matthew 28:18–20; Mark 16:17; etc.).

Finally, some denominations mandate that all deliverances be performed by specifically designated persons, usually priests appointed to that office. While that may appear wise—and I do advise that all Christians obey the policies and commands of their church officers—I have not found this practice to be successful.

According to the biblical principle of the priesthood of believers, all of us are the Lord's priests. And Mark 16:17 does not say, "In My name a few designated ones will cast out demons." Though Jesus was addressing the eleven disciples, His words *those who have believed* mean *all* who have believed; they do not limit the practice to a few, whether priests or men.

Every Christian can deliver others. Some are specifically called and gifted for the office, but that authority is given to "all His godly ones" (Psalm 149:9).

The Body of Christ is maturing into the fullness of her calling. Let me say, then, speaking prophetically, that we *must* come to understand and do deliverances. For as the world turns more and more from God to occultism and satanism, more and more people will require deliverance. We will even need to comprehend deliverance for our own protection, to say nothing of the greater calling to help others.

We are an army. The army must be equipped. Nor are we playing some childish video game. The warfare is real. We must know how, when and where to fight.

Read on!

# 3

## What Inner Healing Is

Inner healing, like deliverance, is as old as the Bible. One can see it in Jesus' encounter with the woman at the well, as I pointed out in chapter 1, when she told her fellow villagers, "Come, see a man who told me all the things that I have done" (John 4:29).

Jesus Himself advised those who follow Him to dig deep and lay their foundations on the rock (Luke 6:48). If He had been speaking only of the need to be evangelized, as though conversion alone were enough, He would not have said to dig deep! No, He was addressing those who already called Him Lord and asking them, "Why do you call Me, 'Lord, Lord,' and do not do what I say?" (verse 46).

### Why Don't We Do As Jesus Says?

This very question should pin us to the wall. Why *don't* we do as He says? In fact, there are a number of reasons, which suggest some of the biblical definitions of inner healing.

#### *Discovering Bitter Roots*

Often the reason we do not do as Jesus says is that we have not yet dug deep to find those aspects of our "old man" that can

49

defile and undermine Jesus' character in us. Nor have we brought these defilements to death on the cross and rebuilt on the rock of His nature.

The New Testament writer commands us to "see to it that no one comes short of the grace of God; that no root of bitterness springing up causes trouble, and by it many be defiled" (Hebrews 12:15). When we first received Jesus as Lord and Savior, His finished work on the cross (John 19:30) became ours. Our sins were washed away; our sin nature was dealt a death blow.

The problem is, our sin nature refuses to stay dead. This is what *springing up* in the Hebrews passage means. Every bitter root within us died when we invited Jesus into our heart. But we are commanded to see that none of these roots springs back to life to defile us and others.

This is exactly what inner healing is: the discipline of digging deep, under the guidance of the Holy Spirit, to discover whatever roots might be springing back to life, and to bring them to effective death on the cross. We will see some dramatic examples of this later in this chapter.

### Evangelizing Unbelieving Hearts

Another reason we do not always do as Jesus says is that deep in our hearts remains some measure of unbelief. Inner healing is obedience to another command in Hebrews to "take care, brethren, lest there should be in any one of you an evil, unbelieving heart, in falling away from the living God" (Hebrews 3:12).

Hidden parts of the heart of every one of us did not believe the good news that our mind and spirit heard and responded to when we were converted. Those parts have refused the grace of Jesus, becoming "an evil, unbelieving" part. *So inner healing is actually evangelism, a ministry to bring the Gospel to those parts of a believer's heart that have not yet believed and received salvation.*

Some years ago the Lord said to me, "John, you didn't understand that Scripture."

"What Scripture, Lord?"

"The one you quote every time you try to win someone to Me—Romans 10:9–10. Let Me show you how you mistranslate it."

And He read it to me, changing it as I will indicate by italics:

If you confess with your mouth Jesus as Lord, and believe in your *mind* that God raised Him from the dead, you shall be saved.

The Lord said, "John, I didn't say through Paul that those who believe with their *minds* shall be saved. It is belief in the *heart* that brings salvation."

And He went on to say that many Christians cannot live the Gospel because they have believed only with the mind. Their faith has not yet totally conquered their hearts. The work of inner healing is to reach the tardy hearts of born-anew Christians with the good news of salvation.

Jesus went on to call my attention to verse 10: "For with the heart man believes, *resulting in righteousness*, and with the mouth he confesses, resulting in salvation" (italics mine, to indicate where our Lord put the emphasis).

"John," He said, "in your years of counseling, you have learned that in any area of a man's heart where he truly believes, My work on the cross has been effective. In that part of his nature, he has truly died with Me and can therefore manifest My righteousness. But now turn that around and you will see a corollary: In that area where his heart has not believed the good news, he has not allowed My cross to be effective. Therefore, he cannot manifest the fruits of the Spirit. He cannot 'result in righteousness.'"

Thus I learned that the work of inner healing is to evangelize the unbelieving hearts of believers. It is the application of the blood and cross and resurrection life of our Lord Jesus Christ to those stubborn dimensions of believers' hearts that have so far refused the redemption their minds and spirits requested when they invited Jesus in.

### The Process of Crucifixion

A third reason we do not always do as Jesus says is that we have not fully died to ourselves. Inner healing is the continual process of daily dying to more and more areas of our sinful hearts as the Lord reveals them.

"I die daily," Paul wrote in 1 Corinthians 15:31. And in Galatians 2:20: "I have been crucified with Christ." And in Galatians 5:24: "Those who belong to Christ Jesus have crucified the flesh with its passions and desires." In the second verse our Lord crucifies us with Him. In the third verse we crucify ourselves, that we might be found in Him, not having a life of our own.

Inner healing is one way to crucify ourselves to whatever blocks His nature in us. By inner healing we invite Jesus to complete our transformation by crucifying us.

### A Major Tool for Sanctification

Fourth, we do not always do as Jesus says because our minds have not yet been renewed and we have not yet been transformed.

Included in transformation is the process of sanctification, in which inner healing plays a major role. Sanctification is not striving to be holier than everyone else. It is the process by which the Holy Spirit brings us more and more to death on the cross and to new life in Jesus. "Do not be conformed to this world, but be transformed by the renewing of your mind, that you may prove what the will of God is, that which is good and acceptable and perfect" (Romans 12:2).

Transformation is the process by which the Holy Spirit changes every wrong thing in us into blessing. Our deserts are transformed into gardens, our weaknesses into strengths (2 Corinthians 12:9), our degradations into glories (Isaiah 61:3). Transformation means that Satan has won no victories whatever, that Romans 8:28 is indeed true: All things do work together for good to those who are called for His purpose.

Inner healing does not erase a memory or change our personal history. Rather, it enables us to cherish even the worst moments in our lives, for through them God has inscribed eternal lessons onto our hearts and prepared us to minister to all who have suffered in the same way (Hebrews 2:18). We know we are healed and transformed when we can look back on everything with gratitude. However we have sinned or were sinned against, God has written wisdom and knowledge into us so that now we can help others (2 Corinthians 1:4).

Sanctification and transformation are God's intention for everyone. He purposes to accomplish them through many means—private prayer, Bible reading, trials and testings, good works that write lessons onto our hearts, the witness of brothers and sisters, teachings, sermons, etc. One of the primary means He uses to sanctify and transform is inner healing.

## The Aim of Inner Healing

As I said earlier, *inner healing* is a misnomer. Healing suggests fixing something that is broken, whereas God has no intention of "fixing" our soul. That would be like putting a new patch on an old garment, whereas God has but one answer for sin: death. "The soul who sins will die" (Ezekiel 18:4).

The good news is that our Lord Jesus has become death for us. So when we discover a sinful structure within a person's heart, we do not merely comfort and forgive. We "reckon" that structure as dead on the cross with Christ (Romans 6:11). God wants to slay our old habits and replace them with resurrection ways.

There is no "healing of the soul," unless by that we mean death and rebirth into newness of life. Without the cross there is no healing at all. The way to life is the way of death (John 12:24; Matthew 10:39). Thus, inner healing should really be called "counsel and prayer for the sanctification and transformation of all Christians."

Some have referred to inner healing as the healing of damaged emotions, the healing of memories or the healing of wounded hearts. None of these is adequate. We are not merely comforting or healing an emotional bruise, as 2 Corinthians 1:4 refers to. We are evangelizing, sanctifying and transforming. We are converting character into the nature of our Lord Jesus Christ. We are "speaking the truth in love" in order that the Body of Christ may "grow up in all aspects into Him, who is the head, even Christ" (Ephesians 4:15).

The aim of inner healing is to change individuals—and indeed, the entire Body of Christ—into "a mature man, to the measure of the stature which belongs to the fulness of Christ" (Ephesians 4:13).

## How Inner Healing Is Done

Inner healing is effected by our listening to one another until God allows us to see whatever quirks in our old nature have not yet found their death on the cross.

There may be areas in which our outer person thinks we have forgiven others—especially those most formative to us in childhood—but counsel and prayer reveal that such forgiveness is far from complete. It may be that coping mechanisms from childhood are causing us still to act and react in childish ways (1 Corinthians 13:11). Or bitter roots may have sprung back to life, causing us to defile others and reap harmful consequences that we cannot, without counsel, even explain.

Countless experiences and our reactions to them have formed who and what we are. But when old, dead ways beguile us into behaving as though they were still alive, inner healing is one of the Lord's most effective tools for bringing these ways to death.

### Seeing and Repenting

Seeing old feelings or ways or "structures" in the heart that need to be redeemed is the first step in inner healing. The next step is repentance. (We will look at this in more depth later on.) We must come to a decision to change, for the right reasons— that is, for the sake of our Lord and others around us who are being afflicted by our undead ways.

### Going to the Cross

The next step is prayer aloud for forgiveness and to bring to death on the cross whatever practices we have seen (Colossians 3:9–10).

Even so, these ways do not usually die easily. It takes determination on the part of the one being healed and the counselor in Christ. Paula and I have a friend who wears a T-shirt that reads, *The trouble with living sacrifices is they keep crawling off the altar.* It takes patience and persistence to hold a thing to the cross long enough for it to die to its control of our feelings and actions.

### Ripeness

Ripeness means coming to such vivid hatred of our sin that we are willing to let it go and are ready to pay the price of change, whatever that may be. Ripeness means wanting to become the good soil Jesus talked about in Luke 8:5–15, soil that can hold on-to the seed of His Word and bring forth fruit with perseverance.

Becoming ripe requires receiving enough love to stand and change. The toughest work of counseling in inner healing is to give unconditional love again and again until the other *does* become good soil. In another sense it is not tough at all, since it is Jesus alone who can love people to life, while we have the joy of participating.

### Loving People to Life

People do not grow at a steady upward rate. We grow, hit plateaus, fall back, surge again, plateau and fall back again. Guess who, other than ourselves, suffers and hurts during these times? Whomever the Lord uses to love us back to life, someone who will grieve and be on his or her knees constantly in inter-cession. Paul addressed the Galatians as "my children, with whom I am *again* in labor until Christ is formed in you . . ." (4:19, italics mine). Plus, when we don't really want to come alive, we tend to attack and criticize whoever is committed to trying to love us to life.

How many times? As often and as long as it takes for the other to mature and grab hold of his own life, so that he, too, becomes a father in Christ rather than a child.

## The Four Scriptural Laws

At Elijah House, all diagnosis in counseling is reduced to four basic laws in Scripture. The Bible tells us, in fact, that diagnosis is one of its fundamental purposes:

> For the word of God is living and active, sharper than any two-edged sword, piercing to the division of soul and spirit, of joints

and marrow, and *discerning* [*able to judge*, in the NASB and NIV]
the thoughts and intentions of the heart. And before him no creature is hidden, but all are open and laid bare to the eyes of him
with whom we have to do.

Hebrews 4:12–13, RSV, italics mine

The Word of God is not composed of men's thoughts, but eternal, unchanging revelation, relevant for every people in every
age. God's laws are absolute; they describe the way reality
works. The immutable laws of God, therefore, are the clear
scope by which we see into every life.

### *Honoring Parents*

The first scriptural law we use for diagnosis in counseling is
based on the only commandment of the Ten with a promise:
"Honor your father and your mother, as the Lord your God has
commanded you, that your days may be prolonged, and that it
may go well with you on the land which the Lord your God gives
you" (Deuteronomy 5:16).

This is a description of reality. In any area of your life in
which you could and did honor your parents—in that very area,
life *will* go well with you. In more than thirty years of counseling, I have never seen an exception to this law.

To honor means to obey, to try to respect. It means to love and
cherish and forgive. Some parents are not honorable, but God
calls us to try from the heart.

The inverse of this law is equally true and gives us the basis of
diagnosis: In whatever area and degree you could not, as a child,
honor your parents, life will not go well with you.

Whenever a person comes to us for counseling, for whatever
problem, our route to healing is always the same. We listen to
the details of the present problem, then look to see in what corresponding area the person failed to honor his father or mother.
Either the Word of God is true or it isn't. If the person had honored his or her parents, life would have gone well. If he has any
problem for which he is in any degree responsible, then in some
way he dishonored one or both of his parents.

At its root, counseling is that uncomplicated. The absoluteness of the laws of God grant surety (see Psalm 19:7–14). When
we depart from a simple basis in God's fundamental law—in this
case, honoring parents—confusion enters.

### Judging

The law of honoring parents found in Deuteronomy 5 links up
with the second law: "Do not judge lest you be judged. For in the
way you judge, you will be judged; and by your standard of measure, it will be measured to you" (Matthew 7:1–2).

The Lord spoke here of a particular kind of judging. We rightly
judge a friend's driving ability when we choose to ride in his or
her car. We rightly judge the trustworthiness of those in business. We appraise one another in nearly every situation in life—
relationships, friendships, dating, competition, business, etc.
Appraisals made from a heart of understanding and compassion
do not activate the laws of retribution. Paul said that Christians
"will judge the world" and will even judge angels (1 Corinthians
6:2–3).

But when we judge others with impure hearts—with blame,
condemnation, anger, envy, jealousy or rancor—then God's
immutable laws are set in motion to bring recompense.

To judge a parent with an impure heart is to dishonor, and
both laws are activated. Our judgment will be meted back to us,
and life will not go well with us.

### Sowing and Reaping

These two laws combine with a third law: "Do not be
deceived, God is not mocked; for whatever a man sows, this he
will also reap" (Galatians 6:7). There are no exceptions. Law is
law. Every good deed sows blessing and will reap blessing, and
every evil deed sows harm and will reap harm.

"For the one who sows to his own flesh shall from the flesh
reap corruption, but the one who sows to the Spirit shall from
the Spirit reap eternal life" (Galatians 6:8). This means we cannot ever lose our reward, but neither can we escape our fleshly
deeds. Those who think they have gotten away with something
fleshly will nevertheless reap harm. In fact, the longer a sin goes

unrepented, the greater the reaping will be. "They sow the wind, and they reap the whirlwind" (Hosea 8:7).

Children do not understand the best-intended parental discipline, let alone mistaken and abusive parenting. They react sinfully, dishonoring fathers and mothers, judging them from impure hearts. Children are, after all, sin—clothed with soft skin and angelic eyes, but still sin! And they have set into motion forces that will come back on them.

Not immediately. We do not reap at the time we sow, nor when the plant comes up from the ground, nor when it blooms, nor yet when there is unripe grain in the ear. Reaping may come only after many years, long after the deed has been forgotten, if we were aware of it at all. Consequently, adults reap awesome results from sins sown against their parents when they were but infants and children.

That seems unfair—and, of course, it is. God is just, but ever since Adam sinned, life is not. God knew from the ground plan of salvation that because of the infection of Adamic sin, even children would set into motion forces that could later destroy them.

At the right time, therefore, God sent the Lord Jesus, who went to the cross to bear the results of all of our sinning. His mercy awaits one thing—our seeing and confessing the sin that planted the seed we are now reaping or will reap.

Thus, the necessity for counselors, for as David wrote, "Who can discern his errors? Acquit me of hidden faults" (Psalm 19:12). None of us sees clearly into his or her own heart. Nor can we perceive our own hidden motives: "A plan in the heart of a man is like deep water, but a man of understanding draws it out" (Proverbs 20:5). It is the Lord, through His Holy Spirit, who reveals what needs to be forgiven and brought to death within us: "I am conscious of nothing against myself, yet I am not by this acquitted; but the one who examines me is the Lord" (1 Corinthians 4:4).

Counselors are the Lord's servants through whom He can reveal what is hidden and extend His mercy to stop, by way of the cross, our reaping of childhood sins.

### Becoming What We Judge in Others

The fourth law is becoming what we judge in others: "Therefore you are without excuse, every man of you who passes judgment, for in that you judge another, you condemn yourself; for you who judge practice the same things" (Romans 2:1). *I have found it to be a law that whoever judges another dooms himself to do the same thing*, or something stemming from the same root.

A young man came to me who was born again, loved his wife and enjoyed good marital sex. But James confessed that he went to bars compulsively and, while there, would meet some woman with whom he would go out and commit adultery.[1]

"I don't understand myself," he told me. "I love the Lord. I love my wife. I want to be faithful. I don't even like the taste of alcohol! And the sex with these women is so bad it's repulsive. Why do I do what I don't even want to do?"

You will remember Paul's identical words in Romans 7:

> For the good that I wish, I do not do; but I practice the very evil that I do not wish.
>
> Romans 7:19

It was no surprise to me that James' father had been an alcoholic and a woman-chaser. As a boy James had hated that and judged his father for it.

Now remember that God's laws are absolute. The boy had dishonored his father. Life would not go well with him in that area, and the same judgment would be meted out to him as he had meted out to his father. The fourth law took effect: He would do what his father had done until repentance set him free.

I taught James these simple facts. He understood and repented of his judgments against his father. And from that moment on, he was free. Nor has he suffered another moment's compulsion to sin in those ways.

In my own childhood, I worked hard on our small farm but my mother could not bestow compliments. I judged her for this and swore up and down I would never treat my kids that way. But when I became a parent, I could not seem to muster whatever it took to give our children the compliments they needed and deserved.

What prevented me? The inexorable laws of God. Until I repented and was forgiven, I was doomed to do as my mother had done.

Later we will discuss how inner vows compel us to sinful actions. But in this case, because I had judged my mother, my inner vow worked in reverse. It helped propel me to do as she did. As children, we may not like the way our parents discipline us. But if our vow to do differently is combined with a judgment, the law will cause us to treat our kids the very same way!

Truly there is no escape from God's immutable laws other than the cross of Christ.

## The Principle of Repentance

Psychologists believe we are conditioned by what happened to us in childhood—in essence laying the blame on parents. But we believe that as Christians we decide how we will react to what happens to us. We ourselves are responsible.

Scripture says God looks on His children with compassion (Psalm 103:13). He does not blame a child who judges a reprehensible parent. Nevertheless, law will inevitably institute the principle of sowing and reaping, and God does not want His children to bring destruction on themselves. Most of the time they will be set free if they know what they need to repent of. So God sends counselors and He moves on hearts to enable repentance.

It does little good to identify the sins of childhood unless repentance follows. Thus, repentance is the primary tool of Christian counselors.

Repentance is not feelings, nor buckets of tears. To repent is to be sorry for the hurt we have caused the Lord and others by what has lodged in our hearts and by what we have done; it is being willing to die to what we have been, and allowing God to change us into what He wants us to be.

It is not enough to see sin and be sorry, as important as this is. Nor is it enough to forgive and be forgiven, as important as these are. No, the habits we have formed in reaction to those who have hurt us must actually come to death on the cross.

Many in inner healing understand the necessity for forgiveness from the depths of one's heart, and for the acceptance of God's forgiveness—but they stop there! That leaves the manufacturing plant of sin in place to produce more sinful thoughts and actions. Two verses are critical regarding childhood hurt and anger: "I have been crucified with Christ" (Galatians 2:20) and "Those who belong to Christ Jesus have crucified the flesh" (Galatians 5:24).

As children under duress, we developed habitual, sinful ways of coping. These ways must be brought to death on the cross. How? By reckoning them as dead. Jesus has died on the cross in our place. So we crucify those sinful ways within us by believing that Jesus has already died *with* those ways on the cross. They have no more claim on us once we have seen and repented of them.

This requires coming to a perfect hatred of the evil that has gripped us. For a while I kept trying to quit a particular sin. I prayed about it repeatedly, to no avail. Finally I got angry at God.

"How come You aren't helping me with this?" I demanded.

"You aren't disgusted enough yet."

"What do You mean, Lord? You know I hate this sin."

"No, son. If you hated it, you'd quit it. You love your sin. That's why you keep doing it."

Repentance means coming to sufficient hatred of our sins and sin nature that when we reckon them as dead, death *happens*, because we really do not want them any longer. For this reason Paul wrote, "Abhor what is evil" (Romans 12:9).

Repentance is a gift of grace. Only when our Lord reveals to us how much our sins hurt His heart and wound others can we come to sufficient hatred to turn about and let Him change our heart, and allow our sin nature to be truly crucified with Him.

Demons work to keep us from hating our sins and from the fullness of death on the cross. When it becomes obvious that a blocking spirit is preventing true realization and repentance, deliverance is necessary.

## The Most Common Sinful Practices

I lack space to present here the full gamut of sinful practices we deal with in inner healing. This has already required several books. Our readers can find most of these practices discussed in two books I wrote with Paula: *The Transformation of the Inner Man* and *Healing the Wounded Spirit*.

But for readers who know only the deliverance side of ministry or who are unfamiliar with our teachings, here is an exposition of four of the most common sinful practices:

### Bitter Root Judgment and Expectancy

The most common and powerful practice in the old nature that Christian counselors must work to bring to death is bitter root judgment and expectancy.

Bitter root judgment operates by the power of law; we *will* reap what we have sown (Galatians 6:7). This is spoken of by the writer to the Hebrews: "See to it that no one comes short of the grace of God; that no root of bitterness springing up causes trouble, and by it many be defiled" (Hebrews 12:15).

Bitter root expectancy, on the other hand, is merely psychological. It is self-fulfilling prophecy: "I expect life to go in a particular way and it usually does." Whether or not it really does, we look at life through the lens of our unconscious expectations and treat others in ways that tend to bring back on us what we expected in the first place.

Linda's father was gone most of the time. When he was home he scarcely noticed and rarely complimented her. Linda's response: to develop a bitter subconscious expectancy that all men would treat her like that.

Later, when men began to notice her, they were puzzled as to why they did not treat her as courteously as they did other women. Intended compliments got left unsaid, somehow, or were spoken so awkwardly they seemed like put-downs. Men forgot to phone her, though they planned to and doing so was their normal pattern. Why? Because Linda's bitter root expectancy was preventing them.

But bitter root expectancy does not possess the power of bitter root judgments. We can actually affect the behavior of others by what is in *us*. That is how bitter roots defile others. By law, judgments bring reaping.

The following account is hard to believe but true, and a good example of the power that bitter root judgments have to affect the behavior of others.

A woman came to me whose father had made her work the family farm like a field hand, although she was a child, while he stayed in the house and got drunk. When Betty came in from the fields, exhausted, he accused her—especially as she grew into adolescence—of having sexual affairs with one or another of the farm hands.

Betty grew into a beautiful woman, then married, unaware that she had made a very bitter root judgment against her father. It was not long before her husband lost his job. But instead of looking for another, he made her go to work while he stayed home and drank. When she came home, he would accuse her of having sex with men at the office.

After several years of this hell, Betty divorced him. It was not long before she found another husband. But within six months he had quit work and she had to find a job to support them both. Incredibly, he, too, began staying at home drinking and—when she came home—accusing her of adultery. No amount of scolding, pleading or arguing on Betty's part made any headway. Secular counseling only increased her determination to divorce him, which she did.

Along the way Betty became a Spirit-filled Christian. Although she had never expressed forgiveness toward her father or brought that pattern of judgment to death on the cross, she thought her anger was all taken care of. And now that she was a Christian, she thought she had grown at last into some wisdom. So she searched carefully, found a Christian man, who happened to be quite rich, and married him. She thought she had it made.

Within a year he made her go get a job. More incredible yet, although he had never been a drinker, now he began to stay at home and get drunk. And—you guessed it. When she came home, he began to accuse her of illicit affairs at work.

Do you see the power that bitter root judgments have to defile others and affect (even, in some cases, control) their behavior?

You remember, of course, the story Jesus told of the servant forgiven his debt of ten thousand talents who would not forgive his fellow servant of a tiny sum (Matthew 18:23–35). When we are forgiven all our sins at the cross, but continue to harbor resentments against others, we bring all our debts, like those of the unforgiving servant, back on ourselves! Can there be any more compelling reason for inner healing?

Remember, too, that it does little good if awareness is not followed by repentance. By the time Betty came to see me, she was so mad at men that she resisted seeing the causes of her problem—partly because she would have to admit her role in it. When she finally did see, she did not repent. It only made her angrier at men. She blamed the men in her life: They should not have gotten drunk. They should not have falsely accused her.

Of course they should not have. They *were* at fault. Marital problems, however, are *never* ninety percent one person's fault and only ten percent the other person's fault. The fault behind marital problems is almost always fifty-fifty. But Betty was unwilling to see how her bitter root judgments and expectancies had defiled the men she had married.

The facts were all on her side, but God looks on the heart to reveal motives: "Therefore do not go on passing judgment before the time, but wait until the Lord comes who will both bring to light the things hidden in the darkness and disclose the motives of men's hearts; and then each man's praise will come to him from God" (1 Corinthians 4:5). Betty was passing judgment before the time of the Holy Spirit's coming to disclose her own motives. Had she been able to repent, God would have praised her for standing and trying to do what was right, despite her history.

Betty would not repent and left without receiving healing.

Sam was having difficulty with authority figures. His boss never seemed to affirm him. And though Sam did overall a better job than those around him, when the boss came to scold the crew, he seemed to pick most of all on Sam. Sam had lost several jobs in the past and developed a "thing" about employers—"They use you up and then fire you."

It also seemed to Sam that preachers preached directly at him, condemning and blaming, and never seemed to have anything good to say about all the volunteer work he was doing for the church. And he thought his father-in-law often made snide, critical remarks about him to the rest of the family.

By now you ought to be able to tell what Sam's father was like when Sam was growing up—critical, demanding, controlling, unable to affirm.

That is not, however, the most important thing. Had Sam not judged his father, his past would not have had such a negative impact on his life. But his judgments and expectancies had so affected his bosses that they themselves could not understand why they treated him as they did.

Once, for example (as Sam learned later), his boss approached his office thinking, *I'm going in there and telling Sam what a fine job he's been doing.* He started out to do that, but found himself inexplicably ripping Sam up one side and down the other before he left his office. He came out smacking himself on the forehead, thinking, *What did I do that for? I went in there to compliment him and all I did was criticize him. What's the matter with me?*

Defilement was the matter. Sam was due to continue reaping that kind of treatment until he could see and repent. Fortunately he did see and repent. We brought that pattern to death on the cross and asked God to give him a new heart, one that could expect and draw respect and proper treatment from authority figures.

The last I heard, Sam had kept his job for a number of years and enjoyed a good relationship with his boss.

Josie's father died when she was four. Her oldest brother, who became like a father to her, died when she was nine. By her twelfth birthday, her other brothers had married and left home. Children's hearts are not as magnanimous or understanding as their minds, and Josie's forlorn little heart made bitter root judgments and expectancies that all the men in her life would leave her.

Josie grew to be a beautiful woman and married a faithful man. But after several years of normal marital ups and downs, her husband unaccountably left her—and stayed away.

It did not take me long to see how Josie the child had formed bitter root judgments and expectancies that were presently defiling her husband. A little teaching showed her what was happening. Josie repented of unconsciously dishonoring her father and brothers, and especially for hurting her husband through her judgments and expectancies. On behalf of the Lord Jesus I pronounced Josie forgiven, and together we reckoned that pattern as dead on the cross. We prayed, asking God to give her a new expectancy that the men in her life would want to be with her.

Two weeks later Josie phoned me in great glee. "My husband's come home! He says he doesn't know why he left me; he always loved me. And now he's sent the kids off to the neighbors for the weekend, and we're having a second honeymoon!"

I wish all healings could be so quick and complete!

Josie's husband told her later that after their marriage, he had found himself annoyed continually by thoughts that someday he would have to leave her. He loved and respected her and could find no fault in her sufficient to make him think that way. But after a few years, feelings began to arise to reinforce the persistent thought that he should leave her. At last he obeyed those impulses and left. He couldn't understand why he had done it and was miserable without her, but still he stayed away.

What a remarkable illustration of the defilement that bitter root judgments cause!

What about free will? Are we simply controlled by other people's roots? Of course not. We have free will and are responsible for our own actions. We can never get away with saying "it was her/his bitter root that made me do it."

But the power of the law in root judgments and expectancies is so great that resisting their defilements is like trying to stand against a gale, which pushes us one way when we are trying to go the opposite.

Some patterns are not always obvious. Janelle's father had been an alcoholic who never came straight home from work. Short "stop-ins" at the pub lasted hours. He had no time for his daughter except when, in a drunken rage, he became abusive.

Janelle married a teetotaling pastor who was always kind and loving. It seemed she had escaped. But she still reaped her judgments. Her husband became a workaholic who was never there for her; he gave all his time and energy to the Lord and the church. Over the years, as fatigue and strain set in, he remained kind and loving to the members of the church, but was often cross with Janelle, especially when she complained about his absences.

Since her heart belonged to the Lord, it was easy for her to see what her bitter root judgments were doing to defile him, making his workaholism worse. She repented and brought those bitter roots to the cross. Subsequently, her husband heard her concern for him for the very first time when she remonstrated about his working too hard. Defiling roots were no longer blinding him. He decided to stay home on his days off, and began to find special ways to make Janelle feel chosen and appreciated.

We do not sow oranges and reap apples. We reap what we have sown. Our spouse often "becomes" our parent whom we judged, only worse. Without counsel and teaching, few married couples understand this simple fact.

Most divorces take place because people are blindsided by forces they have no awareness of. They do not know why they act as they do or why they react so angrily at one another. They are driven by bitter root judgments and expectancies. They fight about present issues and have no awareness that the river needs to be dammed at the headwaters.

Demons take advantage of bitter roots to tighten their grip and add to their effects. Most of the time, however, the problems are caused not by demons but by hidden motives and structures in the heart. We may have to deliver and heal, but let's remember that demonic activity in these cases is an *effect* of the reaping, rather than the *cause*. Counsel and prayer are incomplete until the habit structures of judgment and expectancy have been replaced by positive anticipation that our Lord will cause life to go the opposite way—to blessing rather than harm.

One question faces every couple in every kind of relationship: Will they get better living with each other, or worse? Will they drink from one another's strengths and enable the other to be better, or will they drag one another down? The answer lies solely in whether they will let the Lord get at their roots and set one another free to become the most they can be in Him.

### Inner Vows

Inner vows are determinations we make as children, determinations that become "computer programs" within our nature. They energize our brains to reproduce repeatedly whatever the vow calls for. These vows are called "inner" because we make them as children and then forget them. They actually have more power by virtue of their hiddenness. (Vows made later in life are not very effective, as anyone can attest who has made New Year's resolutions only to see them soon wither and die.)

Inner vows resist change. We can determine with our will to act differently, but those vows haul us adamantly back to habitual practices. We can receive Jesus as Lord and Savior, but find ourselves defeated continually.

I discovered inner vows when a woman came to me who wanted to give her husband a son and could not. Fran could get pregnant easily and had carried girls full-term. But each time she got pregnant with a boy, she miscarried. Her gynecologist said there was nothing wrong with her. She ought to be able to carry a boy full-term; the problem had to be psychological.

I asked my usual questions: "What was life like with your father? Was he kind to you? Did he give you affection?" It turned out her father had been unusually kind and affectionate.

Her brother, on the other hand, had bullied and picked on her continually. He told lies about her to their parents and her friends and teased her viciously (not as brothers tease who love their sisters).

Then Fran recalled walking beside a stream sometime between the ages of ten and twelve, picking up rocks, hurling them into the stream and exclaiming, "I'll never carry a boy child! I'll never have a boy baby!"

That was an inner vow. It worked like a program in her inner computer—never mind that her outer self now wanted to bear a son. About the third or fourth month, that inner vow would kick into action, and her body would abort the boy child.

Fran repented of her judgments against her brother, and we pronounced forgiveness in Jesus' name. Then we took authority in Jesus' name and broke that inner vow. We spoke directly to Fran's body and loosed it from that wrong order to abort male children, based on Matthew 16:19: "I will give you the keys of the kingdom of heaven; and whatever you shall bind on earth shall be bound in heaven, and whatever you shall loose on earth shall be loosed in heaven" (see also Matthew 18:18). Subsequently Fran carried easily and gave birth to a baby boy.

All inner vows are not that dramatic. Most are small ones— such as the time we were embarrassed in school and vowed we would never again speak in public. Now, when the pastor asks us to teach a class or read Scripture to the congregation, we break out in a cold sweat, our voice quavers and we redouble our vow not to do that again. A second or third child may vow never again to wear hand-me-downs and then, as an adult, buy new things compulsively he or she doesn't even need.

There is a common inner vow men make who were raised by mothers who tried to control them. Boys soon learn something many married men live with: Women have elephantine memories. You cannot remember what you said five minutes ago, but your wife can remember what you said two hours ago, five months ago and ten years before that! Fighting with women is unfair, because you always fight on their ground. They can remember what everyone has said, and you cannot even remember what you said.

Boys soon grow to be faster and stronger than their mothers. So how does a small domineering woman control her son? With her tongue. She learns how to put him under guilt and make him jump. Boys soon realize, "Every word you say can and will be used against you in a court of law." So they decide it is necessary to hide from Mama: "Don't never tell the woman nothin' about nothin'!"

When at last they have broken free from Mama's control so that they can now be friends, such men remain unaware they carry a strong vow that will become debilitating to their marriage. At dating age, they find a girl they can talk with about anything. "This must be my spouse!" So they marry. For a while everything is great. They still talk and share their hearts openly. He proclaims his wife as his best friend, which she is.

Then she becomes a mother. Immediately his inner vow kicks into action and he stops sharing.

She still greets him at the door. "Hi, honey, how did your day go?"

"Fine. It went just fine."

"I know it went fine, but tell me some details. What happened today?" She can feel tension and hurt in his heart. Something is bothering him.

"Oh, it was like any other day. It was O.K."

"Tell me what went on. I know something's bothering you. You never tell me anything anymore."

"Yes, I do. I'll tell you anything you want to know."

"Well, then, tell me how your day went."

"It was a good day. About like any other day."

He cannot see that his heart has no intention of sharing his secrets with her. He has regressed to reacting as he did to his mother. That inner vow now rules him.

She may squawk so loudly that at last he hears enough to go with her to a Marriage Encounter or counselor. There he learns that he must share, and he obtains some skills for opening up and communicating. She breathes a sigh of relief. He's back, they can talk again. But after only a few months he has reverted. The vow is too strong for him to continue to resist.

If a Christian counselor sees the vow, he traces it to its root in the man's judgments against his mother (and probably his sisters, if he had any). A female "snitch" in his primary school might be part of it, or a girl cousin, or a particularly critical woman teacher. Once forgiveness is accomplished, the counselor breaks the power of the inner vow by his authority in Christ, and the man is set free, to remain free.

Girls, on the other hand, look to their fathers for their sense of self-worth. Every girl knows in her heart she is a gift of God to ravish her daddy's heart. If she cannot do that—if he won't notice her, for example—she is undone. She may become a beauty queen, but if her father failed to affirm her, she will not feel beautiful inside. But if he told her she was pretty, she will feel confident, even if in reality she is as ugly as a mud fence. Some girls who preen before their daddies, as they should, to "practice their wares" where it ought to be safe, are ignored or, worse yet, taken advantage of sexually. Neglected girls may vow something like this: "I'll never risk myself like that with a man again. It hurts too much when he doesn't notice." In adulthood such women hang back, afraid to be aggressive in love play or unwilling to let their beauty shine. Molested girls make stronger vows: "I'll never let a man take advantage of me again" or "I'll never again be vulnerable to a man."

Usually these vows translate into promiscuity before marriage and frigidity in marriage, since neither affords a real meeting of the other in openness and trust.

The inner vows made by both boys and girls are based in fear and hurt. Demons may make use of roots to strengthen the vows and their effects. Some deliverance may be necessary. But neither healing nor deliverance is complete unless forgiveness and authority shatter the inner vows.

### *Parental Inversion*

Parental inversion occurs when one or both parents are immature, sinful, absent or when they fail for one reason or another, and one of the older children takes over to parent his parent(s). Parentally inverted children (P.I.'s) usually become very responsible adults. They have learned how to discharge duties well—but at a great price. The following list of symptoms fits most, if not all, adults who were parentally inverted as children: They cannot trust the Lordship of the Lord Jesus Christ—or any authority, for that matter. The authority figures in their past have failed to be responsible; bitter root judgments and expectancies tell them (unconsciously, of course) that God will fail, too, so that they have to help Him hold His universe together.

They cannot rest. As children they learned to stay alert lest chaos break out—a drunken father beating the mother or the other kids, or quarrels and shouts erupting between the parents or the children—and people in their family be hurt.

P.I.'s have learned not to expect nurture and comfort from primary people. I was parentally inverted. I learned to be on guard around my hypercritical mother, and found comfort only with my cow and my dog. These friends loved me and never talked back. But as an adult, I could not find rest and comfort where God designed that I should—with Paula. I would find nurture away from the home, with friends, which was nothing less than spiritual adultery, until I brought that to death on the cross and learned to open up to Paula as my first and best human comforter.

Parentally inverted people develop hearts of stone: They are frequently loving and helpful to others but cannot let anyone inside their own heart. They become noble martyrs fond of saying, "Well, if nobody else will, I'll do it."

People around P.I.'s seldom become whole and free. P.I.'s have learned to define themselves as loving by ministering to weaker people. Unconsciously they don't want dependent people to become whole. Then they would no longer be needed.

P.I.'s do not usually know how to enjoy life and just have fun. They feel guilty and out of place somehow if given an extended vacation or put on sabbatical.

Finally, P.I.'s are controllers. As children, they built into themselves ways to control a family in emotional chaos. Those practices are so automatic that as adults they can preach eloquently about freedom, and even pray for others to be set free, only to control their own family without realizing it. When I played cards with my family, they used to tell me, laughing ruefully, that they could all get up from the table and I would go on playing everybody else's hand and not even miss them!

Parental inversion is dealt with by enabling the person to forgive his parents. Often he will have protected one parent while reacting against the failings of the other.

It was painful for me to admit that both my parents had failed, so I held resentment against my hypercritical mother while excusing and covering my father's sins of alcoholism, absenteeism from the home and lack of taking authority to calm my mother's volatile nature. Coming to wholeness meant I had to see each of my parents as sinner and saint, and forgive both.

God wants to honor those who take responsibility and try to help their families. The flip side of that coin is that P.I.'s have usurped their parents' position. They need to receive forgiveness and then resign the general managership of the universe. It is often a shock for them to learn that God can take care of things quite well without their help!

### *Performance Orientation*

Performance orientation (P.O.) occurs in homes where stringent demands for behavior have not been tempered with enough affection. Performance orientation is a lie accepted by children and built into their natures: "I am loved only if I can perform well enough to earn my parents' love." In adulthood this computes into "I belong only if I can please people and live up to their standards."

At the heart of performance orientation is fear—fear of failure, fear of rejection, fear of not being loved, fear of not measuring up to the standards of people who matter.

Nobody in a P.O.'s home is allowed to rest. Discipline is administered not purely for the child's good, but because the child didn't make the parent look good. P.O.'s maintain a facade of togetherness because they have accepted this lie: "If people know what I am really like, they will not love me."

Performance-oriented children grow up to be nervous and striving. P.O.'s are always judging how well they and others are doing; usually nobody measures up. They tend to be critical and demanding.

But P.O.'s themselves cannot take criticism. Even a gentle reproof means they are not loved. Paula, who was tremendously performance-oriented, used to say when I would offer a bit of constructive criticism, "You're saying I don't love you!" I would pull my hair and think, *Now where did this lovely creature get that?*

It went this way: She thought that if she loved me, obviously she would do everything right for me. So if I told her she was doing something wrong, I was really telling her she didn't love me.

Every time I tried to talk with her about something, she would throw it back on me: "Well, you're not doing so great yourself!"

"I know, Paula," I would respond. "I do lots of things wrong. But we're not talking about me right now. We're talking about you."

"But I'd rather talk about you. You do this and this and this. . . ."

To admit fault is terrifying to P.O.'s because it means they will or should be rejected. Living with them is difficult because you will be managed and controlled, measured and judged, whipped into line, on guard all the time lest you step into some miniscule misbehavior that must be criticized and set straight (lest you make the P.O. look bad).

Because the security of non-P.O.'s is in the Lord, they can blurt out something in a group, knowing that if it is wrong, they will be loved anyway. But because the center of value and decision-making for P.O.'s is not in themselves but in what people think of them, they will sit quietly until they have figured out the rules. Then they will offer something carefully, within the guidelines. P.O.'s are usually calculating and self-controlled. They find it difficult to be spontaneous.

The Pharisees were totally performance-oriented. That is why they were furious at Jesus. He accepted sinners who had done nothing to earn the right to be loved. They themselves, by contrast, were the "righteous ones" who had done everything according to the rules and were more worthy of love than these "low-lifers."

Among born-anew Christians the root of performance orientation is unbelief. The heart does not really believe the good news of the free gift of salvation, although the mind and mouth may be preaching it to others.

One performance-oriented woman to whom I ministered was the evangelist of the church. Midge never missed church, where the Gospel was preached every Sunday, and the prayer group met weekly in her home. But each time we entered counseling, she would actually say, "If I don't do right, God won't love me." This came from Midge's relationship to her father, who had withheld expressions of affection whenever he wanted to control her. And when she was violently raped, her father blamed her, shouting, "You did something to attract it. You're a slut!"

Midge's heart had been rigidly programmed. To be set free, she needed to see her inner resentments and be willing to let them go. Now, at last, Midge does believe with a full heart that God loves her unconditionally, no matter what she does.

It should be added, lest this seem an open door to license, that although God still loves us when we sin, terrible consequences result. His continuing "foolish" love (1 Corinthians 1:18–21) does not mean we get away with anything at any time; His laws are absolute.

Entire churches for whom performance orientation has become a religious spirit of striving, jealousy and rancor can need deliverance.

It takes a combination of deliverance and inner healing, however, to set individual P.O.'s free, since they have been laid hold of by spirits who specialize in jealousy, criticism, rancor, self-righteousness, fear, condemnation, false guilt and rejection. Counsel must reveal what deprivations of affection created the reaction that became performance orientation. Then forgiveness and healing are needed to reassure fearful hearts that they will not be rejected for shortcomings. Perfect love casts out fear, but love has to be administered patiently over a long time before a P.O.'s heart can truly believe Jesus loves him or her without requiring performance.

Although dozens of other practices in the old nature could be discussed here, practices that Christian counselors must try to bring to death, I hope these few basic structures are enough to reveal what inner healing is and does.

Many practices have to be dismantled one by one on the cross. Demons may be involved, especially where hate has been masked. Both inner transformation and deliverance may be needed as the long process of healing continues. Wise counselors are amenable to the guidance of the Holy Spirit to know which is appropriate and when.

By now I hope you can see that inner healing is a fully biblical way of reaching to the depths of wounded hearts, to enable people to truly "walk the walk" they have been *talking*.

# 4

# What Inner Healing Is Not

Now that we have gone into some depth exploring what inner healing is, let's take a look at what inner healing is not.

## Inner Healing Is Not Psychology

Misinformed critics have often accused inner healers of being psychologists. We are nothing of the sort. Psychology can at best only chronicle the deceits of the flesh while offering no solutions, whereas Christians have the answer in the blood and cross and resurrection life of our Lord Jesus Christ.

Inner healing may make use of psychological insights, but it does not stand on psychology. Rather, applying biblical principles to understand and heal the heart, inner healing stands solely on the Word of God. (Please take time, now or later, to read appendixes 2–5. You may be surprised to discover that inner healing is not only found within the Bible; it is a major theme!)

Psychologists want to restore people's capacity to function. This is not necessarily a Christian's aim. Christian counselors know that God will put a person "between a rock and a hard place" in order to write something on his or her heart. If the person escapes the situation too soon, God will have to put him or her into another. A wise proverb warns us not to cast water on a fire God is building.

Nor should we comfort another too soon lest we miss God's larger purpose in his or her life. "For momentary, light affliction is producing for us an eternal weight of glory far beyond all comparison, while we look not at the things which are seen, but at the things which are not seen; for the things which are seen are temporal, but the things which are not seen are eternal" (2 Corinthians 4:17–18).

Psychologists want to restore a person's self-image, believing that a person who sees himself or herself in a good light will have the confidence to perform well.

To be sure, we all work to make ourselves acceptable to others. We want others to see that we are doing well and affirm us. But once we have built a good image, we must strive to live up to it. That is hard work, and perhaps one reason Jesus said, "Come to Me, all who are weary and heavy-laden, and I will give you rest" (Matthew 11:28).

In addition, a strong self-image creates confidence in the flesh, whereas the Bible teaches that the arm of flesh will fail, and that we are to put no confidence in the flesh (see Philippians 3:4–11). When we receive Jesus as Lord and Savior, one of the most important deaths we die is to the nurturing of our self-image.

We have, instead, a Christian identity—altogether different from a self-image. Our identity is a gift we did not build nor must we strive to maintain. We are children of God, sinners redeemed by the blood of Jesus. In Him we can "crush a troop [and] leap over a wall" (Psalm 18:29, RSV). "I can do all things through Him who strengthens me" (Philippians 4:13). Confidence rightly placed is confidence in what the Holy Spirit will do through us. True strength lies not in what *we* are, but in who and what Christ is in us. Self-image gives *us* the glory. Whatever we do in our identity as Christians gives *God* the glory.

Christian counselors work, therefore, to slay self-image on the cross and to fill men and women with the realization of their new identities in Christ. Any Christian who labors to build self-image works against the power of the crucifixion.

Psychologists are trained, for the most part, to believe in conditioning—that we are whatever life writes on our consciousness. That way of thinking began with the seventeenth-century mathematician and philosopher Rene Descartes, who stated that we begin life as a *tabula rasa* (literally, an erased tablet or slate) onto which experience writes what we become.

This theory was buttressed by cultural determinists like Emile Durkheim and psychologists like Pavlov, who conditioned animals to salivate at a given signal and theorized that human beings were similarly controllable. That is why some psychologists become softheaded about criminals: "You couldn't help it. Your parents and society conditioned you to become what you have. We are to blame, so we should turn you loose."

Christians, by contrast, believe that human beings can choose how we will react to what forms us. We are not innocent victims who must be reconditioned; we are guilty and need forgiveness.

To most secular psychologists, guilt is an enemy barring people from freedom and happiness. To a Christian, guilt is a friend. If we do not recognize our guilt, we cannot get to the cross. So Christians work to make people feel *properly* guilty, since that is the route to repentance and being set free in Christ.

## Inner Healing Is Not Imagination

Critics have often accused inner healers of making false or magical use of imagination. We at Elijah House have never espoused such techniques. Having studied the occult before I came to Christ, I know how imagination can be used and how powerful it is. The Flood itself happened because of mankind's evil use of imagination: "And God saw that the wickedness of man was great in the earth, and that *every imagination of the thoughts of his heart was only evil continually*" (Genesis 6:5, KJV, italics mine).

Simply picturing, in the flesh, what we want and using "prayer power" to make that vision happen is magic, strictly forbidden by the Lord (Deuteronomy 18:9–13). And we are to beware of those puffed up in their own minds, taking their stand on visions and not holding fast to the Head, who is Christ (Colossians 2:18–19).

But we are not to let the mistakes of some deter us from the right use of the blessed gift of our imagination. When God grants a vision, that is another matter entirely. If the Holy Spirit gives us a picture in our mind while we are counseling or praying for another, that may be holy and righteous guidance from the Lord telling us what is wrong or how to pray for the person's healing.

God often shows me what has happened in a person's life. That is one way the gift of knowledge operates in the Lord's servants—as a holy and powerful diagnostic tool. Or God shows me what He wants to happen, so I can pray that He will achieve those purposes in the person's life. My son Mark is very effective as a counselor because he remains humble and open to the Lord's guidance by the pictures he is given through his imagination.

Years ago Ruth Carter Stapleton, the sister of the then President, was catapulted into prominence in inner healing before she had a chance to mature and sift error from truth. Consequently she wrote a book in which she taught Christians the wrong use of imagination. If a person had a brutal father, for instance, the counselee would be led into prayer in which he pictured Jesus coming to him, the hurt child, and saw the father as kind and gentle.

That was a lie. The father had not been kind and gentle. But this pretense, well-intentioned as it was, avoided repentance in the counselee for the sin of judging his father. It did not require his dying to sinful practices in his own heart. It merely buttressed the person's "pity party."

Stapleton would take groups of seminar attendees on imaginary trips in which they were to meet and talk with the Lord, trips that were often nothing but soulish mind games. Hearing of her errors, much of the Body of Christ confused Stapleton's methodologies with all others in inner healing and got soured on right practices.

The Holy Spirit uses imagination wonderfully, whether in inner healing or deliverance or any other endeavor. We do well to purify our hearts so that His employment of our imagination may result solely in His holy purposes.

## Inner Healing Is Not New

Inner healing has always been practiced in the Church, though by other names or no names at all. In *The Testaments of the Twelve Patriarchs* (thought to have been written circa 192 A.D.) Gad, one of the twelve sons of Jacob, described his jealousy and hatred for his brother Joseph. Then the second-century Christian author put these words into Gad's mouth:

> These things I learnt at last, after that I had repented concerning Joseph. For true repentance after a godly sort destroyeth unbelief, and driveth away the darkness, and enlighteneth the eyes, and giveth knowledge to the soul, and guideth the mind to salvation: and those things which it hath not learnt from man, it knoweth through repentance. For God brought upon me a disease of the heart; and had not the prayers of Jacob my father intervened, it had hardly failed that my spirit had departed. For by what things a man transgresseth, by the same also he is punished. For in that my heart was set mercilessly against Joseph, in my heart too I suffered mercilessly, and was judged for eleven months, for so long as I had been envious against Joseph until he was sold.[1]

Isn't this description, written 1,800 years ago, just what many in inner healing have been saying?

Or try the First Letter of Clement for an excellent examination of the effects of jealousy on the human heart.

Our ancestors in the faith were incisive about character defects and how these were to be brought to death on the cross. Treatise after treatise from the early Church Fathers speaks of the necessity to conform human nature to the character of Jesus, seeing transformation as an essential part of being made fit for heaven. Quite a contrast to the "gimme-gimme" gospel of today, proclaiming only what Christ will do for us!

Inner healing is a tool in the Lord's hand calling us back to self-sacrificial ministry for one another that alone can reshape our character for fellowship with the Father.

Inner healing began to be rediscovered during the second World War. Agnes Sanford (no relation to us) had been given the gift of praying for physical healing. As a hospital "gray lady," pushing a cart carrying gum, candy and newspapers, she called on wounded soldiers and prayed surreptitiously for them. Miraculous healings resulted.

Then she found a young Jewish man, Harry Goldsmith, from whose leg three inches of bone had been blown away. She prayed for Harry and taught him how to pray. Instead of having an amputation, he regrew three inches of bone! And along the way he became a Christian.

But while studying to become a Christian psychiatrist, he asked Agnes in a letter why he still had occasional unaccountable rages. He would fly into a fury, he wrote, and throw his typewriter against the wall.

Knowing he was now born again, Agnes puzzled over his problem. Then the Lord showed her that Harry had often been persecuted and beaten by gangs of Gentile boys when he was about ten. The grown man had tried to forgive but he could not reach the heart of that ten-year-old. So Agnes prayed that the little one within be enabled to forgive.

It worked. Gone for good were Harry's unaccountable rages. And a door of understanding opened for Agnes Sanford, who began to see that many Christians could not maintain their walk because of old grudges lodged in their hearts.

As an Episcopalian, she first viewed inner healing as an extension of the office of the confessional. Agnes and her husband, Ted, an Episcopal rector, started a school to teach what they were learning about praying for healing. Many who later became leaders in the charismatic renewal attended her School of Pastoral Care, where she pioneered the teaching of what came to be called (against her will) "the healing of memories."

In 1959 she was scheduled to teach in the then mecca of fundamentalism, Evangel College in Springfield, Missouri. She asked Father Wilbur Fogg and his wife, Alice, of Streator, Illinois, to sit in the audience and intercede so that she might be heard. The Foggs invited me to go along. I, too, prayed fervently that her audience would hear, since they believed that once a person is saved, he or she is transformed and has no need to look at possible unbelief and sin deep in the heart.

Agnes opened the Bible and the minds of many in that meeting to wondrous truths. Afterward the Foggs asked her to pray for physical healing for my back. She knelt and laid hands on my back. Wonderful liquid warmth poured through my frame. But she also prayed for me to be enabled to forgive my mother, with whom I had endured a terribly wounding relationship (which I mentioned earlier).

I had forgiven my mother, in an emotional scene at age thirteen, for her critical tongue and harmful ways. Since then we had enjoyed a close and loving relationship. So I could have told Agnes, "No, I've forgiven my mother long ago." But I had read Agnes' books. I knew she was praying for the boy from birth to age thirteen, the boy I could not reach, to be able to forgive as well.

I was able to forgive from deep within; and thus began the healing of both my back and my heart.

Subsequently I began to teach with Agnes and others in the Schools of Pastoral Care. Together we pioneered the rediscovery of the healing of the inner man.

## Inner Healing Is Not Just Comfort

Agnes and many who attended her schools saw inner healing as a great gift to the hearts of hurting people. But my first mentors in the faith, other than Father Wilbur Fogg (who had prayed for Agnes at Evangel College), were evangelicals and Pentecostals who drove me into the Bible and evangelical theology. I saw that the Lord was interested in more than simply restoring people to function.

From my seminary studies in Church history, I had seen the need for transformation after conversion, evidenced in the spiritual disciplines of many of the Lord's most prominent missionaries. I came to believe that inner healing belonged in the larger context of the Lord's work to purify and sanctify His Church. So Paula and I attempted to ground the movement of inner healing in evangelical biblical theology.

Through our own efforts and those of others, the Church has begun to receive inner healing as a valid and necessary ministry.

## Counterattack

But Satan struck back! A number who entered the field of inner healing were neither wise nor well-grounded in Scripture. They began to employ imagination in ways too close to the occult.

Some taught grievous errors, such as the one I mentioned earlier—visualizing a cruel father as kind and loving. That kind of visualization was a lie and avoided the cross, while forgiveness was needed, along with death to any bitter root judgments and expectancies (see chapter 3).

Some practitioners merely soothed people. They confirmed personal stories of woe and self-righteousness and failed to confront people with their sins and bring them to repentance.

Some practitioners employed various techniques in a mishmash of psychology and faith.

Then, in the 1980s, apologists for the faith began to write polemics against not just these few, but against all who had ever been involved in inner healing. Christian apologists are always needed to correct error in the Church and defend the faith against attack. But whoever sets out to chastise the faithful should determine to follow exacting biblical disciplines, examining what he sees and going to his brother first, so that the Body of Christ is edified.

Unfortunately, this was not done. Agnes Sanford (who had by then passed on to her reward in heaven) was written off as a champion of the occult—a great irony and injustice since Agnes hated the occult. I was with her when she stumped through churches and camps driving out occult beliefs and practices. But not one apologist checked with any of us who had worked with Agnes for years, to ascertain whether his understanding of what she believed and said was accurate.

Paula and I were accused of being occultists and New Agers, although we have been among the foremost to identify and warn against the deceits of the occult and the New Age.

Apart from the sloppy scholarship of these apologists, I was appalled that many Christians do not follow the scriptural admonition not to accept an accusation against an elder except as confirmed by two or three witnesses (1 Timothy 5:19). Since any two or three can join in accusing an innocent person, Jewish law provided that those witnesses had to present their case in the presence of the accused so that he could defend himself.

That so many in the Body of Christ would believe charges against many of the Lord's true servants, without following through to read and ask questions, is a shame and a stench in the nostrils of the Lord, for which many need to repent before Him and ask forgiveness. Many Christians have been turned away from the healing they desperately need simply because they accepted libelous and shoddy scholarship.

## A Word About Pioneers

Pioneers have no well-trodden paths to follow. They do make mistakes. But they blaze trails that others can continue to clear. Certainly in heaven, but perhaps someday here on earth, credit will be given to Christian pioneers who have rediscovered ancient paths to walk in (see Isaiah 58:12). Those of us in inner healing have been neophytes, trying to find out how to apply the blood and cross and resurrection life of Jesus Christ to the heart where it counts. Let us forge ahead, undaunted by the confusions of men.

Someone has said, "Greater revelations yet hath God to break forth from His holy Word." If we must err, let us err on the side of searching for truth for the healing and salvation of men and women. This is part of the Great Commission to carry the Gospel to all people.

Let's be among those who carry not only the Gospel of redemption but the good news of healing and transformation—unafraid of what men may think or say—into the fullness of all that God intends us to be.

# 5

## A Christian Can
## Be Demonized

Sweat beaded on Steve's forehead as he clung to the pew. He gritted his teeth and promised himself, *This time I'm going to make it through the service.*

Then, as happened every Sunday, the voices came: *There is no God! You're wasting your time.*

Steve tried to shut them out and concentrate on the sermon. All around him people sat attentively, drinking in Pastor Jamison's words. Steve looked at the pastor as intently as he could. His mouth was moving but the words seemed to tumble out in disjointed clusters. Steve could hardly make them out, what with the cacaphony of other voices that grew ever louder in his head. *Don't listen to what he says. Satan is king!*

Steve glanced at a woman sitting to his right. Her face was soft and tranquil. Steve's stomach hurt. Perversions and blasphemies flooded his mind, then thoughts of hate and anger. His hands began to shake. Sweat was now pouring off his brow. *There is no God! You are God!*

"I can't take this," he mumbled. Choking back tears, he got up, excused himself clumsily and stumbled out the back door of the sanctuary.

He lingered in the narthex, however, until after the service when everyone had gone. As Pastor Jamison was putting on his coat, Steve approached him timidly.

"Pastor, can I talk to you a minute?"

The reverend turned and saw Steve's flushed face and red eyes. "Yes, of course," he replied with concern. "What is it, Steve?"

Steve took a moment to steady himself. "I don't know how to say this." He stood in silence, afraid to go on.

"I'm listening," the pastor reassured him.

"I—" Steve gulped. "I couldn't sit through your sermon!" Then he saw a flicker of embarrassment in the reverend's eyes. "No! I don't mean I didn't like your sermon. I just—" Steve's voice trailed off.

Pastor Jamison's concern was deepening. "Please tell me. What's wrong?"

Another silence. Then Steve blurted out, "Do you think Christians can be possessed? I hear these voices, and—"

The look in Pastor Jamison's eyes stopped him cold. Steve regretted opening his mouth, especially when the pastor, after an awkward pause, began a long, theological explanation about the efficacy of salvation.

"In the first place, Steve, that doesn't square with the doctrine of salvation. We belong to Christ, not Satan. And second, it goes against my understanding of the doctrine of sanctification. Paul says in 2 Corinthians 5:17, 'If anyone is in Christ, he is a new creation; the old has gone, the new has come!' How can demons find a place in that new creation?"

Steve was torn between trying to listen politely and wanting to leave. He managed to pay attention to scattered phrases—". . . Belong to Christ . . . new creation. . . ."

*I know that verse*, he thought, *and I believe it. But that doesn't make the voices go away.*

Pastor Jamison was saying something about Christians being Christ's possession forever when Steve interrupted him. "But what about the voices? How many times do I have to pray the sinner's prayer to be saved? Or am I just crazy?"

In fact, Steve knew he wasn't crazy. A psychological test had shown him only to be troubled.

The pastor stopped a moment to ponder the words *demon-possessed*. Having had precious little teaching on demons and deliverance, he reached into the recesses of his memory banks and came up with the only scriptural example of demon possession he could remember with any clarity—the story of the man with "Legion," several thousand demons, who ran around naked day and night among the tombs, screaming and cutting himself. Ghastly!

Nature abhors an intellectual vacuum. Something will always fill the empty space. Several other images lurked just below the level of the pastor's consciousness. Although he didn't realize it, they filled in the blanks, rounding out his conception of what a demon-possessed person would look like: guttural voice, head spinning round, green vomit. . . . What was that movie he had seen back in college? *The Exorcist*.

Pastor Jamison took a long, hard look at the young man. He appeared flustered, but nothing like the images he had come to associate with possession. So the reverend had dug deep into his far larger store of teaching on salvation and sanctification to demonstrate, biblically and conclusively, that Steve could not possibly be suffering from the same malady as the girl who was demonized in the movie.

"Have you been under a lot of stress lately?"

*Yeah, from Satan*, Steve thought. His life wasn't particularly stressful. He had been involved in the occult, of course, but that was before he had gotten saved. A lot of people thought of him as arrogant. But no big deal! He had long ago decided not to care what people thought. It did bother him, however, that his attitude didn't go over well with women.

"Well," he said at last, "it *is* hard for me to keep a girlfriend."

Jamison smiled for the first time. "Satan can't have any power in a Christian's life, Steve. All he can do is attack you by getting you to think he can. You just need to know who you are in Christ, and learn to stand in that."

Steve endured another list of verses, thanked the pastor politely and made his escape.

He did return the following Sunday morning, tormented once again in the pew. Then he decided not to come back.

## True "Possession" Is Extremely Rare

Pastor Jamison had been partly correct. Steve was not possessed. But he needed help the pastor couldn't give. Jamison could have helped him if he had known, first of all, that the man with "Legion" was the only scriptural counterpart of the young woman in *The Exorcist*. In fact, the descriptions in our English-language Bibles of people as "demon-possessed" are a mistranslation. The term *demon-possessed* is not even found in the Greek text of the New Testament.

Instead, three other terms are used. Some passages say *to have* a demon. Others say *to be in* a demon. The most common term is *demonized*. (See *The Most Dangerous Game by* Don Basham and Dick Leggett, Don W. Basham Publications.) The three terms mean essentially the same thing and are used interchangeably in the account of "Legion" (who was possessed; Matthew 8:28–34; Mark 5:1–20; Luke 8:26–39). None of these terms, in and of itself, indicates total ownership or control of a host. They simply mean the person is in some way affected.

Pastor Jamison, you remember, had two objections to the idea of a Christian being demon-possessed. One objection was the biblical doctrine of sanctification—that demons cannot lodge in a Christian as a new creation. My father has addressed this already in chapter 3, "What Inner Healing Is." He spoke there of the need to evangelize the unbelieving heart of the believer. His teaching about inner healing is also true of deliverance.

As for the other objection, that we are Christ's possession and cannot be indwelled by an evil spirit, Mr. Jamison might not have raised it had he done a thorough exploration of demonology.

I can hardly fault him for that. Until recently, the Church has not viewed demons with great concern. Demons, like the supernatural gifts of the Holy Spirit, have been relegated solely to Bible times. How peculiar that Satan's warriors would curtail all activity after the first century A.D., when Scripture states plainly that in the last days evil will increase (2 Timothy 3:1–5)! Yet in my own three years at seminary, I cannot recall enough teaching on demons to fill half a class period. Fortunately, a good number of recent books are making up for that lack. Still, we see some common errors, which we will address later.

For now, I speak not only to laypersons, but to the "Pastor Jamisons" who continue to rely on their seventeen minutes of seminary training.

## Demons Specialize

All examples in Scripture, with the exception of "Legion," involve people like Steve, beset in some way by demons but not completely taken over and controlled. This is because it takes an entire legion of evil spirits to possess a person totally. All one demon alone can do is specialize, attacking its host in a particular area.

Some will afflict physically, as with the woman "who had been crippled by a spirit [literally, a 'spirit of infirmity'] for eighteen years" (Luke 13:11), or the "deaf and dumb spirit" (Mark 9:25), which also caused epilepsy in a boy (Matthew 17:15), often throwing him into fire or water. (This is the only example in Scripture, incidentally, of a demon specializing in two tasks at once.)

Other demons specialize in mental deception. Hymenaeus and Philetus, who taught the false doctrine that the resurrection had already happened (2 Timothy 2:17–18), were in "the trap of the devil, who has taken them captive to do his will" (verse 26). And Paul alerted Timothy, "The Spirit clearly says that in later times some will abandon the faith and follow deceiving spirits and things taught by demons" (1 Timothy 4:1).

Still other demons specialize in emotional turmoil, like the spirit that terrorized Saul with what, in modern terms, appears to have been increasingly virulent anxiety attacks (1 Samuel 18:10–12). Paul warned the church at Ephesus not to allow Satan to make use of their festering anger: "Do not let the sun go down while you are still angry, and do not give the devil a foothold" (Ephesians 4:26–27).

Demons can specialize even in relationships. Abimelech incited the citizens of Shechem to enable him to murder their rulers (his seventy brothers!), whereupon they made him king (Judges 9:1–6). In retribution for their mutual treachery, God sent an evil spirit between him and the people of the city, which caused the Shechemites to forsake him and follow King Gaal. To retaliate, Abimelech destroyed the city of Shechem, setting fire to a temple crammed with helpless refugees. Later, in a battle against the city of Thebez, he himself was killed when a woman dropped a millstone on his head (verses 53–54).

Every one of the Bible characters just mentioned, apart from the demons' areas of specialization, was otherwise in control of his or her faculties. The woman crippled by a spirit, for instance, had no mental or emotional infirmity. Nor did Saul have a physical ailment. Each still had a sense of his or her own identity and thought processes.

But the man with "Legion" had lost control of both mind and body. He could not bring himself to wear clothes or live in a house (Luke 8:27). He could not restrain his own will, nor could he be restrained, even by chains. He had been driven into isolation, away from the company of friends and family (verse 29). He could not refrain from self-mutilation (Mark 5:5). This poor soul owned nothing of himself, neither his actions nor his thoughts. When asked his name, he could not even recall it.

Instead, the demons made their identity his, calling him by their name, *Legion*. (See my father's explanation of the giving of this name in chapter 2.) To completely possess their host required an entire legion of evil spirits. (A Roman legion, according to *Harper's Bible Dictionary*, contained from 5,400 to 6,000 footsoldiers.)

To possess Steve, then, would have required several thousand demons. If he had had only one demon or even a few dozen, they could have done no more than lodge in some portion of his being.

My father elaborates on demonic specialists in chapter 12.

## Attack Versus Demonization

The Bible states clearly that a Christian cannot be possessed, for we are called "God's own possession" (Ephesians 1:14, NASB). But the Bible says just as clearly that demons can gain a foothold. In Ephesians 4:27 the Greek word for "foothold" is *topos*, from which we derive the geographical term *topography*, according to the *Theological Dictionary of the New Testament*.

This does not, in the Greek, describe a momentary demonic action. It is, rather, a place Satan has secured, a semi-permanent station on some corner of the map of a Christian's life.

That is what the demons did with Steve. He had long since concluded that this was not merely an attack from forces outside himself. He had often rebuked them away, but they had always swiftly returned. For a season, not just a moment, these male-factors had come to make their home with him, though he could not understand why.

The answers Pastor Jamison did not—indeed, could not—give Steve were, first, that demons rarely possess; more often they specialize; and second, that an attack is different from demonization.

The apostle Paul was beset by a "messenger of Satan" (2 Corinthians 12:7). And for a time Satan hindered him from visiting the church at Thessalonica (1 Thessalonians 2:18). Was Paul demonized? Jesus was sorely tempted by Satan (Matthew 4:1–11), but we certainly wouldn't call that demonization! These two were merely under attack.

What differentiates attack from demonization is sin. As Dad explained in chapter 2, demonization occurs wherever unrepented sin invites Satan to work his will. Christ was, of course, sinless. Paul was not. But his attack was allowed "to keep me from *becoming* conceited [not because Paul was conceited already] because of these surpassingly great revelations" (2 Corinthians 12:7, italics mine). Nor was Paul prevented from visiting the Thessalonians by any fault of his own. There was no sin, so there was no demonization.

## Biblical Instances of Demonized Christians

Scriptural examples abound of Christians demonized because of their sin.

Paul warned, as we saw already, that unresolved sin can open the door to Satan (Ephesians 4:26–27). In the last days some Christians will become demonized through the sin of heresy (1 Timothy 4:1). Paul directed Timothy to gently instruct those who had become apostate, so that "they will come to their senses and escape from the trap of the devil, who has taken them captive to do his will" (2 Timothy 2:26).

The apostle handed Hymenaeus and Alexander "over to Satan to be taught not to blaspheme" (1 Timothy 1:20). And Paul admonished the church at Corinth, "I am afraid that just as Eve was deceived by the serpent's cunning, your minds may somehow be led astray from your sincere and pure devotion to Christ" (2 Corinthians 11:3).

In the Greek, *be led astray* is past tense; Paul worried that they might already have given Satan an open door. He warned them about false apostles, noting that "Satan himself masquerades as an angel of light" (verse 14). And he lamented, "If someone comes to you and preaches a Jesus other than the Jesus we preached, *or if you receive a different spirit from the one you received*, or a different gospel from the one you accepted, you put up with it easily enough" (verse 4, italics mine).

Some early Christians became demonized by deceiving. When Ananias tried to hide what he had done with part of the proceeds from a piece of property, Peter said to him, "How is it that *Satan has so filled your heart* that you have lied to the Holy Spirit . . .?" (Acts 5:3).

Others became demonized through perversion. When a man carried on a sexual relationship with his father's wife, Paul instructed the Corinthian church to "hand this man over to Satan, so that the sinful nature may be destroyed and his spirit saved on the day of the Lord" (1 Corinthians 5:5). Satan does not destroy the sinful nature; God does. But sometimes a man will not let God be fully in charge until he has hit bottom in his sojourn with sin and demons.

Demons are even connected with the sin of nonresistance. Peter warned believers to be "self-controlled and alert. Your enemy the devil prowls around like a roaring lion looking for someone to devour. Resist him, standing firm in the faith, because you know that your brothers throughout the world are undergoing the same kind of sufferings" (1 Peter 5:8–9). James offered a similar exhortation: "Resist the devil, and he will flee from you" (James 4:7).

If we do not resist, Lucifer may dog our steps permanently.

## The Kinds of Sin Demons Use

Pastor Jamison might have protested, "To say that sin invites demonization would make everyone susceptible, since everyone sins."

But not every passing sin gives demons a foothold. It takes a sin as weighty as having sex with your father's wife, or "lesser" sins that are indulged over time. Entertaining a momentary heretical thought does not make a person demonized. The people about whom Paul warned Timothy had embraced it; some even taught it as truth. Furthermore, not just any resentment opens the door to Satan, but anger the sun has gone down on.

Nor was it a "little white lie" that got Ananias into trouble. In the Hebrew culture of Jesus' day, a man might spend the better part of an afternoon dickering over the price of a bushel of wheat. To sell a piece of land, he would barter for months. The public actually gathered to watch these bargaining sessions as a form of entertainment! Ananias must have had to scheme for some time to fool the public by keeping hidden the true price he sold his land for.

So, too, Steve had become demonized through weighty sin. In his teens he had gotten involved in occult pursuits—astrology, seances, spell-casting and witchcraft. When he got saved, he repented of those sins. So why did the demons return after he rebuked them? Because more was involved than just the sin of witchcraft.

Psalm 91:1–4 says that when someone trusts in God, "He will cover [him] with his feathers, and under his wings [he] will find refuge." A person who trusts in God is hidden from Satan. But when Steve entered the occult, he exposed his entire being to the powers of darkness. The demons moved into lodgings already well-prepared for their purposes. Steve had long practiced lies that ultimately motivated him to dabble in the occult. And those very lies became the niches where the demons built their nests.

Steve's lies grew out of a lifelong feeling of powerlessness. He was the youngest of five kids, the runt. He and his siblings had been expected to perform flawlessly in everything they did. Four A's and a B were not good enough. Even when that B came up to an A, he never got the *Attaboy!* he longed to hear. It would be held out as the carrot for the next challenge.

"That's what we expect from you, anyway" was as close to a compliment as Steve ever got. A baseball game in which he batted three home runs was apt to be followed by some fatherly tips on how he could have avoided his only strikeout. A flawless performance in a school play was greeted by qualified plaudits: "You did O.K., son," Mother said. "But next time why don't you try to project your voice a little farther?"

The goal of perfection seemed even more unreachable since his older siblings had already broken the records for excellence. His two sisters were straight-A students, and his two brothers, the school's leading athletes. Steve spent every ounce of his energy running to catch up, to elude the shame prodding him from behind: "Sissy. Coward. Do you want people to think you're a weakling? Why can't you be like your brothers or sisters?"

In this family, power came through surpassing achievement. Without that, he might as well give up. Steve had to find a power that no one else had.

He found it in the occult. Through the secret sciences he could learn what none of his siblings or friends had ever dreamed of. So he asked demons to enter him and give him their power. Through them he could cast spells and make things happen that no one else could. He could even make his competitors ill or cause his Little League opponents to strike out or drop his fly ball. He could levitate objects or listen in on conversations three miles away.

Steve reveled in the thought that this power was his to command. In fact, he believed a lie. He had actually come under Satan's power. Perhaps he would not have believed that, were he not already so accustomed to being dishonest with himself. Countless times he had felt the disappointment of praise withheld, or suffered the humiliation of an unfavorable comparison with an older sibling, or felt the shame-filled sting of name-calling. But he had never admitted to himself that he felt hurt or angry about it. That would have been less than a straight-A performance. So he had chosen to believe lies: that his parents' demands were fair, that he felt no anger about withheld rewards, unfair comparisons or shaming labels, that he could use power to escape shame, that he could feel good about himself by taking power over others.

Satan is the "father of lies" (John 8:44). So when Steve swallowed the lie that he could command Satan's power, Satan took power, not only in that lie, but in all the lies preceding it. They became the foundation stones on which the demons built their homes.

Steve eventually accepted Christ and renounced witchcraft. But that was not enough to make the demons leave. They had entered via the one lie of witchcraft. Since then, they had found many other lies to cling to. Until Steve repented of those lies, demons would continue to find a place in him.

Thus, his arrogance continued; he could never admit he was wrong. He lost friends because he refused to compromise. He could never apologize. Whenever a girl got close to his heart, which threatened to expose his vulnerable inner child, he would always find some fault with her—she was too tall, too short, too emotional, etc.—and dump her.  Just as he had done in the occult, he continued to control others by vaunting himself over them, and his demons happily continued to assist him.

Even so, Steve was blessed with enough persuasion to convince a few others to join him in his delusions. When he became a born-again, Holy Spirit–filled Christian, they came to see him (despite his youth) as a kind of prophet, exposing the ills of the Church. When he exercised his "gift" without tact or compassion and was rebuked, he wouldn't hear it. Long ago he had vowed that no one would ever again "ace him out" in the game of life. (That had been the promise that got him into witchcraft in the first place.) And even though Steve was now out of the occult, that inner vow remained, and he would not break it for all the blessings of heaven.

So his demons remained, for they had found a home through witchcraft and "rebellion is like the sin of divination" (1 Samuel 15:23).  Though Steve was now a believer, demons shouted in his head, repeating the lies he had never relinquished: "There is no God. You are God!"

When Steve approached Pastor Jamison, he was nearing the bottom. With a deeper understanding of inner healing and deliverance, the pastor could have identified Steve's inner vow and enabled him to break it. Steve could have faced and dealt with the bitter roots that had motivated him to make that vow and later to enter the occult. The demons would have lost their home. Then, finally, Steve could have received from his heavenly Father the comfort he had been denied with every report card and after every ballgame.

## Breaching the Wall of Denial

"Steve" is actually a composite of several individuals I have counseled. Some, like him, were prideful and overtly power-hungry. Others had learned to hate themselves and used the occult to boost their egos. Most responded to counseling and faced the bitterness inside. A few did not.

Those who did not respond were chained by the most powerful lie of all: denial. It would have been a fearful thing for them to discover the depth and breadth of the lies they had founded their lives on. So instead they became like the town drunk everyone has seen intoxicated who himself cannot admit he is an alcoholic. (All of Steve's acquaintances had suffered his arrogance, but he was so addicted to his straight-A illusion that he would sacrifice any truth to preserve it.)

Whether we are hooked on a substance or simply the lies we use to justify our old nature, God is kind to let us "bottom out." It breaks us out of our denial.

After our salvation experience, many of us went through a "honeymoon" period. Later, how many of us hit a phase when we feared we were becoming less righteous, and not more? The truth is, we were only beginning to see the sin that our denial had long hidden from us. That sin is the demons' dwelling place. As the Holy Spirit fills our hearts and exposes sin, His presence will torment any demons that might have found repose there, and they will make themselves known.

Pastor Jamison considered the idea of Steve's hearing "voices"—actually, demons screaming in his ears—contradictory to belief in a God who conquers sin. On the contrary! He should have known that the Lord Himself was undermining the foundations of Steve's denial. By shouting his own lies to him, the demons were making one last, frantic bid to hold onto what Steve was close to facing and repenting of. They did not want to lose their happy home!

In recent years, we have seen the same thing happen to the Church at large. We have long been ensconced in a theology of denial, marked by a lopsided view of sanctification and an ignorance of demonology. We have fooled ourselves into thinking that we have "arrived," that the work of sanctification is finished.

But God is too kind to let us remain in denial, for the longer we deny our sins, the worse they can grow. As we have "kicked against the goads" of His call to continued repentance, our denial and the powers of hell have conspired to create such spectacles as renowned Christian leaders exposed for embezzlement and sexual perversion.

Because of the naïve counsel of the "Pastor Jamisons," it may take the "Steves" of the world a lot longer to find their breaking point. I hope it does not give them time to become the next spectacle. I want them to hit bottom before it is too late. We write this book in hopes of a softer landing.

# 6

---

# Deliverance and Inner Healing Meet at the Armor

Finally, be strong in the Lord, and in the strength of His might. Put on the full armor of God, that you may be able to stand firm against the schemes of the devil. For our struggle is not against flesh and blood, but against the rulers, against the powers, against the world forces of this darkness, against the spiritual forces of wickedness in the heavenly places.

Stand firm then, with the belt of truth buckled around your waist, with the breastplate of righteousness in place, and with your feet fitted with the readiness that comes from the gospel of peace. In addition to all this, take up the shield of faith, with which you can extinguish all the flaming arrows of the evil one. Take the helmet of salvation and the sword of the Spirit, which is the word of God.

Ephesians 6:10–12, NASB, 14–17

Steve, from the previous chapter, asked me why, for him, the armor of Ephesians 6 seemed so ineffective. Morning by morning he had asked God to outfit him with each piece, yet his tormentors' arrows had not been extinguished.

His bewilderment revealed a warped understanding of God's grace. He was steeped in a doctrine that minimizes or eliminates the need for sanctification beyond the born-again experience. To him, therefore, the armor was no more than a magic wand to dispense with evil. I explained to him that the armor is rather an expression of our trust in God, a trust that must grow daily to supplant the defenses in which we have previously trusted. The one wearing the breastplate of righteousness, for example, is saying, "I don't have to trust in my own goodness. I trust Jesus to be righteous for me." To wear the helmet of salvation is to say, "I don't have to worry about what others think. I know who I am in Christ. The helmet of salvation covering my head protects my thought life from worry."

It was clear, then, why Steve's morning prayer had been ineffective. He had not trusted Jesus to be his righteousness. Instead, as I wrote in the last chapter, he had defended his own "goodness" by never compromising, apologizing or heeding rebuke. Nor had he trusted God to protect his self-image. He had covered up his insecurities by thinking of himself as better than others. Steve already had a breastplate and a helmet of his own making. When Steve asked for the armor, therefore, he received nothing, for the only way he could have taken up the true armor was to pray for the grace to lay down the false.

As it was, Steve's "armor" was not only ineffective; it became the very weapon demons wielded against him! St. Paul describes demons as having been empowered by both our sin and the law:

> When you were dead in your sins and in the uncircumcision of your sinful nature, God made you alive with Christ. He forgave us all our sins, having canceled the written code, with its regulations, that was . . . opposed to us; he took it away, nailing it to the cross. And *having disarmed the powers and authorities*, he made a public spectacle of them, triumphing over them by the cross.
>
> Colossians 2:13–15, italics mine

If demons have been disarmed by the forgiveness of sins and cancellation of the written code, then Steve provided them ways to rearm, for he refused to repent of some sins and justified himself before the law.

Since demons reenter by way of unrepented sin, it would follow that the sin of the host provides the demonic armor of Luke 11:21-22:

> When a strong man, fully armed, guards his own house, his possessions are safe. But when someone stronger attacks and overpowers him, he takes away the armor in which the man trusted and divides up the spoils.

The context states that unrepentance will invite the exorcised demon to return, with seven others, armed as before.

Satan obviously used Steve's unrepentance as a weapon against him. To protect himself from shame, he used the breastplate of arrogance. To protect himself from feeling powerless, he used the shield of power over others. But his arrogance only tempted others to shame him, and his power-lust only incited others to fight back. Demons of arrogance and lust for power enabled him to fight ever harder, inviting ever more shame and interpersonal strife. He (and the demons) met this with still more arrogance and more force, as he was drawn into a downward spiral.

I do not propose that with every deliverance we should try to correlate the sin involved with one particular piece of counterfeit armor; that would seem rather contrived. But I do believe that where there is demonization there is a sinful defense, and the armor of Ephesians 6 does provide a handy metaphor. However we describe it, Satan has a broad array of fleshly defenses at his disposal. Let's look at case studies for two more possibilities.

## The Shield of Mistrust

The sins Satan finds most potent and enduring are bitter root judgments, expectations and inner vows (which my father examined more closely in chapter 3)—the most practiced and trusted defenses of the flesh. The defenses we acquire in adulthood are seldom ingrained so powerfully as those we learned in childhood, which stamp themselves far deeper into the soul. The following accounts of Peggy and Jenny illustrate this principle, and the faulty shield of faith.

Peggy stumbled into a couple of sour romances. Her beaus proved to be smooth operators, wolves in sheeps' clothing. Each plied her with charm and roses, hoping to "notch her virginity onto his bedpost." Overwhelmed by the pain of double betrayal, she vowed never to trust another man.

But through the comfort of good friends and the sweet release of tears, Peggy was able to regain the perspective she had developed over a lifetime. She remembered kinder men—gentlemanly dates, a teacher who had regarded her schoolgirl crush with respect, affectionate uncles who had teased her gently and, most importantly, a dad who surpassed them all.

Peggy remembered a few bad apples, too, but she simply tossed the two most recent fellows into the barrel with them. "That's part of life," she thought, managing to forgive them. "At least I know what kind of men to avoid!" And throwing off the faulty shield—her vow never to trust a man—she picked up God's shield of faith, which eventually brought her a true gentleman.

Jenny experienced betrayal at a much earlier stage. When she was a child, her father arrived home late every night after stopping at the tavern, then demanded dinner. When her mother asked if he could come home sooner to share supper with the family, he barked an excuse. Mom pleaded. He cussed back at her. Mom cried. He flew into a rage.

At other times she overheard her mother urging him to "take Jenny to the zoo" (or the Dairy Queen or the park). He would promise lamely. But when the time arrived, he would yell some angry excuse. Jenny held her breath if her mother pleaded too long. Dad had a breaking point beyond which he exploded at one or both of them with name-calling and violence.

So Jenny closed her heart to her father. She made sure her friends didn't visit so she wouldn't be embarrassed by his rudeness and profanity. "I don't need Daddy anyway," she told herself. And without saying it aloud, without even being especially conscious of it, Jenny made an inner vow not to trust men. After all, despite the occasional visits of an attentive uncle (the exception to the rule her father portrayed every day), all men must be like Daddy.

That vow became for Jenny a shield of faith, an attempt at invulnerability.

When she reached her teens and dated a bad apple who plied her with false charm, the years of stored pain and betrayal erupted. As a child Jenny had shielded herself with the inner vow never to trust men. Now she began to raise the shield of mistrust to men other than her father. Time and time again she used this shield to ward off disappointment, embarrassment and abuse. In time it became automatic.

The trouble with fleshly defenses is they actually *invite* demonic attack. Jenny thought her vow never to trust a man would protect her from being hurt. In fact, it brought the opposite.

Since it was based on a lie Jenny had chosen to believe—"No man is trustworthy"—she forfeited the ability to discriminate between trustworthy and untrustworthy men, and her "shield of faith" kept her from finding men who would have proved trustworthy. To protect herself from further betrayal, Jenny scrutinized the best of men for their faults—even the gentlemanly dates, respectful teachers and her attentive uncle—and used the slightest hurt as a pretext to put up her shield.

Lonely Jenny did venture from time to time into a relationship and was burned every time by real or imagined betrayal. Each disappointment, however slight, confirmed her belief that no man could be trusted. This strengthened her resolve for a season. Then she would cave in to her loneliness and be burned again.

In one sense Jenny's shield grew ever weaker. Because Satan is the father of lies, Jenny's "shield of faith" became his own. God's shield of faith would have protected her, but now a demon of bitterness began to shoot darts through her faulty shield. It reminded her of past hurts. It sharpened her awareness of the many weaknesses of the male sex, until even the thought of men brought pain and revulsion.

Jenny's pain was not like Peggy's. Peggy possessed a lifetime of memories of good men against which to balance her present misfortune, while Jenny knew few other men. Peggy went on to find a fulfilling relationship, while Jenny remained trapped. Peggy could open up again with relative ease, while Jenny had few men she could turn to. Even if she could find one, what would she say? Unlike Peggy's dad, Jenny's dad had not taught her how to put her hurt into words. Nor had he even allowed her to admit she was hurt.

Peggy's vow was an adult's temporary stop-gap against pain, while Jenny's childhood vow became a permanent defense.

## Girding the Loins with Lies

I have counseled many like Jenny who have become locked in a hopeless war. They battle with increasing despair as Satan turns their own weapons against them.

Frank learned he could never please his castigating mother, so he told her what he thought she wanted to hear. He learned he could not entrust her with the honest cries of his heart. And to protect himself against rejection and criticism, he learned to gird his loins not with truth but with lies. A lying spirit helped Frank become more adept at covering up the lies that were becoming compulsive.

Later in life, his friends caught him in lies and, feeling betrayed, rejected him. He made new friends. They eventually caught him, too. But since Frank was becoming more clever at covering his tracks, these new friends had more time to draw closer. This only delayed the inevitable: They felt all the more betrayed and rejected Frank all the more vehemently.

Frank then tried harder to cover his lies. The lying spirit was growing stronger.

## The Armor We Give Our Children

Perhaps if Jenny and Frank had been dressed in the armor of trust by their parents, they would have found it easier to put on the armor of God when they came of age. My father says that parents "body forth" to their children who God is. Never having seen God, and not being old enough to conceptualize, children can see God only within the small frame of reference that parents provide.

Thus David wrote, "You made me trust in you even at my mother's breast" (Psalm 22:9). Isaiah echoed that thought: "Can a mother forget the baby at her breast and have no compassion on the child she has borne? Though she may forget, I will not forget you!" (49:15). Isaiah assumed that whatever the Israelites had learned through their earthly mothers would influence their view of God. Solomon penned the words of a godly parent to a child: "My son, if you accept my words and store up my commands within you . . . then you will understand the fear of the Lord and find the knowledge of God" (Proverbs 2:1, 5).

How hard it is for children to trust in God's armor when their parents, by their words or actions, have lied to them about who God is! Jenny's father taught her that her heavenly Father could not be trusted to keep His promises, and so failed to equip her with the shield of faith. Frank's mother taught him that God could not be trusted with the honest cries of his heart, and thus did not gird his loins with truth.

How tempting, then, for each child to devise his own defenses! To make matters worse, God Himself must have looked an awful lot like the enemy. And since each child learned to protect himself with lies, the father of lies deceived each into regarding him as their friend!

## We Cannot Blame Parents . . .

Scripture makes it clear, however, that Jenny's and Frank's parents were not to blame for the sins of the children or for their becoming demonized.

True, parents' failings offer ready opportunity to sin. Parents need to heed this warning: "If anyone causes one of these little ones who believe in me to sin, it would be better for him to have a large millstone hung around his neck and to be drowned in the depths of the sea" (Matthew 18:6). But ultimate responsibility for each child's actions lies with the child: "Fathers shall not be put to death for their children, nor children put to death for their fathers; each is to die for his own sin" (Deuteronomy 24:16).

Jesus Himself grew up with sinful parents in a sinful world. But Scripture says of Him, "[He] has been tempted in all things as we are, yet without sin" (Hebrews 4:15, NASB). Further, no parent can compel a child either to sin or to act righteously. Thus, it was their own sinful reactions that caused the three children to err.

Scripture promises children that if they turn to Jesus, they will come to know the truth and the truth will set them free (John 8:32). Jenny could hardly blame her father for her stony heart, since she noticed even in childhood that all men were not like him. Her uncle and a few others did "body forth" a gentle God able to sympathize with weaknesses (Hebrews 4:15). She could have chosen to disbelieve her father's lies, forgive him and open her heart to other "fathers."

If we always blame conditioning, every generation would blame the one before, and no one would take responsibility for his or her own actions.

## Nor Should We Shame Ourselves . . .

Some readers, on the other hand, might feel anger that such a heavy load be placed on children. Some might take what I just said as unfair, even Pharisaical. Some, like Jenny, have been abused by those who should have embodied God's protectiveness. Some have been beaten with boards and belts and hairbrushes until their bodies were covered with bruises. Some have been seduced or raped by the ones who should have enfolded them in God's protective love.

"Are we to understand," they might ask, "that as small children, without the aid of counselors or mentors, we should have chosen to forgive? How were we supposed to believe that an invisible God was really there, holding us in arms we could not feel, singing lullabies we could not hear? Were we supposed to know to take refuge in the God whose true nature is the opposite of everything our parents demonstrated? Only now, as adults, do we begin to see what we have become. How can we be blamed for our past?"

They cannot, of course, be blamed for their past. But it seems the cruelest of ironies that we who did not choose to be born sinners are destined by Adamic sin to fall into bitterness and judgmentalism. If this is our common fate, how can an abused child be expected to do anything but judge his or her parent? Nonetheless, the Bible is clear: Every person is accountable for his or her own actions.

Many give lipservice to God's grace while their hearts cannot truly believe that He can and does sympathize with children trapped in bitterness. In the name of sound doctrine, Pharisees have always rubbed salt into the wounds of sinners, and sinners have always feared that God might do the same.

But God does not relish punishment. Jeremiah comforted sinners, "For he does not *willingly* bring affliction or grief to the children of men" (Lamentations 3:33, italics mine). The Hebrew text defines *willingly* as "coming from the heart." And Jesus assured a humble Pharisee named Nicodemus that "God did not send his Son into the world to condemn the world, but to save the world through him" (John 3:17).

Never in Scripture was God angry at someone who wanted to repent. Jesus got angry only at Pharisees who exulted in their own fleshly strength. God is not anxious to rub our noses in shame. He only wants us to know that our fleshly defenses stand between us and Him—weapons that hurt us more than the perceived attackers we wield them against.

So my answer to the tough questions above is this: It is hard to swallow, but according to Scripture, no matter how unfair the circumstances that cause a child to become bitter, it is still his bitterness and no one else's. And although he is instructed to make his confession with the help of a brother (James 5:16), he is the only one who can ask God to remove the bitterness.

What makes this palatable is that rather than condemn us, God wants to take care of our problem, and in fact has gone to extraordinary lengths to do so:

> You see, at just the right time, when we were still powerless [over sin], Christ died for the ungodly. Very rarely will anyone die for a righteous man, though for a good man someone might possibly dare to die. But God demonstrates his own love for us in this: While we were still sinners, Christ died for us.
>
> Romans 5:6–8

The ramifications of sin are more than any of us can carry. So Jesus shoulders our bitterness for us, if only we will carry it the short walk to the cross.

## Nor Can We Blame Demons!

Since sinners receive the benefit of the cross only by recognizing that they alone are responsible for their sins, I find it troubling that some, in the name of healing, blame demons for their problems. Some deliverance ministers cast out anger, fear or malice as if these were demons rather than the sour fruit of sinful hearts. Others deal in a token way with the flesh but still identify demons as the primary culprits.

I lived once near where many deliverance ministries were headquartered. People often came to me for counseling who had gone elsewhere first for help. For the most part they had found these ministries praiseworthy. They had been touched by the Holy Spirit's power and felt relief.

But many had also experienced "the revolving door syndrome." Demons had been cast out, only to return again and again and necessitate further deliverance. They felt condemned when deliverance ministers, standing rightly on biblical principles, insisted that their sin must have allowed the demons to return. But they saw no way out of that condemnation when the ministers could not name the specific sin.

The problem was, some ministers had not learned to regard repentance as the foundation for deliverance. They were skilled at rebuking demons but had little understanding of the depravity of the heart. So they spent token efforts calling for repentance, as if that were an afterthought, "just in case they try to come back."

To be fair, I counseled only the dissatisfied. No doubt many others had no complaints. And it might be argued that Jesus Himself did not spend much time dealing with individuals about their particular sins before delivering them. (This wasn't possible for Him in any case as a "traveling evangelist.")

Still, Jesus considered healing and deliverance secondary to His teaching, which was a call to repentance. Those who heard

Jesus' call were to search their hearts for specific sins that stood between them and a delivering Savior.

If repentance is foundational to deliverance done in momentary encounters, how much more foundational is it in the context of discipleship (of which counseling is one method) when the discipler takes time with the individual? The fleshly habits of some people are so ingrained that they cannot see the hidden motives of their own hearts without a season of in-depth discipling, or time spent with someone with keen discernment about the complexities of the flesh.

In preparation for deliverance, we must allow the Holy Spirit to search our hearts for sins, since repentance removes the ground for Satan's attack. We must know, moreover, that demons have not created the sins. They are ours alone. Jesus said, "Nothing outside a man can make him 'unclean' by going into him. Rather, it is what comes out of a man that makes him 'unclean'" (Mark 7:15). Demons cannot defile us unless we have already defiled ourselves. (We noted three means of defilement in the last chapter: anger, nonresistance and apostasy.)

Nor should we assume (as Dad said in chapter 2) that where there is sin, there is always a demon. The only way demons could be involved in every case is if they were both omniscient and omnipresent. No, demons are mere opportunists. For that reason I am continually amazed to find that some people who have sinned heavily need little deliverance, while others with a more innocent past are heavily demonized.

I met a woman of the second type whom I will call Mary. Her personal history was not particularly checkered. To be sure, her heart was filled with bitterness toward a controlling, shaming mother, who had even teased Mary about her body in ways that bordered on molestation. Mary had grown up with a low self-image and struggled with self-condemnation, procrastination and overeating. But her bitterness was not sufficent to account for the hundreds of demons that tormented her.

Then I learned that Mary had been involved in several occult practices she had thought innocent. Unaware of the biblical prohibition against the occult and desperate for a touch from God, she went looking in all the wrong places. A book introduced her to New Age techniques. After limited success with auto-sugges-tion, automatic handwriting and horoscopes, Mary discovered the pendulum. When she held it over her Bible and asked it ques-tions, it swung north and south for *yes*, east and west for *no*.

Mary learned much later that the Bible prohibited occult prac-tices and denounced them. Meanwhile, though, she had unknow-ingly thrown the window of her soul wide open to the powers of darkness. Plenty of demons nearby were ready to jump in.

During this time she was married to a man who was heavily demonized. A pre-surgical transsexual, he was intent on becom-ing a woman. This man so hated his own maleness that he was able to skewer his genitals with a darning needle, feeling no pain. Once, without anesthetic, he partially castrated himself using a razor blade and resewed the incision. His many demons saw in Mary an opportunity, and quickly found homes in every nook and cranny of her bitterness toward her mother.

Later, every counseling session with me was punctuated with deliverances from demons that would object with a shake of Mary's head or a curt "No!" or "Stop that!" If she had not married a demonized man, I believe few demons might have seen that occultic window and flown through it. If she had not opened it at all, she would have had fewer demons still.

## Demonization Is a Process

It can take only a moment to become demonized—for exam-ple, just one seance. The first commandment is, "You shall have no other gods before me" (Exodus 20:3). Deuteronomy 18:10–11 forbids consulting occult sources. One who does so calls on a power other than God. Rest assured that if anyone from the dark side is nearby, it will answer that call with more than we bar-gained for!

Or we need commit only one act of sexual perversion. If there happens to be a demon specializing in sexual sin anywhere in the vicinity (most likely in the sexual partner), it will probably enter. The prostitute Mary Magdalene was delivered of seven demons (Mark 16:9).

So why not deliver all at once? Sometimes a simple deliverance accompanied by a short prayer of repentance will do, which may take no longer than it took to sin. But often deliverance (just like repentance from sin) is a process, since becoming demonized is often a process. For Jenny and Frank, distrust inspired sin. Sin became armor. That armor invited demonic attack. They strengthened their armor against it. Paradoxically, that strengthened the demons. And so began the downward spiral.

It takes a long time to dress oneself in false armor, and it may take some time to strip it off piece by piece. Some people are ready for an instant miracle. But for many it takes a while to learn to trust God enough to take off the old armor. After all, it is theirs alone to relinquish. God never preempts their will. His desire is to heal, not humiliate. So He removes our armor layer by layer, like the proverbial onion.

## April's Story

The need for a gradual healing and deliverance process is hard to comprehend if we have not walked in someone else's shoes for a season. So I give you the story of April. She was more tormented than most, but I recount her story because every person we undertake to counsel is a potential April. Until we have tarried with each, we will not know whether his or her pain is as deep as April's, and we must not rush in too quickly, adding pain to pain.

April came seeking relief from depression, anxiety attacks and low self-esteem. Her present life was relatively stress-free, but she could not escape the pain of her past. When I questioned her about her childhood—she recalled vaguely a molestation by her uncle at the age of four—April drew a fairly typical profile of a dysfunctional family.

Her father expected perfection. April tried hard for the required A's but got C's. Unknown to her and her parents, she suffered from dyslexia, a learning disability. When she insisted she was doing her best, her father replied, "No. You're not working up to your potential. Your sister can do it; why can't you?"

Punishments were strict. For a sibling squabble she had to move a pile of bricks the size of a sofa across the yard, brick by brick, and back again, lining them in tidy rows. If accused falsely she was not allowed to say so, however politely. If Dad ever saw his mistake, he covered his tracks: "Just remember all the times I *didn't* catch you." Never did April hear him utter an apology.

She was not allowed to release mounting tensions through exercise. At seven, after open heart surgery, the doctor forbade her to jump, climb or run. There wasn't much play with the neighborhood kids. After surgery Mom paraded her "living miracle" before her friends. When April complained that she felt like a specimen, Mom pouted, "I'm a good mother, aren't I?"

April's apparent task in life was to make her mother feel good about herself. When she erred, she heard, "How could you do this to me?" The problem with any infraction was not how it broke God's law or how it affected April's own life. It was how it made her mother feel.

April's morality belonged to Mom and Dad, along with most everything else. Interpersonal boundaries were few. It was Mom's "right" to read April's diary, her mail and go through her private things. Mom and Dad reserved the right to break confidentialities. They could enter the bathroom at any time, even when she was showering. If she protested, Dad called it "false modesty."

April learned to obey the unspoken rules of the house: *Please others, whatever the cost. Be a good reflection on the family. Control yourself emotionally. And relinquish all other control to parents.* Feeling helpless and vulnerable, she learned not to trust her heart to parental figures, earthly or heavenly.

That was probably one reason April forgot so quickly that she had been molested. Also, she had heard her father remark disgustedly that "if a woman gets raped, she was asking for it," and, "Children lie about being molested." Dad didn't mean to blame April. If he had known, he would have blamed Uncle Byron. (In fact, he would probably have torn him limb from limb!) But April felt blamed and unprotected, which increased her distrust tenfold. Alone and in pain, she learned to devise her own armor.

Counseling might have been shortened by many months were it not for another layer of pain and resentment. April had sought help at a "Christian" counseling center and met Erick. With a gentle manner and winning smile, he had built her self-esteem. He made her the secretary and a member of the board. Eventually he even trusted her to counsel a few clients. April thought she had finally found someone who accepted her uncritically. Not daring to lose that, she overlooked the changes coming over him.

Erick gradually increased her workload to 18-20 hours a day, seven days a week. He tormented her with double messages. He promised choice tasks at seminars, then gave them to others. He deliberately gave false instructions, then accused her in front of everyone of ruining a retreat. He allowed her no privacy. When she was out of his presence, he actually tracked her every move with extrasensory perception, making her afraid to run. After Erick won her heart, he systematically broke her will through these and other cult brainwashing techniques. As she was increasingly weary, her judgment began to falter. Little by little she gave her mind over to Erick.

In counseling, Erick used sarcasm and name-calling. He screamed at her, his face inches from hers, to confront hidden sins. "What sins?" she pleaded. "You know," he smirked. For days she fretted, searching to no avail. As punishment for "stubbornness," he prayed that her spirit would be locked in a box where she could no longer access the feelings of her inner child.

God did not answer that prayer—but a demon did. Thereafter April could not feel sadness, anger, even joy. She wanted to talk out the memory of her molestation slowly, but Erick cranked her for information. If she didn't share everything right now, he threatened, God would make her relive every detail with physical sensations! She spilled just enough to appease him and tried to hide her fear.

Exhausted and bewildered, April could not fight what came next. Erick asked her to be his third wife! She was appalled at the thought of bigamy, but he made it sound downright biblical. She had been taught wrongly that the way to get guidance was to ask others to pray without giving them details, to avoid personal bias. April's friends responded that whatever the issue was, it was her choice, but that God wanted this for her. She felt uncertain, but obeyed their "discernment." Meanwhile, Erick told her to keep their new bigamous relationship hidden from an "unenlightened public."

Again he used brainwashing techniques. Soft touches progressed to rough treatment. Calling it her "wifely duty," he coerced her into degrading acts, abusing her with objects and watching pornography of all kinds. She would tremble as she watched his eyes change from light brown to black as demons of sexual violence overcame him.

"What are you good for, babe?" he would ask. "Loving," was the hesitant reply. "No, you're my brood mare. You're only good for one thing." She mustered meager resistance. "No, I'm not. I'm good for loving." Erick would answer with a stinging slap and rough sex. In her confusion, she could only wonder what she had done to provoke him. It was years before she realized this was rape. Obviously Erick was no Christian counselor. He was a sociopath who reveled in abusive power.

One day Erick went a step too far. He sent her to buy food for a staff gathering. Because he had underestimated the need, she bought more than requested. He berated her before the entire group, his neck veins popping. But when the meat ran low, he berated her again. When she protested, Erick spewed profanities. April could take no more. She grabbed a kitchen knife and stabbed it into the table, inches from his hand. He froze. She had finally drawn a line. He did not move and did not speak; she was standing, knife in hand, at the breaking point.

Soon after, April packed her bags. Through an impromptu "underground railroad," friends spirited her out of state and out of harm's way.

## Some Common Lessons for the Process

In the first months of counseling, I spent much effort trying to undo Erick's damage. To regain trust, I had to supply April with several assurances that I have found to be standard fare for the healing process:

**No need to "navel gaze."** I assured her that, contrary to Erick's teaching, she was innocent until proven guilty. She did not need to fret for days over unknown sins. That was the Lord's job:

> I care very little if I am judged by you or by any human court; indeed, I do not even judge myself.
>
> 1 Corinthians 4:3
>
> My conscience is clear, but that does not make me innocent. It is the Lord who judges me. Therefore judge nothing before the appointed time; wait till the Lord comes. He will bring to light what is hidden in darkness and will expose the motives of men's hearts.
>
> 1 Corinthians 4:4–5

**God will set a pace you can keep.** I would not force April to face memories too soon. God would be a "light for [her] path" (Psalm 119:105), proceeding at a pace she could keep. My father once brought home from Israel a lamp that a shepherd of old would carry along the path. Nestling in his palm, it would shine just enough light to place his next footstep. I would not rush April on into the darkness ahead, but allow her to find secure footing in the one step He would illuminate each day.

**You don't have to "relive every ugly detail."** That would be to deny the work of the cross. We know from Isaiah 53 that the Suffering Servant "took up our infirmities and carried our sorrows . . . and by *his* wounds we are healed" (verses 4a and 5b, italics mine).

I shared with April a wise image from Sandra Skinner-Young, one of our staff counselors—that a traumatic memory is like a bushel of sour cherries. The molestation had been too much for April as a child to stomach, so God took the memory away. Now she was strong enough to face the pain. But not all of it, as Erick had insisted. By sampling only a few cherries, she could come to know their sticky texture and sour flavor. By sampling only a few memories and their corresponding feelings, she could step out of denial and experience the full bushel of God's comfort.

Perhaps Jesus would give her a big bagful of cherries to taste, or a small handful, or none at all. He would give her only what she could handle. Then, on the cross, He would "eat" the rest and suffer the ill effects for her.

April forgave Erick by increments. With each forgiveness and each repentance, Christ swallowed a few more sour cherries for her. Trust grew. The memories began to surface.

They came randomly, though in each session they seemed to weave themselves into a theme. Brief flashes, isolated snapshots of terror, placed side by side, told a gruesome story. I reminded her that she need not see any more than she could handle. But as she became accustomed, courage grew; she wanted to know more. Knowledge gave a sense of control. She realized that the monster you see in the light is not as scary as the one you imagine lurking in the dark. Still, to spare April undue pain, God revealed some of the scariest memories to me by vision, for which she expressed a deep and tearful witness.

Her Uncle Byron had molested her as revenge on her father for some unknown slight. She recalled his threat: "If you tell, I'll rape you in front of your mother, kill your parents and then you. Nobody will believe you anyway. They'll think you're crazy and lock you up." She felt overwhelmed. Inner rumblings foreshadowed a picture far worse than she had imagined. There was too much hurt, too much rage. How could she ever forgive?

**You don't have to feel forgiving.** Erick had taught April rightly that she was not a hypocrite for not feeling forgiving. Hypocrisy, she learned, is acting contrary to your beliefs, not your feelings. Saul tried to murder David for years. But each time David had an opportunity to kill Saul, he said instead, "I shall not touch the Lord's anointed," and he forgave. Yet all the while he was not afraid in the Psalms to admit outrage. Forgiveness is not the cessation of feeling. In that case it would depend on us. No, it is God's work, a gift of grace.

I have often used this word picture to explain it: Bitterness is like a splinter under the skin. Anger is like poison collecting around it. You can drain the poison, but if the splinter remains it will produce more. We extract the bitter root through prayer.

Afterward sometimes there is still anger to drain. But in the end there is no bitterness left to produce more. As Ephesians 4:26 says, "'In your anger do not sin: Do not let the sun go down while you are still angry, and do not give the devil a foothold." After a forgiving prayer, the original anger might resurface, this time requiring resolution. But it no longer has to continue indefinitely.

## April's Story Continued: The Process Unfolds

Before leaving Erick, and impatient with God's seeming lack of justice, April had fantasized a chilling plan. As he slept, she would pin him to the couch with a butcher knife and skin him alive, taking special delight in castrating him. Then she would remove all evidence, returning a few hours later to "discover" a mysterious murder.

But what if he didn't die? She panicked about how Erick might retaliate—and the fantasy shattered.

April found Erick's insight freeing that she was not a hypocrite for not *feeling* forgiving. But Erick's abuse had undone his wise word. "Like a thornbush in a drunkard's hand is a proverb in the mouth of a fool" (Proverbs 26:9). When a person opens up only to be crushed, he or she will be slow to open up again.

But April "white-knuckled it" and forced herself to open again to God. She knew the only real answer was forgiveness. "But I don't want to let him off the hook!"

*You're the one on the hook*, God seemed to answer. *You're the one I want off the hook.*

After tormented deliberations and a large slice of humble pie, she gritted her teeth and relented: "All right. I'll choose to be willing to be made willing to forgive Erick."

A still, small voice answered, *That's good enough.*

Eventually April ventured to pour her rage into prayer, or to a friend, or to the wind, and then forgive. At other times she forgave first. We did whatever seemed appropriate at the moment. Gradually the Lord freed her from having to mold her feelings to suit others. A demon of emotional stifling lost its stranglehold. With no shield of control to hide behind, it stood naked under God's scrutiny and fled.

April dreamed she was running frightened from strangers. They caught up, and a young, dark-haired man sprayed something into her face, sapping her energy. She lost her breath and gave up. Then she recognized him as a friendly person from her past. The young man spoke comfortingly: "She will rememeber when she can and as she can." No urgency.

I recognized the young man in April's dream as Jesus. In her heart of hearts she was getting reacquainted with this true Gentleman who, unlike Erick, stood at the door of her soul and knocked.

As counseling progressed, Satan's plan for April became apparent. Both Erick's and her uncle's abuse had been diabolically designed to repeat and reinforce her childhood trials, retrenching her in the dysfunctional family rules: *Always please others. Reflect well on the family. Always be in control. Yet relinquish control and privacy of thought, feeling and will to those who have power over you.* Thus stripped of proper defenses, April had learned time and again to wield whatever counterfeit armor she could muster.

*Snapshot:* Uncle Byron's clammy hands on her throat. Gasping, she thought, *I can't breathe*, but the words were trapped in her chest. Uncle Byron slapped her. Cold sting. A pillow across her face. "Don't make any noise." Blackness.

*Snapshot:* Erick taunting, teasing her to tears, so that he could comfort her. Then he could be the strong one, the hero.

*Snapshot:* Dad despising her tears. "Go to your room until you can stop being a crybaby."

For each memory now, tears were cherished. The child April was comforted and enabled to forgive. She dropped her shield-like inner vows: "I'll never lose control." "I won't be vulnerable." "I'll share my feelings with no one, since they will disrespect them."

After Erick had broken April down by invalidating her feelings, he took greater power, cornering and sexually conquering her frightened child.

Uncle Byron: "This is all women are good for. You had better get used to it."

Erick: "What are you good for?"

I had a disquieting prompting. "April, I know this is embarrassing, but do you abuse yourself with an object?"

"Yes," was the squeamish reply.

Erick had raped her with the handle of a hammer. By doing the same, her heart said others had been right to defile her. After healing prayers, she repented and promised to stop, ungirding her loins of that lie.

Jesus said that nothing going into a person defiles him; what comes out defiles (Mark 7:18–20). But April had believed the lie that she, the victim, was unclean. That lie had lodged especially deep when she felt abandoned to her uncle's torment.

*Why did Mommy and Daddy leave me at Uncle Byron's house?* she had asked herself. *I don't think they'll ever come back to get me. I'll be here for the rest of my life. Why is this happening? It must be because I'm a bad girl. I made this happen.*

April prayed, recognizing who was truly accountable, and took another step of forgiveness. Since she rejected the lie that she herself was to blame, the father of lies lost his hold. I rebuked a demon of defilement and it fled.

Still, much of April remained shattered. Her mom and dad had returned and she had felt relieved. But secretly she had told herself, *They don't love me. So I don't want to be with them.* Bonding was broken; then the disunity extended inward. She avoided feelings of shame by allowing Satan to drive a wedge between her and parts of herself she had come to identify as shameful.

God cleansed each part like a soiled quilt and stitched it back into the glory that was April. One part was her physical self. Erick had supposedly sent away a demon named "Abaddon," the destroyer. But Erick himself was a destroyer. So Abaddon continued to fracture the bond between April and her own body. Health problems abounded: heart problems, arthritis, headaches, sore joints, intense stomach pain, female problems.

When I sent Abaddon and several lesser demons of infirmity away, April began to heal. Her joints ached much less. Backaches and stomach pains subsided. Headaches ceased. PMS symptoms greatly decreased.

Her uncle's mocking had created ready compartments for those spirits to enter: "Don't you have beautiful hair?"—as he spat on it. "You are uglier than the dog____ on the bottom of my shoe." "I should fillet your face." "What do you think your father would think of his pretty little girl now?" He graphically and gleefully described gutting, drawing and quartering her, as he slid a knife-edge gingerly across her skin from part to part.

April had come to believe her uncle's words. She felt she was obliged to feel all the physical pain Abaddon dished out. But fearing it, she had become expert at shutting out pain. Her chiropractor later was shocked at the extreme tightness in her back and shoulders. April was shocked, too. She had not even realized her back was stiff!

On the way toward forgiveness, we again established accountability for the abuse with the defiler, not the defiled. She was accountable only for her own bitterness and the lies that gave Satan access: that her body was bad, that somehow she had brought it all on herself. We prayed that April could feel God's wholeness and blessing on each part, bestowing acceptance on head, stomach, legs, feet, hands, etc., as one would welcome back lost children.

April chose to be willing to be made willing to forgive. Satan lost his access. We rebuked a demon that caused her to feel as if she were floating in space, her spirit disconnected from the body she had so despised. She repented of a false shield against pain, an inner vow to no longer "be here" in this physical existence.

In a vision I saw her eyes occasionally dimming, even going blind for moments at a time. "Yes," she said, "for a period in my life, that really happened, though it has stopped." And April recalled Uncle Byron threatening to poke out her eyes with a knife. We sent away a demon of failing eyesight, and she received her eyes as a gift from the Creator. (See my father's discussion of "encapsulated" demons in chapter 2.)

April had become as divorced from her inner self as from her outer self. Memories surfaced revealing the reasons.

*Snapshot:* Her uncle calling her "Princess." "Whore." "Lousy little piece of trash." "No one will ever want you."

As the Lord revoked the power of those names and restored April's self-respect, she shed a breastplate of unworthiness. A demon of unworthiness fled and, with it, the phrases resounding through her head. Bit by bit she learned to cherish her very self—her beauty, femininity, intelligence; her crafts and creative cooking that she had neglected.

*Snapshot:* Uncle Byron kicking, chasing April: "Go ahead, leave." Then blocking the door.

*Snapshot:* Erick: "Oh, you can leave anytime you want, babe." Then tracking her down with ESP.

*Snapshot:* Mom reading her diary. Dad muttering something about "false modesty."

Inner healing gave April a voice. She learned to say, "No! None of those people had the right to trap or own me. I won't believe that anymore." She forgave Erick and Uncle Byron for enslaving her, and her parents for unknowingly teaching that they had a right to do it. God forgave the adult April for girding her loins with that lie. Satan lost another foothold.

Then I got a picture of a spirit of captivity, jaws agape, a snake large enough to swallow a man. She replied that she had often dreamed of that gigantic snake, watching her like a cornered mouse, waiting for opportunity to devour her. We sent away a "devouring" spirit, as April took another step to reclaim her will.

As present stresses no longer struck negative chords from the past, April's life came back into balance. She "reclaimed" her parents. Unlike Erick and Uncle Byron, Mom and Dad were not deliberately evil, just blind and dysfunctional. As much as they were able, they had truly loved her.

Now she recalled the hours spent in Dad's workshop where he had taught her eagerly about cars, electronics and gardening. He had shared with his children the wonders of nature and the dangers of rattlesnakes and poison oak. She had adored his sly grin and infectious humor.

Mom had loved being Mom. April remembered baking little pies as Mom baked big ones, and it didn't matter one bit if some fixings ended up on the floor. They made Christmas ornaments of glitter, glue and sequins—"the world's ugliest," she recalled with a laugh—but not to Mom, who displayed them with pride.

April was read to on a warm lap and taught how to can fruits and vegetables in a steamy kitchen.

Long ago little April had awakened to see two figures standing in the hallway. It was Mom and Dad. But no, their eyes glowed yellow. They had no feet; they hovered a few inches from the floor. She hurled a pillow at them. It went through them and hit the wall. She flung the covers over her head and curled into a tight ball, not daring to call out or even to breathe.

Now the memory of her parents was no longer overlaid with the image of those demons. They were just Mom and Dad, two aging children, broken and frail, like April.

But as the first light of memory flooded the darkness of that bedroom, April came to realize that the one she had feared most was that frail little girl. Slowly and tenderly God and I had pulled back the covers of shame. Now big April was meeting little April and they were fast becoming friends.

As I write, God paints a vision of little April. In the full light of day she stands unashamed bouncing a little pink ball. But snow begins to fall and soon the ground is covered, too soft to bounce her ball. So she runs to the top of a hill and rolls it down, watching it track through the white expanse. To her dismay, the ball collects snow and twigs and rocks as it rolls, growing bigger with each turn.

Little April runs down the hill after it. At the bottom there stands a great white globe, far taller than she. Somewhere deep inside is her beloved little pink ball. She digs until her fingers are red and numb, but the ball seems hopelessly lost. With darkness coming on and the temperature dropping, she gives up and trudges home without it.

Little April forgets that ball, but the sun does not. In the spring it warms the white globe. Layer by layer the snow melts, releasing rocks and twigs as it recedes. Bit by bit I see April's heart melt, and demons nestled between the layers cast away.

One day a woman named April strolls near a hillside.

In the grass, in a jumble of rocks and twigs, she spots a little pink ball. "Have I seen this before, a long time ago?" she asks. Suddenly she recognizes it, picks up the little ball and heaves a deep, shuddering sigh.

Faintly she hears a whisper from within: "I have suffered much; preserve my life, O Lord, according to your word" (Psalm 119:107).

Now at last April can sit in church without the urge to flee in tears. Her depression has lifted and anxiety diminished. She has regained confidence in her ability to discern God's voice. Once, as she sang a song of praise, she sensed God's hand on her shoulder. "It was," she said, "the strongest, most muscular arm in the universe." God's protective presence shines through intermittently, like sunlight when a cloud cover breaks.

## A Lesson to All

April's story is extreme, yet not unlike our own. "We all, like sheep, have gone astray, each of us has turned to his own way; and the Lord has laid on him the iniquity of us all" (Isaiah 53:6). It is not the depth of our wounding, but the depth of of our sinful response, that makes us Satan's prey. I have met many persons far less wounded who were far more bitter and demonized. April's story is for everyone; we are all at risk.

Erick's story is also for everyone. In my flesh I, too, am a tormentor. I can imagine myself meeting April for the first time. She briefly recounts her troubled life. "Stop," I say. "I don't need to hear anymore. Christ has already paid for that; it's all under the blood." I pray that she will forget and put it behind her. I tell her she needs only to praise the Lord that she is a new creature. After a heroic effort, she returns the following week with the same complaints. I scold her for lacking faith. And in this way I begin to demand that April live up to the perfection of the resurrected life without first walking with her to the cross.

But if I did this, I would be binding her to denial, and possibly to a breakdown and utter disillusionment in her Savior; while the cross, although already accomplished in our lives, is also a present reality. "By one sacrifice he has made perfect forever those who *are being made* holy" (Hebrews 10:14, italics mine). For those who die daily, resurrection is a daily blessing.

Or I can imagine myself attempting to deliver her of all her demons in one marathon session, with no process of in-depth healing and repentance. Again, she returns the following week with the same complaints. I accuse her that she is not standing in faith to keep her deliverance.

But for the grace of God. . . . I shudder to think of the harm I could have done. Lord, direct my paths.

For April, as for Jenny and Frank, becoming demonized was interwoven with the process of becoming wounded and trapped in bitterness. As I said earlier, the law teaches that in spite of April's predicament, she alone was responsible for the bitter roots. And it was her own false armor that gave the demons access. If I had made her face all her issues at once, she would have drowned in guilt and self-loathing; and Satan, armed with accusation, would have had a heyday.

If inner healing and deliverance meet at the armor, let's not give Satan a chance to meet us there, too. Deliverance is a process, proceeding at the Lord's gentle pace for repentance and healing.

The Prodigal Son, unlike April or us, had a perfect father. Yet even the Prodigal fell from grace. But when he returned, his father met him where he was and, without a hint of shame, restored him to more than his former place in the family of God. Let us do the same for all who are thus afflicted.

# 7

# The Do's and Don'ts of Deliverance

Sandy's eyes welled up with tears as she made her way to the front of the church. The speaker had shared gently how God heals the rejected and she was suspended between fear and hope.

Three years before, Sandy had remarried her husband of seven years, but had since learned that the candlelight and lace of a second ceremony was not enough to chase away the pain of rejection. Though Sandy and Jim had made up, he did not know how to talk with her about her pain, so it lingered. Old wounds still bled. Until they healed, her heart could not open to her husband again. Maybe tonight she would find an answer.

When the speaker and his wife laid their hands on her, and they and several others prayed in tongues, Sandy flinched. No one had ever prayed for her this way before. Standing in fear, it was all she could do to stay and submit.

That night she sensed God's presence and felt a little relieved. But she needed more. She had heard that the speaker and his wife would be ministering something called deliverance at a couple's home nearby. Unaware that this meant deliverance from demons, she had taken it to mean freedom from troubles, and expected their prayer to relieve her pain and help her forgive her husband.

The couple's schedule was full all week, she learned, but they would contact her in the event of a cancellation. That would be the sign, she felt, that God was opening the door for her to go.

There *was* a cancellation. But when she arrived, the couple, with no exploratory questions or explanations, immediately rebuked a spirit of fear, which promptly knocked Sandy to the floor. Terrified to think she might be inhabited, Sandy began to cry. Fortunately, rather than start bellowing at the demons, the couple spoke quietly. They lifted her onto the chair and resumed praying against the spirit of fear.

The fact was, Sandy was afraid of deliverance itself. But since they had asked no questions, the couple viewed her terrified look as another manifestation of the demon. Sandy left the house dazed.

That night she was awakened by mocking laughter. Hideous voices taunted, *You belong to us now.* She lay scared and motionless beside Jim. She wanted his protection but could not risk asking for it. He was not even a Christian. But she did not know how to send the demons away. So she lay like a cowering child cornered by bullies in a schoolyard.

The following day Sandy made a frantic phone call and was relieved to discover that the couple was still in town and would be all week. She returned, exhausted, for another appointment, hoping the couple would chase the bullies away.

Rather than command the voices to cease, however, they seemed almost gratified to learn of them. While they did pursue her tormenters, they required manifestations as signs that further deliverance was needed. Later it seemed to Sandy that the voices had added some excitement to the chase for her deliverers, at her expense.

The couple commanded the demons, using Sandy's voice, to name themselves. They urged her to cough the demons out and told her not to be afraid to vomit. Once again the demons knocked her to the floor and tossed her about. The couple also questioned her about her husband. When they discovered Jim was not a Christian, they warned her not to tell him of the day's events—advice she later regretted.

That night Sandy could not eat. Her stomach began to cramp. She became nauseated and suffered a bout of diarrhea. The voices returned worse than before. She was afraid to return for another session, but she was more afraid not to return. Who else could stop the terrifying voices?

So the next day she dragged herself to a third deliverance session, feeling more drained than before. The couple looked for more manifestations and got them.

Sandy returned twice more. Each time the manifestations continued. Each time she lost more control of both body and mind. And at night the voices and physical nausea grew worse.

By the last day she felt utterly crushed and confused. Like a child who submits trustfully to abusive parents, she had submitted to the couple, suppressing doubts and ignoring her pain. Now, weakened by torment and lack of sleep, her pent-up rage fused with the fury of the demons and she exploded at the deliverance team. It took two men to hold her down. The couple rightly saw the angry demons in her, but not the angry and hurting child. They ignored her deep wounding and continued to rebuke the demons.

Although at Elijah House we teach that sin gives demons access, we also make it clear to our counselees that a demon is not a part of them. When we rebuke demons, then, counselees don't feel we are chastising *them*.

Sandy's deliverers explained that distinction to her. But by requiring manifestations, they undid their own efforts, giving Satan so much opportunity to display his power that Sandy could not separate her own thoughts and feelings from his.

This could have been avoided if the ministry team had made Sandy, rather than her demons, the focus of their efforts. Fascination with demonic fireworks distracted them from seeing her heart. When they discussed the demons, they often spoke as if she was not even present. At one point, as the minister stared intently into her eyes, he cursed a demon: "You pig, come out of her!" He did not know that Sandy's childhood schoolmates had called her by that name. But if he had truly seen her, he would have seen the shame his words elicited.

"There is something lustful in you," he said at another point. In response, her body manifested an alluring posture. To this day Sandy is unsure whether a demon was truly manifesting or whether she was merely complying, doing what was expected. The couple gave no explanation as to why lust was there, nor did they ask any probing questions to find out.

Sandy struggled to keep her composure, barely concealing fear and guilt behind a red face. *Lust? I didn't know there was any.* She shuddered at what other hidden sins might lurk inside her. No one noticed her anxious look. They had their sights set on their prey. Years later Sandy would still find it difficult to dress fashionably or put on makeup without feeling dirty and questioning her own motives.

On the night after her last deliverance session, she lay in bed in a stupor, hardly able to sort out the week's trials. The cramping in her stomach was almost unbearable.

*I thought God told me to go to those people. But that wasn't God's work. Or was it? Or is there something wrong with me that kept me from receiving from them?*

Sandy could no longer trust her own discernment. Could she even distinguish God's voice from Satan's? They seemed equally punishing. And how could she tell where she ended and Satan began?

A few years before, desperate for help but unaware of the Gospel, she had prayed, "Whoever needs to come into my life, please do it." Our dear Lord had obliged, after which He had led her to others who explained the meaning of the born-again experience.

Now a vision came to Sandy in which she saw herself asking that question. But it was Satan who answered. He caused a black cloud to enter her, then said, "You are an angel of light." He was attempting to rewrite history in order to steal not only the healing Sandy had sought from the deliverance team, but any assurance of God's grace.

The following morning she called the ministry team, who were preparing to leave the area. They prayed at length with her and advised her to praise the Lord as a weapon of faith. Then they went on their way, leaving her in the care of the couple whose house they had used.

As Sandy praised God, the physical symptoms stopped. But emotionally she was still in a quandary, wondering what she had done wrong, whether she could ever again trust her own discernment, whether she had ever really been saved.

For two years Sandy wandered in a haze. Terrified of demons, she thought she saw them in everyone and everything. She felt cut off from God. And for a while, whenever she attempted to read the Bible, the cramping returned.

Sandy was later to describe her week with the ministry team as "spiritual rape." She had come to the couple in fear. But as they tried to cast out the spirit of fear, they subjected her to the fright of her life. This gave the demon opportunity to return with its entourage. By insisting on demonic manifestations, the couple had left her less able to resist.

Then, at an Elijah House seminar, Sandy felt drawn to John and Paula by their gentle manner. And she found wise counsel through "Fletch" and Betty Fletcher, who were doing prayer ministry. As they helped her peel away layers of pain and bitterness, they became "Mom and Dad" to her. They dealt with the issue of Jim's former rejection, the emotional shock of the week of deliverance, and the childhood memories that had made her especially vulnerable to these traumas.

In one session, Betty held her and prayed tenderly in the Spirit. Sandy saw the vision again. But this time when she asked, "Whoever needs to come into my life, please do it," Jesus came to her in a special way.

Sandy knew as an adult that she was saved. She knew her beliefs could not rest on visions and supernatural experiences. But the child inside had a hard time connecting what her head knew with the fear in her heart.

Jesus went the extra mile for Sandy and reaffirmed His written Word. In a vision she became a small child. He picked her up, banished the black cloud, threw back His head and let out a gleeful laugh. Sandy saw it was a joy to Him to free her from the dark powers. As she basked in a shower of His joy, Jesus showed her His nail scars and banished forever her fear of not being saved.

The ministry team that first "delivered" Sandy were, unlike Erick in the last chapter, truly attempting to do God's work. Both Sandy and the couple in whose care she was left have since come to a more balanced understanding of deliverance. But Proverbs 19:2 warns, "It is not good to have zeal without knowledge, nor to be hasty and miss the way."

God can heal anything. But lest others miss the way, here are two scriptural rules of thumb for deliverance ministry that reiterate and develop some of what Dad said in chapter 2, followed by some general do's and don'ts.

## Rule #1: Do Not Give Satan a Stage

It is true that Scripture often speaks of noisy, action-packed exorcisms. When Philip cast out demons in Samaria, they came out "shouting with a loud voice" (Acts 8:7, NASB). Jesus often encountered fitful demons, as when He delivered the man at the synagogue at Capernaum: "And throwing him into convulsions, the unclean spirit cried out with a loud voice, and came out of him" (Mark 1:26, NASB).

But nowhere does Scripture make this a necessary evidence of ministry.

### Do Not Require a Manifestation

Most deliverance passages mention no manifestations at all. (This is not to say that none occurred; only that if they did, they were not recorded.) About the girl delivered from a spirit of divination, we read simply that "it came out" (Acts 16:18, NASB). In the healing of the dumb man, the only recorded sign of the demons' leaving was that the man could now speak (Matthew 9:33).

In the case of the boy suffering epileptic fits, Matthew 17:18 mentions no manifestation, while the corresponding account in Mark 9:26 does: "And after crying out and throwing him into terrible convulsions, it came out" (NASB). But even here Jesus downplayed the manifestation. The spirit had seen Him coming and knew it would soon lose its host. In a last-ditch effort to draw attention to itself, it "threw him into a convulsion, and falling to the ground, he began rolling about and foaming at the mouth" (verse 20, NASB). When Jesus saw that a crowd was beginning to gather (verse 25), He cast out the demon quickly lest it gain a larger audience.

In Sandy's case the prayer ministers, by insisting on manifestations, encouraged demons to frighten her. They were so fascinated that Sandy became almost incidental. After that, until she met Fletch and Betty, her picture of God was smaller than her picture of Satan, as if Satan had more power. When we grant Satan a stage, he is adept at creating that illusion.

At Elijah House we probably see fewer and milder manifestations during deliverance than most ministries, for the following reason: Repentance enacted through inner healing robs demons of their power. Disconnected from their energy source, they often come out with a whimper instead of a bang. By not insisting on manifestations, we provide them no megaphone by which to amplify their dying cries.

If our focus is truly on God, not demons, we should find the whimper more thrilling than the bang!

### Do Not Converse with Demons

Demons love to draw attention to themselves. When I was still in school, some friends tried to deliver a man involved in sexual perversion. Ignorant of scriptural principles, they foolishly engaged a demon in lengthy conversation. It stalled for time by lamenting (through the man's voice) that it yearned to get back to heaven, if only there was forgiveness for such a fallen creature. My friends promised to pray for its salvation, if it would promise to leave. In the end it only faked an exit.

My friends would have spared themselves a fruitless evening if they had remembered there is no repentance for fallen angels (2 Peter 2:4). Nor is there any scriptural allowance for bargaining with demons. We are not to *ask* them to leave; we are to *command* them. That is why the demon only pretended to vacate its host.

Most important, my friends should not have been conversing with demons at all. Nowhere in Scripture does any minister of

God ever talk with a demon. In fact, Jesus invariably shut them up. Demons often tried to disrupt Jesus' perfect timing to reveal Himself as the Messiah by announcing it prematurely. So Mark 1:34 states, "He would not let the demons speak because they knew who he was."

In Acts 16:17 the girl with a spirit of divination followed Paul and Silas shouting, "These men are servants of the Most High God, who are telling you the way to be saved." No demon wishes to proclaim the Gospel! This one was actually trying to water it down. In the Greek text, the demon's word is *a* way of salvation, not *the* [exclusive] way—a handy heresy in a polytheistic culture. So Paul cast the demon out.

Demons have no wisdom to offer us. One who encourages demons to speak invites them to disrupt God's plans.

### *Do Not Curse Demons*

To curse a demon can be counterproductive, as Sandy discovered. When the ministry team leader looked into her eyes and called the demon a pig, it served only to heap shame on her.

Even if the cursing does not harm the person, it is still wrong. We often hear of deliverance ministers scourging demons with words like these: "I know who you are, you wretched, vile creature. You may have tormented this child of God for a season, but just remember, your torment will be much worse when you burn in the fires of hell."

It all sounds so spiritual, except that Scripture prohibits such railing. 2 Peter 2:10–11 forbids us to "slander celestial beings," warning that even angels are constrained from doing so. Jude offers the same caution and provides an alternative: "Even the archangel Michael, when he was disputing with the devil about the body of Moses, did not dare to bring a slanderous accusation against him, but said, 'The Lord rebuke you!'" (verse 9).

God's Word lists no reasons for the prohibition, but I would venture two. First, reviling demons fosters the very hatred on which they feed. Second, it puts the focus on demons rather than on God and demons simply do not deserve that much attention. We would do well to copy the ministers of Scripture and spend our time praising God. A simple rebuke will suffice.

## Do Not Command Demons To Name Themselves

It is understandable that Sandy's deliverance ministers and many others have taken Jesus' question while ministering to the Gadarene demoniac—"What is your name?" (Mark 5:9)—as a precedent. It seems obvious.

But they do it mistakenly. As Dad pointed out in his discussion of this passage in chapter 2, the Greek text shows that Jesus directed His question not at the demons (which would have required the plural *your*) but at the man (with a singular *your*). This eliminates the only possible scriptural precedent for asking a demon to name itself.

Besides, why would we expect demons to tell us the truth about themselves? They are liars by nature (see John 8:44). If we want to know their names, how they found entrance or anything else about them, we do well to consult the Holy Spirit.

Some might protest that they have commanded demons to name themselves and real deliverance has resulted. They might point out that "Legion" did, in fact, rightly name itself.

Wrong! In the Greek of both Gospels, it was the man ("he") who answered, "My name is Legion." At this point some might object that in Mark 5:8 the "evil spirit" was in fact singular. So couldn't the "he" in question have been the evil spirit? The answer is that wherever the pronoun "he" or "him" is found prior to this, it refers to the man, not the demons.

That means that either the man had confused his own identity with that of the demons, or else he was being forced by the ruling demon (as my father suggested in chapter 2) to speak as their mouthpiece. In either case, Jesus had asked for the man's own name; "Legion" was a lying answer.

Even if the practices of some are not quite sound theologically, God can keep us from botching His work. He is in control and has the power to coerce demons to name themselves. But if we know better, we should take heed. Demons will create enough ruckus on their own. They don't need another excuse to show off their puppet tricks through the bodies or voices of hurting souls.

## Rule# 2: Make Relationship Your First Priority of Ministry

Relationship is something Jesus wants from us that He does not want from demons. For this reason, Jesus always silenced demons but never their victims. God is so interested in relationship, in fact, that He insists we tell Him what He already knows: "You do not have, because you do not ask God" (James 4:2). The context following this verse suggests that asking God is part of what it means to submit to God, and that by so doing, we will "resist the devil, and he will flee from you" (verse 7).

When Jesus met the Gadarene demoniac, His concern was not for the demons but for the man. By asking him his name, Jesus was (as Dad already suggested) giving him a simple reality test. It was also the only attempt at establishing relationship that the demoniac could have understood. But even if he did not understand, the crowd would have. It must have been years since any of them had spoken to this man on his own terms! Thus, Jesus encouraged them to receive him anew with respect as a man and not the weird alien most of them thought him to be.

Healing always begins by establishing relationship. It ends with restored relationships. When Jesus met a man whose demonized son had suffered epileptic fits from birth (Mark 9:14–29), He could have chosen to cast it out immediately but did not.

The father must have been disheartened after years of watching his child suffer. When Jesus' disciples could not cast out the demon, his discouragement probably deepened. So before delivering the boy Jesus asked the man, "How long has he been like this?"

"From childhood. It has often thrown him into the fire or water to kill him. But if you can do anything, take pity on us and help us."

Jesus knew He was dealing not only with a boy's demon, but with a father's attitude toward God. So He answered, "If you can? Everything is possible for him who believes."

As if embarrassed that his words had revealed his doubts, the father blurted out, "I do believe." At the same moment, compelled by conscience to be fully truthful, he added, "Help me overcome my unbelief!"

Jesus then cast the spirit out of the boy. To make up for the father's admitted lack of faith, He commanded it never to return. This cleared up any possibility in the father's mind that his lack of faith could undo God's work.

Thus, the father found a relationship with a God who requires faithfulness, yet sympathizes with our weaknesses and wants to come close to us. I can imagine the father holding his son, weeping and feeling closer to him than ever. His son had been healed and he, too, had been delivered from his own kind of infirmity.

### *Begin with an Interview*

Not all deliverance needs to be done in the context of ongoing inner healing. But some kind of rapport needs to be established first.

Sandy's ministers did not do this. Their primary purpose was to contend with demons; Sandy herself felt like a pawn.

It is a pity the couple did not ask her a few opening questions on the night she first came forward. Like the father of the epileptic, she might have revealed secret doubts, and the couple might have had a chance to respond as Jesus had. If only they had noticed her body language (her trembling, her downcast eyes), they could have asked her what was wrong. She might have told them that having hands laid on her and being prayed over in tongues was new and frightening. They might have learned that Sandy needed to be approached with more care.

The couple missed another opportunity at the beginning of the first deliverance session, when they had more time. If they had asked her what she needed from them, they would have found that she was not expecting deliverance; indeed, that she did not even know what the word meant. More thorough teaching might have kept her fear of deliverance from compounding the fear and hurt for which she sought healing.

Since the ministering couple did not establish a relationship with Sandy through an interview, they continued to miss her heart throughout the remaining sessions. They did not attune their senses to where she was emotionally and failed to see her fear of the demons that had bullied her the previous night.

Instead, in the thrill of the chase, they ran roughshod over her fears. Even when they looked directly into her eyes, they did not catch Sandy's response of shame when they called her demon a pig. When they identified a demon of lust, they could not read the puzzlement and guilt etched on her face, and did not think to offer her an explanation.

When Sandy's inner child, hurt by their insensitivity, finally reacted in rage, the couple heard only demons shouting through her. When they pinned that child, with the demons, to the floor, they unwittingly bound her over to her tormentors. No wonder the demons returned (if they had ever left)! No wonder Sandy came to believe that her original prayer for salvation had been answered by Satan, for the couple had unknowingly protrayed God also as a tormentor.

## *Be Yourself, and Appropriate to the Person*

God does not bypass human personality. Every book in the Bible is colored by the character of its writer. We can hardly miss the passion of David, the sternness of James, the energy of Paul, the scholarly wisdom of Luke, the compassionate, mystical nature of John. Each wrote in the style, vocabulary and images of his own personality and culture.

The Gospel has always been enacted in ways appropriate to individual hearts. Jesus drove the moneychangers out of the Temple with whips, and called the haughty Pharisees "whitewashed tombs." But to the woman caught in adultery, frightened and ashamed, He said gently, "Neither do I condemn you. Go now and leave your life of sin" (see John 8:11).

God meets us on our own terms through very human ministers acting (naturally!) like themselves. Jesus came to earth in human flesh. We have nothing to fear from acting in a human way.

Yet many think they must act differently, even weirdly, as though this indicates they are being "spiritual."

I heard a man give a talk in a normal conversational tone, using natural gestures. But as soon as he began to do deliverance he shouted in a quavering voice. As he laid his hands on a girl to pray, he shook her so violently I wondered if she would keep her balance. She became ill at ease, but the man didn't seem to notice. As he thundered at the demons, railing on in King James English, accenting each exclamation with a shuddering spasm throughout his body, she jumped and her eyes flashed in fear.

"Why?" I mused. "Aren't his natural body stance and daily language spiritual enough?"

Strange posturing and vocalizations do not draw people toward God; they separate them from Him. Viewers infer that God is not part of their daily routine. It is as if they must enter another galaxy to find Him when, in fact, God and His servants are accommodating. "I have become all things to all men," wrote the apostle Paul, "so that by all possible means I might save some" (1 Corinthians 9:22).

For that reason I will not shout as I pray over a timid person. I will refrain from shaking when I lay hands on someone reserved. I will not use evangelical cliches when ministering to an intellectual, nor King James English to street kids. And I will spend enough time with each individual to discern how he or she needs to be met.

At the same time, without compromising tact and diplomacy, I will be myself, talk like myself and pray the way I talk.

## Do Not Idolize Methods

There are times when God really does cause people to tremble as they pray. Sometimes God's Spirit does prompt us to shout or do things we would not normally do.

But when we enshrine those experiences, we begin to miss God's purpose for the person. We think that if a technique worked once, it will work again. Maybe Sandy's deliverance ministers prayed aloud in tongues over another individual and it bore good fruit. But it was inappropriate for her and caused her to freeze in fear.

Once, at the start of a counselee's initial session, I was prompted to share with him that he was demonized. It served to establish instant rapport. He said he had known for a long time that he had demons and was relieved that at last someone believed him.

Feeling high on the success of the moment, I decided that this must be the way to minister. I enshrined the approach of being candid and up-front. Soon after, a woman brought her twelve-year-old daughter for counseling. Although (as I discovered later) they had no prior teaching on demons and deliverance, I informed them immediately that the girl was demonized. They sat polite but nervous through the remainder of the session. As they left, I watched them through the window. Stepping into their car, they glanced at each other with expressions that said, "Boy, was that weird!"

They never returned, and I don't blame them. I had no right to expect them to worship the idol I had created.

There are several deliverance methods the Body of Christ has enshrined. Some can hinder relationship; others are just not always necessary. Let's look at a few.

### Shouting at Demons

One method that can sometimes be hurtful is the practice of shouting at demons. Rightly asserting authority over demons is not measured in decibels, but by the character of Christ as He shines through the speaker.

Scripture does not say that Christ always spoke to demons in a raised voice, nor that He always spoke to them quietly. In the story of the epileptic boy we looked at earlier, when He rebuked the demon quickly before a large crowd gathered (Mark 9:25), it stands to reason that He would have spoken quietly, lest he seem to beckon the crowd.

Sometimes a raised voice is appropriate. With Anne I felt prompted to rebuke a tormenting spirit loudly. She smiled and remarked later how healing it had been to hear that. All during her childhood her older brothers had teased her mercilessly. She thought that by loathing herself, she could get them to take pity and back off. But this piece of faulty armor only invited more attack from her brothers. It had given the tormenting spirit a target as well. Anne had always wished that someone would really tell them all off, and finally someone had!

Jay responded differently. He came for counseling because his conscience weighed too heavily on him. He had no tolerance for his own mistakes. For every mishap on the job or the slightest faux pas, he could not keep from berating himself with names like *stupid*, *idiot* or *numbskull*. I discerned that a demon of self-condemnation was joining him in that effort, and proceeded to rebuke it in a normal tone of voice.

But as I added some forcefulness Jay cringed slightly. When I asked him why, he said it reminded him of his father, who used to thunder all the names Jay was now calling himself. I saw that Jay had put on a faulty breastplate, thinking he could force himself into being righteous by treating himself as his father had. I did not wish to repeat the abuse. So I rebuked the demon again in a less threatening voice. Then, prompted by the Holy Spirit, I asked Jay if he himself would be willing to rebuke it loudly and sternly. He did. By so doing, he gained a voice of his own and knocked the wind out of Satan.

No matter how softly it is spoken, Christ's name carries enough authority to make demons cringe. We need not yell ourselves hoarse as a habitual approach. Unless the Holy Spirit prescribes it, it will make no difference. Demons have no eardrums. The authority Jesus Christ has over Satan does not depend on sound-waves.

### Being Vocal or Silent Before Demons

For that same reason I disagree with those who insist that we must always bind demons vocally. There are times I have worked with people who were not ready to deal with the sins their demons fed on, nor even to believe that the demons existed. At the time, then, I could not bind them aloud. But I needed to get the demons out of the way so the people could be free to respond to counsel. So for the time I bound them silently.

Some hold that this was ineffective because the demons could neither hear me nor read my mind. Others say that we are safe from demons so long as we keep our mouths shut. If we disclose personal information to someone else, the demons will learn about it as well. These people make it a practice not to reveal anything about themselves to those who come to them for deliverance. They figure that if the demons don't know anything about their spouses, children, homes, daily lives, etc., they won't know how to attack.

This is a deception that stands in the way of establishing rapport with counselees and preventing them from hearing the wisdom we have gained from our struggles.

Just what do demons hear? Jesus made it clear in a rebuke to the Pharisees:

> Why is my language not clear to you? Because you are unable to hear what I say. You belong to your father, the devil, and you want to carry out your father's desire. He was a murderer from the beginning, not holding to the truth, for there is no truth in him. When he lies, he speaks his native language, for he is a liar and the father of lies.
>
> John 8:43–44

What demons hear is lies. Truth is a language they do not understand. I take Colossians 3:3 literally: "For you died, and your life is now hidden with Christ in God." If we walk in truth, our thoughts are hidden, and even our spoken words, for demons cannot understand truth. In another country where no one speaks our language, we can say anything in front of anybody and not worry. Similarly, in the face of our spiritual enemy, we need not be frightened into silence.

Colossians 3:5 goes on to say, "Put to death, therefore, whatever belongs to your earthly nature." If we continue to walk in the lies of our former nature, demons can hear and understand those lies, even if we live our lives in silence.

The only truth demons hear and understand is that the name of Jesus is invincible. Many Christians have reported being attacked at night in their beds by suffocating spirits. Prevented from calling out, they rebuked them silently and the demons fled. In the majority of cases, of course, we do rebuke aloud. But with or without sound waves, their spirit ears hear and they flee.

There are five other practices some insist on as a matter of course: that we always bind the demons before casting them out; that we pray against any possibility of transference of demons from one person to another; that we refrain from laying on of hands; that we command the demons, when we cast them out, to go to the pit; and that we command them never to return.

Are such practices biblical? We do well to avoid any ritual that detracts from the flow of the Spirit and from communion with the hearts of those for whom we pray. Let's look at each of the practices in turn.

### Binding Before Casting Out

Should we be careful to bind demons before sending them away? Matthew 12:29 and Mark 3:27 say that no one can enter a strong man's house unless he first "binds" or ties up (from the Greek *deo*) the strong man. Luke 11:22 uses a synonymous Greek term, *nikao*, meaning "to attack and overpower" or "to have victory over."

None of these references identifies casting out as the second step in the process. Nor is there any instance in Scripture where Jesus or His disciples followed a two-step method. Since casting out implies "having victory over," it follows that casting out constitutes binding, that the two are one and the same.

There is, however, a kind of binding (aside from casting out) that is biblical. When Jesus commanded demons to be silent before He cast them out (e.g., Luke 4:35), He was commanding them to stop a particular action that might hinder deliverance. In persons not yet ready for deliverance, I have found it helpful to bind demons ahead of time. Commanding demons to cease from their activities makes it easier for people to face the sin that has given the demons access. Repenting of the sin, in turn, causes the deliverance to hold.

Others are ready for deliverance. For them, binding beforehand is an unnecessary formality.

I have found this approach to bear good fruit. Some prefer to bind *every* time beforehand, and with mostly good fruit. The only bad fruit comes when some insist that their method be written in stone, and condemn those who disagree as heretical.

### Binding Spirits in Order to Avoid Transferences

Should we pray against the transference of spirits? Although there are no scriptural examples, Luke 11 says that a demon will sometimes try to return to its original host. It can just as easily find another host. I have seen this occur in a number of instances.

Since Scripture does not mandate a routine prayer to guard against transference, it is up to the individual. In any case, we ought to be aware when the Spirit prompts us to pray this way. And there is no harm in making it routine, if it is not done in fear.

I knew a man who rebuked the transference of spirits whenever he came in contact with a "suspicious" character. Soon his life was filled with suspicious characters, and he was afraid even to open his mail before rebuking spirits that might transfer from the writer!

One church allowed only the elders to pray over its people for fear of transference. This fostered an elitism that took deliverance out of the hands of the laity, while the Lord mandated it as a ministry for all (Mark 16:17).

In both cases, relationship was hindered.

### Prohibiting Laying On of Hands

Some believe we should refrain from the laying on of hands during deliverance, in order to prevent transference of demons. But demons can easily traverse an interpersonal space of a few feet. It is not touch that gives them access; it is unrepented sin.

Wholesome touch is not sinful. Jesus laid hands on the woman crippled by a spirit for eighteen years (Luke 13:13).

Once again, we should be aware of the Spirit's leading in each case. But to forbid the laying on of hands as a rule would be to close another door to relationship.

### Sending Demons to the Pit

This is clearly unbiblical. In Matthew 25:41, Jesus said that demons will not go to hell until He Himself dispatches them at the final judgment. He never sent demons to the pit. When we exorcise one, "it goes through arid places seeking rest and does not find it" (Luke 11:24). Even when "Legion" feared being cast immediately into torment, "and they begged him repeatedly not to order them to go into the Abyss" (Luke 8:31), Jesus consented to send them instead into a herd of swine.

It might not hurt to order demons to the pit; they will simply go to dry places. This represents the mild distraction of an extra bit of unnecessary methodology. But it might puff up our egos to take to ourselves a power that is Christ's alone.

### Commanding Demons Never to Return

There is only one instance of this in Scripture, where Jesus cast the deaf and dumb spirit out of the epileptic boy (Mark 9:25). In that case, as we said earlier, He seemed to be bolstering the faith of the boy's father, who had confessed his unbelief.

In no other case did Jesus or anyone pray this way. Indeed, it would seem pointless, for if sin is not repented of, the demon will return no matter what we command.

## Discover Your Own Gift

Where Scripture mandates a particular procedure, we must always follow it. Where it does not, we should follow the Spirit's leading. Otherwise we can become overly careful about procedures, which is not conducive to attuning ourselves to the Holy Spirit and to the heart of the individual.

This is also true of the gift of discernment of spirits. Some watch how others discern spirits and try to copy them, as though their methods had scriptural precedent, while the Bible sets forth no specific way in which spirits must be discerned. Following others slavishly can detract from our own relationship with God, who does not speak to everyone in the same way.

In the absence of a strict scriptural precedent, each should strive to discover the unique ways the Spirit chooses to speak to him or her, which may be different at different times.

When a demon is present, I sometimes feel a sudden pressure or discomfort around me. Sometimes I see a vision (though not usually with my physical eyes). Sometimes that vision relates to something in the person's memory.

As I was praying for one woman, I "saw" a demon cracking eggs over her head. This seemed too silly to mention, but in obedience to the Holy Spirit I did. She responded that in her childhood, her sister would often tease her by cracking eggs over her head—a small reminder of the much larger picture of abuse and molestation she had suffered from others. The demon did not break literal eggs, of course, but it was a metaphor for the shame it continued to heap upon her as an adult.

Sometimes I feel in my body the same psychosomatic symptom the demon has produced in its host. With one woman, I felt a mild pain in my stomach, which she confirmed as her own, and which I discerned as a spirit of hostility. (There is a reason we say sometimes that we cannot "stomach" someone!) When I cast the demon out, my pain—and hers—ceased immediately.

Or I simply "know," through the gift of the Holy Spirit, about a person's psychosomatic symptom. I was talking with a boy about his mother's haranguing. Suddenly I knew there were times that his physical hearing shut off. He actually experienced minute-long periods of full deafness. This sounded weird to me, but I shared it. The boy affirmed that, yes, this did happen. I sent away a demon of deafness and took the opportunity to deal with his anger toward his mother, which he had been suppressing, along with the sound of her nagging voice, under a false helmet of denial.

At other times I simply know that a demon is present and I send it away. Or I feel the emotion it plays upon in its host, whether hate, anger, envy or whatever.

There are many avenues for discernment. My brother Loren says he often feels the hair on his body stand on end and a righteous anger rising in him toward the demon. Carol Brown, an Elijah House staff member, says that in the presence of demons she feels defiled and unclean or dizzy. Sandra Skinner-Young, one of our counselors, feels a force rush against her face, or a dizziness. Others say they feel a whirling sensation.

I could go on. Each one experiences the gift in his or her own way.

## The Sum of the Matter: Will We Be Healers or "Mechanics"?

A pediatrician told me once he detested the kind of doctors he dubbed "body mechanics." From his days in medical school, he recalled overhearing conversations between doctors who referred to patients as "this 42-year-old gall bladder" or "this 37-year-old spleen," sometimes while the patient listened, feeling about as significant as a throat culture in a Petri dish. These doctors, he sputtered, were not in the business of healing people. They were in the business of fixing bodies.

The couple who ministered to Sandy were acting like "soul mechanics." They were there to fix a problem, not heal a person. So Sandy felt less significant than her problem.

The story of Sandy's "deliverance" is a recent twist on that quintessential tale of problem-solving therapy gone sour—the book of Job. Like Sandy, Job had been crushed by misfortune. His livestock had been destroyed. Most of his servants had been killed. His sons and daughters had been feasting when a strong wind collapsed the house on them, killing them all. Finally Job himself was struck with painful sores from head to toe.

When Job's friends Eliphaz, Bildad, Zophar and Elihu came to comfort him and Job poured out his heart—"Why did I not perish at birth, and die as I came from the womb?" (3:11)—it should have been obvious that this was no time to offer advice. When a man is a suicidal morass of rampaging emotion, he possesses little strength with which to follow advice. But being "soul mechanics," they missed the cry of Job's heart and saw only a couple of problems to be solved.

Problem #1: Job was being much too emotional. They had to get him to use his thinker.

Eliphaz: "If someone ventures a word with you, will you be impatient? [Modern translation: "Stop your blubbering and listen to me!"] Think how you have instructed many, how you have strengthened feeble hands. . . . But now trouble comes to you, and you are discouraged" (4:2, 5).

Bildad: "When will you end these speeches? Be sensible, and then we can talk" (18:2).

Job: "What strength do I have, that I should still hope? What prospects, that I should be patient? Do I have any power to help myself . . .?" (6:11, 13).

Ministering couple: "Don't bother us with your emotions, Sandy. We've got a job to do."

Problem #2: What has Job done to bring this on himself?

Eliphaz: "Who, being innocent, has ever perished? Where were the upright ever destroyed? As I have observed, those who plow evil and those who sow trouble reap it" (4:7–8).

When we are more interested in fixing problems than in healing people, sometimes we, like Eliphaz, answer our own questions. When "me, myself and I" have already discussed and drawn our conclusions, a Job can feel positively ganged up on.

Job's response: "If you say, 'How we will hound him, since the root of the trouble lies in him,' you should fear the sword yourselves; for wrath will bring punishment by the sword, and then you will know that there is judgment" (19:28–29).

In our own search for the "roots of the trouble," we who do inner healing can also be soul mechanics. Margie asked Gladys to pray for her; she had been struck on the head and robbed the night before. This was even more traumatic since she had been raped one year prior.

"Tell me about your childhood," Gladys said. "Did your father abuse you?"

"Yes," Margie answered falteringly. Tears began to flow.

Anticipating comfort, she began to melt into Gladys, but was stunned by her reply: "I wonder if you have made a bitter root judgment toward your father that causes you to expect men to abuse you."

Margie backed off and began to panic inside. *Did I cause those men to rape and rob me?* she thought.

But Gladys ignored her startled look. She was already praying to root out that expectation. She also prayed prayers of comfort and healing. But Margie couldn't hear them. She was too busy listening to a little girl inside mulling over the ancient question "What did I do to make Daddy hit me so hard?"

If Gladys had tarried a little longer in conversation, she might have discovered that Margie's bitter root expectation was not that she would be abused. It was, rather, that whenever she was abused, it was her fault. Margie's bad fruit was not repeated victimization, any more than it had been for Job. Rather, it was shame, and Gladys was heaping more on her!

Are we, like Gladys and Eliphaz, interested only in finding roots? Or are we concerned with healing people?

Except for young Elihu, who truly understood, Job was a far better counselor than his friends. He discerned their motives well: "Now you too have proved to be of no help; you see something dreadful and are afraid" (6:21). What were Job's comforters afraid of? *At least of not having the correct solution to his problems.* Whether in inner healing or deliverance, thinking it is up to us to "fix it" can put us in a scary position.

And fear can make us do strange things—like trying so hard to fix our brother's problem that we miss the obvious look of pain on his face or his need to talk it out. Like being so hungry for power that we must "wow" people with bizarre manifestations or railing curses or discourses with demons. Like trying so hard to impress God that we become afraid to be ourselves when we minister. Like wanting so much to do it right that we ritualize healing or try to copy someone else's gift. Like striving so hard to please God that we run ahead of Him, dragging the afflicted behind us.

## A Word from God Does Not Justify a "Fix-It"

But wait! How could Eliphaz have been wrong? He held that God had given him a word for Job:

A word was secretly brought to me, my ears caught a whisper of it. Amid disquieting dreams in the night, when deep sleep falls on men, fear and trembling seized me and made all my bones shake. A spirit glided past my face, and the hair on my body stood on end. It stopped, but I could not tell what it was. A form stood before my eyes, and I heard a hushed voice: "Can a mortal be more righteous than God? Can a man be more pure than his Maker?"

(4:12–17)

Whether Eliphaz's "spirit" was the Holy Spirit, an angel or a demon using a bit of truth to justify his wrong approach, this was the very message God gave Job at the end of the book. And herein lies another lesson for us. Eliphaz used what might have been a true word from God to justify his own methods. Like some deliverance ministers of today, he might have asserted, "I don't need to question Job. I can go straight to the Holy Spirit."

But wise young Elihu involved Job at every step. He also encouraged him to hear God's voice for himself: "Why do you complain to him that he answers none of man's words? For God does speak—now one way, now another—though man may not perceive it" (33:13–14). Then he outlined several ways Job might have heard God.

Unlike his other three friends, Elihu perceived the battered condition of Job's heart. Before confronting the problem, he reassured Job that he would not also bash him: "But Job has not marshaled his words against me, and I will not answer him with your arguments" (32:14). Also: "I am just like you before God; I too have been taken from clay. No fear of me should alarm you, nor should my hand be heavy upon you" (33:6–7).

At every turn, Elihu showed he was interested in what Job had to say, often repeating Job's own words as a sign he really had heard.

Soul mechanics may contend that they are relying exclusively on the Holy Spirit. But here is the sum of the matter: A true healer responds to the hearts of both God *and* people.

## A Few Sessions with Sandy

Although this chapter has been primarily about deliverance, by now you might have gathered that when done with inner healing, the latter is foundational. The deeper a person's wounding and bitterness, the more inner healing will be needed to make deliverance hold. And an Elihu might have to do a great deal of listening before attempting either one. This was the case with Sandy.

She first came to me for three days of counseling sometime after the seminar at Elijah House and her positive ministry time with Fletch and Betty Fletcher, who had moved back East. Her look told me she was still suffering some tremendous stresses. But I began by discussing more "pressing" issues—the weather, her home, her husband's job and the town where she lived. In short, we talked about Sandy and her world. As we did, I "shrank down to her size." She had to perceive that I would be a partner in her healing, that I would cherish her input.

When we got onto the subject of children—since she had already "dipped her toe" into the waters of sharing—the conversation evolved into a more serious discussion of stressors. She wept as she worried aloud about her son who had run away two years before. Where was he now? What was he doing? Was he safe?

Sandy felt alone in her pain. Her husband, Jim, had gotten saved sometime after her bad deliverance experience. Still, he remained guarded emotionally. He would not pray with her or talk with her about her worries. Although he tried in other ways to encourage her, he didn't understand her hurts. And because he had recently been promoted, she no longer got to see him at lunch. Utterly alone in an empty house, Sandy stewed and agonized between anxiety attacks.

As she continued to talk, I asked an occasional question to fill in the broader picture. It helps to get a bird's-eye view before narrowing in on a problem.

Her daughter was no longer running away, Sandy told me, but was now tethered to an abusive boyfriend who manipulated her with rage and jealousy. If Sandy prodded her about it, the daughter lashed out at her and ran straight back to her abuser. The girl had also been charged with possession of drugs, and Sandy had recently suffered through court proceedings. Though her daughter was acquitted, Sandy fretted more than ever about her children's fate.

Part of the reason her children ran, she knew, was precisely because she had always worried so much.

"I've never let my kids go and I still can't," she moaned. "Just as my daughter starts to pull away from her boyfriend, I open my big mouth and chase her right back to him. And my son always hated the way I pushed God on him. I can't get close to Jim, so I've made my kids my life. Now they want a life of their own, and they're having to go about it the wrong way."

I felt prompted to ask Sandy if she had always found it difficult to put her feelings into words. She admitted that she had, and found it especially hard to accept her feelings. "How can I feel sorry for myself when I'm to blame for my children's problems?"

I sensed it was time to narrow our focus to a particular problem. Until Sandy let go of blame, she would not be able to accept her own pain but would hide it under a layer of shame. And unless she accepted her own pain, she couldn't let God comfort her.

When feelings are not allowed, people lose some of their ability to decipher or control their reactions. They become like rudderless ships on a moonless night, fearful of the jagged icebergs that suddenly loom up from the dark. No longer able to bury her pain in home and children, Sandy had run aground on a reef of feelings and was being lashed by waves of anxiety and depression.

In my mind, I heard the Holy Spirit: *It's never all right. Nothing's ever all right.* I asked Sandy if she had ever heard these words. Yes, she had. It was an almost audible voice saying those very words, and others as well: You've fought all your life; why not just get it over with?

It was a demon of despair, not forcing despair on Sandy but acting as a tuning fork. Since Sandy was already tuned to its key, it struck a despairing note and she resonated with it in dark harmony.

We got rid of the demon, after which the hum of her own strings began to fade. But our task was not complete. Sandy still needed re-tuning. We ended our session and reconvened later that day.

"How did your family of origin handle emotions?" I asked her.

"My sister was a lot better at hiding them than I was. Dad didn't want us to have any feelings. He was always badgering me: 'Why can't you be like your sister?' He hated tears. They made him angry."

"Did he ever comfort you?"

"The only time I remember was when I got pregnant at sixteen. He really was there for me. That's a wonderful memory. He himself was very emotional. I was afraid of his anger. It was unpredictable, like a tornado."

"What about your mother? Could you usually tell what she was feeling?"

"Mom never showed much emotion. Her own mother abandoned her when she was little. I don't think she could handle all the pain, so she buried it. I could tell she still hurt, though she tried not to show it. She always told me I looked like her mother. And she couldn't respond to me or put her arm around me."

After a lengthy discussion of her family's emotional history, Sandy summed it all up: "Mom and Dad wanted me to be happy and strong all the time. But I could rarely be what my parents wanted."

Now she was in that same boat again. Because of her depression, she couldn't make herself be what she "should" be. She "ought to" love serving her husband, but she didn't (although he appreciated what she did). A lifetime of faking it had taken its toll. Yet she felt guilty for balking, for she feared disapproval. She had learned that to have the wrong feeling was a sin.

"I know God forgives me," Sandy told me regretfully. "But I can't feel forgiven for being too religious with my son. I drove him away." She had learned not to identify hurt or anger at others. But she knew in her heart she was angry at someone. So she berated herself for her own sins.

Sometimes it feels more "righteous" to turn hatred on yourself instead of on parents or whomever else you really hate. So Sandy had donned a breastplate of false righteousness. Rather than admit anger toward her mother, husband or children, she had tucked all that rage inward.

In order to remove the layer of shame that had hidden her hurting heart, Sandy tearfully faced her anger, and we offered prayers of forgiveness. Only when she admitted her anger could she truly forgive Mom. Just as important, she learned to let Mom be accountable for her own sins.

At last Sandy recognized that she hadn't made her mom be so hard on her. Mom had chosen to do that. God was beginning to comfort the child behind the shame. Before I sent her home for the night, I asked her if she would think about the guilt she had been carrying for sins her children should be accountable for.

But the next morning Sandy had other things on her mind. She had tested the water and it was fine. After wading in, then bathing in the first wave of God's comfort, she could risk sharing her greatest embarrassments.

That morning she had tried to pray and had been attacked by an incubus spirit. An incubus is a type of demon that attacks its host by molesting her sexually. (The type that oppresses males is called a succuba; Dad will discuss that more fully in chapter 12.) Satanists who seek "astral lovers" often purposefully engage such a demon. But sometimes it seduces or attacks someone who has been involved in sexual perversion or has been the victim of rape or molestation.

In recent months, Sandy told me, she had suffered such attacks every time she knelt to pray. Sexual perversions often filled her thoughts and dreams. Sometimes when she closed her eyes at night, she was frightened by a menacing face. And sex with her husband had always felt uncomfortable.

"Were you ever—molested?" I asked hesitantly, hoping I wasn't dropping that bomb prematurely.

Sandy paused, attempting to gather her composure. "When I was three," she admitted in a tearful, high-pitched whisper, "I chased a kitty into my uncle's garage. A neighbor man followed me in. Suddenly he backed me up against the wall. He pushed himself against me and started kissing me all over my neck and mouth and rubbing my body. He was breathing heavily."

Sandy paused to shake off disgust. "It was terrifying. Then he wanted to go for a walk with me. But I pushed away and ran. I told my parents, but Dad started yelling. I know now he was yelling about the man who tried to molest me. But at the time I thought he was yelling at me."

"Did either parent hold you or reassure you in any way?"

"No. They just warned me not to kiss strangers anymore. So I thought I had done a bad thing, that maybe I had caused the man to touch me that way. I stopped crying because I didn't think it was all right for me to cry."

Sandy crumpled into sobs. I put my hand around her shoulder and prayed silently until the tears spent themselves. Finally she gathered herself and managed to squeak out, "I've always been afraid of being raped. Even in my own house, when Jim isn't there, I get so scared."

The sobs resumed. As we sat quietly together, I realized that this memory was the foundation of Sandy's shame. After the incident in the garage—yet another time her parents had told her, in effect, to disregard her feelings—self-blame watered that bitter seed. It grew and flourished until it had dug its roots into the very bedrock of her thinking. It sounded like this: "I am responsible to control everything that happens around me. If someone hurts me, I am responsible since I should have done something to prevent it. If I were a good enough person, bad things wouldn't happen. If bad things do happen, I had better not feel hurt or angry since it's my fault."

Through the years, that mindset had prevented her from properly identifying the pain each time parents, friends, husband and now children offended her. Instead, she buried a little more hurt and anger beneath the shame of the little girl who blamed herself for her molestation.

"Close your eyes," I said to Sandy. "Now picture that man who tried to molest you. Tell him you are not to blame for what he did to you."

"I am not to blame for what you did."

"Now tell him he is guilty."

"How can I do that?" she gasped. "Wouldn't that be judging him?"

"Sandy, when you were little, did your father ever punish you for doing something naughty?"

"Yes."

"If you lied about what you had done, wouldn't he have insisted you were guilty?"

"Yes." Sandy contemplated that for a moment. "I guess he was judging that I had done something bad, but not that I was a bad person. So he wasn't condemning me."

"So was that man guilty?"

She drew a deep breath and heaved a sigh. "You are guilty for what you did. I didn't make you do it. You are guilty."

She crumpled into sobs again, and this time they went on for a long while. When she had regained her composure, she shared the story of her week of deliverance. She shared how she had felt spiritually raped and how she had mostly blamed herself. But just now, as she had said the words "You are guilty," she had shed the last traces of self-blame. No longer bound to turn her anger inward, Sandy embraced the truth that it was the molester, not herself, whom she had always hated. Now, in prayer, she could truly begin to forgive him.

The incubus spirit had lost its legal access, for Sandy's "strings" were no longer tuned to its key. She no longer believed the lie that she deserved that kind of abuse. The father of lies had to succumb to her truthfulness.

Quietly but forcefully I said, "In Jesus' name, I command you, incubus spirit, to leave." Sandy had felt its unclean presence nearby. Now she felt it recede into the distance, and lightness filled its place.

We had breached Sandy's tear-filled dam of backlogged issues. For the rest of our three days, and for many weekly visits thereafter, we continued to identify and resolve the little pains she had not allowed herself to admit nor allowed God to comfort. Having begun to accept that she was not responsible for all the world's ills, she continued to forgive in earnest, beginning with the molester and going on to parents, husband and children.

Later Sandy revealed that after the debacle with the deliverance couple, she had felt shamed and worthless. The couple had rightly identified that her problems with fear and rejection had something to do with lust. But she herself was really not very lustful. The couple was probably sensing but not properly identifying her fear of the molester's lust, which she now echoed only as a mild, morbid fascination.

By saying, "There's something lustful about you," without attempting to clarify, the couple had handed her over to the self-blame that had fed her problems. In reaction, she had thrown herself into a season of sexual perversions, giving ground to the demon of despair, the incubus and a band of others. The shame she had been unable to relinquish was finally dislodged in the flood of healing. She could finally feel the forgiveness she had long ago received.

For good measure, I pronounced forgiveness again. As Sandy bathed in the waters of life, we dispatched her demons to wander arid places.

She still fretted over her children. Who wouldn't? But she made it through with God in the driver's seat. No longer responsible to save the world, she was able to love without smothering. She could trust that somewhere God was caring for her son, and she waited for his return with some semblance of peace. She could believe that God would teach her daughter through her own mistakes. She learned to be appropriately sparing with advice and prodding.

For a season, life remained somewhat troubled but no longer terminally hopeless. Now and then Sandy called me or Fletch and Betty for another counseling session or just a reassuring word. In time her son came home, her daughter found a better man and married him, and her husband grew in spiritual stature and deeper understanding and compassion for her. God had turned her trials into gold.

She had dipped her toe and found the water warm. She waded farther, found refreshment and dove fully into God's grace. As others wade into the living waters, many, like Sandy, will fear drowning because sometime before they have been dunked.

So be gentle and circumspect. Remember, we're teaching them to swim.

# 8

---

# A Balanced Attitude About Mental Illness and Disorders

Some Christians, not understanding mental illnesses or disorders, apply inner healing and especially deliverance in ways that afflict rather than heal. In order to eliminate misunderstanding and the arrogance that drives some to torment the wounded, I would like to call for humility as we all strive for a healthy balance between knowledge of our own limitations and faith in the limitless power of God to heal.

In that spirit, I write this chapter with some trepidation, and with the input of knowledgeable colleagues. I will not attempt to explain how to cure mental illness. Nor will I cover many illnesses, only a few of the most commonly known. Regarding each illness listed, my intent is not to outline a complete healing process. Rather, I wish only to impart enough information to enable readers to recognize each illness, distinguish it from demonization and thus avoid common pitfalls.

I will devote more time to multiple personality disorder. Because of its controversial nature and recent notoriety, and because we who practice inner healing are becoming continually more involved with this issue, I believe it deserves more attention. Since it is a mystery to most people how anyone could have more than one personality, I offer the story of Alice and how her personalities originated.

## A Case of Multiple Personality

In preparation for a recent seminar, I wrote a story about a little girl who had been abused physically and verbally. As I wrote, I felt led to ask God to name the girl. Instantly the name Alice popped into my head.

That's odd, I mused. That's not a name I would have chosen. As I read the story at the seminar, I noticed a woman weeping in the front row. Evidently it held very personal meaning for her. In fact, she seemed so deeply affected that, during some of the story's more emotional scenes, I feared she might run from the room.

Feeling responsible for stirring her up, I approached her afterward to ask if she was all right and, if need be, offer a few moments of counsel and prayer.

"I'm O.K.," she said. Then, "I am Alice."

I glanced at her nametag: Jeannie. "You mean your story is like Alice's story."

"No," she insisted. "My name is Alice. Or at least it was until I was five."

Then and in a later interview, she shared her story.

Jeannie was born "Alice" to a mother who had tried in vain to abort her. She left immediately after her birth, leaving Alice in the care of three sisters, but she came home whenever her husband returned from his job in distant oilfields. She didn't want him to think she had not been at home and hold back his paycheck, so she compelled her three older daughters to help perpetuate the charade. Otherwise she left home for weeks at a time with boyfriends, spending her husband's money on alcohol while Alice's older sisters stole food to keep the family fed.

Alice's grandparents, appalled by the neglect, picked up the girls in Alice's first year of life. They gave them emotional warmth and a stable home. But when she was nine months old, that home burned to the ground. Alice recalled it vividly, her memory seared by the shock of watching the only safe place she had known crash to earth in flames as she lay in a diaper in the snow. Since she had been so young at the time, she wondered if she had made up the memory. Then she met the police officer who had picked her up and wrapped her in his cozy jacket so many years before.

Alice ended up back with her mother. Isolated horrors branded themselves onto her young psyche, each memory confirmed later by Linda, her then ten-year-old sister who cared for her, or by other witnesses. When Alice was two, Linda's appendix was removed. She had just returned home from the hospital and the stitches were still tender. Her mother was angry. Linda had let slip to Dad at the hospital that Mom was gone from home for days at a time.

Mom began beating Linda, and Alice remembered her sister huddling in a ball in the kitchen. Blood was everywhere. Then Mom laid the flat of a knife against Alice's fingers and bent them back, breaking the bones one by one. It was intended to punish Linda, cowering by the refrigerator, watching helplessly. Her mother got as far as her wrist before Alice passed out. She awoke in the hospital, nearly every bone in her body broken, unaware that her mother had been sent to the penitentiary and that her father had divorced her after learning of the latest of her many affairs. Alice convalesced alone in the hospital, thinking for months Linda had died.

In time Alice and her sister healed. A strange man gathered her and all three of her sisters—Alice was overjoyed to discover that Linda, her "substitute mother," was still alive—for a long ride to a "Christian" orphanage. There, a tall, stern matron grabbed Alice's hand and ordered, "You come with me."

She clutched at Linda's hand, terrified at the prospect of losing her again. "I'm staying with my sister."

"No, you're not," snapped the matron. "You're going to get the rules straight right now. You will have nothing to do with her."

Someone whisked her three sisters to another floor. Once again little Alice was torn from her only safe mooring.

When we distance ourselves from painful memories, we exercise a God-given defense against having to remain open to the pain of darker experiences. If we put memories into a compartment in the back of our minds, we can go about our daily tasks, retrieving them to deal with them at more opportune moments. In Ecclesiastes Solomon praised this as a healthy defense, after painting a dour picture of life's bleaker side:

> As a man comes, so he departs, and what does he gain, since he toils for the wind? All his days he eats in darkness, with great frustration, affliction and anger.
>
> Ecclesiastes 5:16–17

Then Solomon encouraged his readers to accept the gift of a defense against futile pessimism:

> Then I realized that it is good and proper for a man to eat and drink, and to find satisfaction in his toilsome labor under the sun during the few days of life God has given him—for this is his lot. Moreover, when God gives any man wealth and possessions, and *enables him to enjoy them*, to accept his lot and be happy in his work—this is a gift of God. *He seldom reflects on the days of his life, because God keeps him occupied with gladness of heart.*
>
> verses 18–20, italics mine

But when our world is shattered again and again, daily routines are disrupted and the pain can be too devastating to push to the background. What can we do?

Alice found another way to survive: She made herself believe that her traumas had happened to someone else. She became "multiple," constructing separate personalities within herself, complete with their own life histories and character traits. These were not separate souls—that would be unbiblical—nor were they demons needing to be cast out. The fracturing was a coping mechanism. Each personality bore for her the pain of a trauma she herself (her "core personality," in clinical language) was unable to face. If she could by some subconscious process fractionalize her inner self into compartments bearing the characteristics of separate beings, she could go about her life as the rest of us do. Not knowing Jesus, it was her only hope for survival and a sense of normalcy.

This was especially true in an orphanage where every minute was regimented. Even potty visits were scheduled. They got to go once before breakfast and once before lunch. If a three-year-old had to go in between, she was forced to wait. If she had an accident, she was not only spanked but beaten, sometimes getting bleeding sores and fractured bones.

Alice had to scrub floors. The stairs were to be scrubbed three times a day. But a three-year-old can hardly be expected to do an adult job. So three times a day she was beaten and scolded with such words as "God doesn't like you because you don't do it properly." Emotions were regimented as well. Children were beaten for laughing loudly or crying. Alice's favorite sister, Linda, managed to sneak down to her floor on occasion to visit, and was beaten when caught. Children were given no toys. There was no play time.

Nor was there any emotional outlet for Alice's unfathomable pain. She developed more "other persons" in whom to hide the hurts. And she hid those "persons" so deep that she would remain unaware of them until she was nearly forty.

Once, for example, Alice was punished by being locked in a dark closet. She was forgotten for 24 hours, which to a child seems like eternity. She split off that memory into another personality who remained frightened for years, locked in the closet, while Alice went about her business in relative calm.

A doctor came every week to examine the children. As often as he could, he molested Alice and her beloved sister. She hid that memory in yet another personality. (Today the doctor, in his seventies, is serving a prison term for sexual misconduct.)

Alice's father came to get her sisters every weekend but left her behind. Because her long hair was light, unlike her parents' and three sisters', he assumed she was the product of one of her mother's many affairs. (Later Alice's hair darkened.) One day he came with his new wife to take his three daughters home permanently. He sent Linda in with a bag of peanuts for her. They would not see each other again until adulthood. Alice was left alone in hell.

Later that year a couple came looking for an eight-year-old boy. Their own son had just died. The mother, unable to face her grief, wanted to hide her feelings behind a replacement. The orphanage had no boys that age, but the matron lied and said Alice was eight. The mother resisted, but the father took a shine to Alice and talked his wife into it.

At last Alice had found a home. But her joy was short-lived. The couple took her to a department store for a new wardrobe, where they removed her old clothes and instructed the clerk to throw them out. They even threw out the necklace her father had given her—her last connection with him. Then they had her long hair cut short. The new mother was so afraid of losing another child that she wanted to make Alice unrecognizable to former relatives who might steal her away.

"Why are you so sad?" her new mother scolded. "If you're grateful for what we're doing for you, you'll smile."

Then came the final blow. On the way home, her new mother informed her that her "brother" had always said that if he ever had a sister, she should be named Jeanne.

"Don't tell anyone you were ever called Alice," she ordered. "If you really appreciate what we're doing for you, you will not speak of your life at the orphanage ever again, or that you ever had sisters or parents before us. From now on your name is Jeanne."

At last "Alice" herself disappeared into one of the dark closets of her past.

Jeanne moved into a house filled with pictures of the dead boy. Her own picture would never be displayed; she could never measure up to her new mother's memory of the perfect boy who could do no wrong.

I could go on about the beatings Jeanne endured from her new mother, the indifference from her father, how she was punished for "lying" about having sisters or a prior life, how she escaped that wretchedness to endure an eighteen-year hell with a physically and verbally abusive and sexually perverted husband. But enough has been said to make the reader understand.

Alice's story is headed toward a happy ending now. Through a psychiatrist, she discovered that she was multiple, though she became aware only of adult "alter personalities." When she came to an Elijah House counseling seminar, she asked my father for prayer. She had always felt bound up, she said, as though there were parts of her locked away inside. When Dad prayed for her, he had a vision of a box on the ceiling of a church in which someone was trapped.

This startled Jeannie (she had since changed the spelling of her name), who had long had a recurring dream of this box on a church ceiling. The matron had often referred to the orphanage as "God's house," and had beaten Alice for being "disrespectful" of it. She had come, therefore, to fear churches. At night she often dreamed of being in a church and climbing up into that box, safe from the horrors below.

It turned out that the box represented multiple personality disorder. It had once been a safe hiding place. Now it was a prison: Parts of Jeannie were hidden away even from herself, and she felt lost and half-missing. When Dad prayed that God would open the box, there was five-year-old Alice, whom Jeannie had forgotten for many years, and behind her the other "children" of her past.

A few weeks later Jeannie heard my talk. It was, more or less, her story. It even bore her name! Through it, God gave Alice back the name and identity she had lost at five.

Lest I make it sound too simplistic, I should say that since then, through a skilled counselor at home and occasional trips to Elijah House, Jeannie continues to reacquaint herself with other "lost children" of her past. One by one they are giving up their separate identities and becoming part of the whole. Even with the speedier recovery that inner healing usually engenders, the process toward full recovery normally takes a few years. But Jeannie is well on her way.

## Alter Personalities or Demons?

Inner healing can be very effective with multiple personality disorder. Each personality has its own set of bitter root judgments, expectancies and inner vows. Deliverance is also often needed. Although the personalities themselves are not demons, some of them may be demonized. Demons take advantage of the false armor multiples use to protect themselves from other individuals or even from other personalities they do not trust, causing them to remain fractured.[1] To complicate matters, a demon may occasionally masquerade as a personality.

Dr. James Friesen offers some tips on how to tell the difference between the two.[2] (Bracketed comments are mine.)

A.  The spirits are usually arrogant and devious, and there is no sense of relationship with them. Alters are likable; even angry ones can evoke empathy. [There are exceptions. "Satan himself masquerades as an angel of light," 2 Corinthians 11:14.]

B.  At a subjective level, the client does not experience them as part of self [except in rare instances, as with the man who called himself "Legion" in Mark 5:9 and Luke 8:30]. Previously unknown alters may initially be experienced as different from self, but soon are accepted as self.

C.  The spirits stir up confusion instead of making things clearer, which one would expect under the proper therapeutic conditions.

D.  The spirits push their way into dominance, perform their evil purpose, and then blame the client! In contrast, alters are usually hooked, and then they try to quietly conform to their surroundings.

E.  The spirits are experienced as only a voice, but upon closer inspection, the clients report that there is no personality experienced which corresponds to the voice.

F.  Bickering alters feel like internal sibling rivalry, but satanic voices bring intense fear.

What makes counseling difficult is that one must have an understanding of the "group dynamics" unique to multiples. Also, whereas some personalities are cooperative and motivated, others resist the counselor's efforts. Some personalities might be psychotic and others sane. Some might be suicidal. Some might even be satanists while others are Christians.

I realize this is a contradiction biblically. A person is either a Christian or not. But we may view this phenomenon as an extreme expression of double-mindedness (James 4:8). If a Christian can have two minds, one obedient and one rebellious, he or she is still a Christian, simply in need of repentance. In the same way, a Christian multiple can have a satanist personality yet still be a Christian.

I am now counseling several people with multiple personality disorder, with much fear and trembling and frequent advice from those with more experience. Even given my own limitations, however, I want to explain at some length how to avoid a common error. Some multiples have been deeply wounded by those who have observed unusual behaviors and assumed they were demonic manifestations.

At one time Jeannie was regarded this way. Some saw her as afflicted by a demon of compulsive lying. In fact, one of her personalities would misbehave, then submerge. Jeannie would resurface, unaware of what the other personality had done. Jeannie's adoptive mother saw her climb a fence in her Sunday dress, for instance, and reprimanded her for it. Jeannie denied it and was flabbergasted that her mother would beat her for lying. Years later she discovered it was "Tommy" who had climbed the fence. In her late thirties, after her divorce, her boyfriend accused her of lying constantly. Because she was unaware of it, he took her to a deliverance minister who "cast out" a small multitude of demons. This bore no fruit. Jeannie was discouraged but not deeply scarred. She chalked it up to experience. No one coerced her to go back for more, and Jeannie was not much the worse for wear.

Many multiples have not been so fortunate. Misty's husband took her to a pastor who identified the radical, moment-to-moment personality changes as demons. For several weeks she was subjected to hours-long deliverance sessions, which accomplished little. Finally, exhausted and emotionally raw, she cried, "I can't take this anymore." Though she had tried desperately to cooperate, the pastor accused her of being rebellious and lacking faith.

Little did he know he was doing the very work of Satan. Shame is one of many reasons personalities split off. Misty had been forced to participate in satanic rituals—acts of violence and sexual perversion for which, in her child's way of thinking, she blamed herself. Through the abuse, the coven had engaged in a practice common in orthodox satanism: get the victim to disown the "children" in her who did those horrid things, locking the memories away in alter personalities, each of which the coven can then hypnotize and control at will.

Misty's recent erratic behavior was a sign of impending healing, not demonic infestation. Those "little ones" were coming out of hiding! By trying to cast them out, the pastor was forcing her to disown those lost parts of herself.

The coven had also heaped verbal abuse upon Misty and, as the matron had done to Alice, demanded performance well beyond her age level. Now, although she was trying heroically to respond, the pastor was accusing her of having a rebellious heart. Once again she could not please.

There is nothing reprehensible about mistaking the presence of a demon. How can one not suspect demons, seeing just a few of the unusual behaviors that multiples sometimes manifest? They might call themselves by different names at different times; make statements like "I feel like I am a lot of people"; hear inner voices; seem to do automatic writing—actually the expression of an alter unknown to the core personality[3]; speak in uncharacteristic speech patterns or accents; or act in exceptionally uncharacteristic ways. These are all possible signs of demonization in its more advanced stages.

Today Jeannie looks back on her experience with the deliverance minister as an honest mistake. But the arrogance displayed by the minister who attempted to deliver Misty was the arrogance of a Job's comforter who acts out of fear.

It can be frightening to see women like Jeannie or Misty whose strange behaviors do not respond to our usual treatment. We feel powerless when we cannot find the answers to people's problems. Job's comforters hid their weakness by pretending to know the answers. He answered their charges with a cogent bit of advice: "If only you would be altogether silent! For you, that would be wisdom" (Job 13:5).

If the pastor had cared more for Misty than for his own ego, he would have discerned her willing heart and might have withheld his censure. It takes courage to face our ignorance. But only then will we recognize our need to learn something new.

## Schizophrenia

Contrary to popular belief, schizophrenia is not "split personality." That term better describes multiple personality. Rather, schizophrenia means to have a mind (*phrenia*) "split off" (*schizo*) from reality.[4]

Opinion differs widely about what causes schizophrenia. It is generally accepted that some persons are predisposed genetically toward the illness.[5] Many theorists believe that schizophrenia is always and only caused by an inherited chemical imbalance in the brain. They say that schizophrenics' childhoods are no different than anyone else's. But since such persons are "chemically fragile," everyday stressors can wear at them until some final straw triggers the illness and causes it to manifest.[6]

Other experts maintain that chemical imbalance alone cannot account for the appearance of schizophrenic symptoms. Some studies (which are hotly debated) suggest that schizophrenics are raised in families where stresses are so heavy that children are unable to retain their grasp on reality.

Contradictory messages, or "double binds," are common.[7] Mom reminds Timmy constantly that she loves him, but always in an angry voice. Or Dad spanks him and will not stop until he cries. Then he spanks him for crying. In most cases, children are not allowed to comment on the contradictions. Their parents try to coerce them into believing that they do not exist.[8]

Some theorists suggest that schizophrenic children elicit double binds. Every parent is somewhat ambivalent. All of us can remember contradictory parental messages from childhood. But normal ambivalence in parents may trigger children predisposed toward schizophrenia to manifest psychotic traits. Confused by these traits and frustrated in their attempts to stop the manifestations, parents can become even more ambivalent. As they try to make the child "come out of the ozone," a feeling of "I love you but you're driving me crazy" may cause parents to express more contradictory messages, sending the child into a downward spiral until the parents realize, too late, that their child is not just out of touch and hard to train but headed toward insanity.[9]

Schizophrenics are often unable to maintain contact with reality, either because of a chemical imbalance or because life (especially childhood) has been a no-win situation, or both. They withdraw, become apathetic. Their attention spans shorten. They may sit in one place and grimace for hours. Some become catatonic. As the condition worsens, inner reality takes over.

We have all had moments when, under stress, we drifted into a daydream or forgot what we were doing. This is called "primary process thinking." For schizophrenics, this kind of thinking becomes the chief mode of operation. Many have described it as dreaming while awake. The ringing in the ears may become extremely loud, sometimes turning into buzzing. Thoughts jump from subject to subject, making it difficult to track a schizophrenic's conversation.

Schizophrenics may perceive hallucinations as real, just as we might think a nighttime dream is real. To schizophrenics, "dream objects" and "dream scenes" can get into the landscape around them. They may engage in bizarre behaviors like collecting garbage or talking to themselves in public. They may break out in inappropriate laughter, tears or anger.

In nighttime dreams any of us may perceive the world as quite different than it actually is. We may live in a mansion or concentration camp or even be the opposite sex. Likewise, more advanced stage schizophrenics may develop delusions about themselves and the world around them. Their speech might become so bizarre that it lacks meaning for anyone but them.

In the latter stages, fully absorbed in the meanderings of their own psyches, schizophrenics become so unaware of the distinction between inner and outer reality that they deny they are ill and often staunchly defend their behaviors as normal. Having lost self-control, they may harm themselves physically. Their hygiene can deteriorate. Some even regress to the point of bed-wetting and soiling, or licking and biting their own hands, accompanied by constant rocking and head-banging.[10]

## A Schizophrenic Episode

Michael had been coming to me for help regarding fairly routine problems—anxiety attacks, depression, marital strife. Some major stressors began to further complicate his life. His back went bad so he couldn't work. Bills began to go unpaid. His wife had to get a job.

Then strange things began to happen. Sometimes his thinking became confused. His ears rang loudly. On occasion, for no apparent reason, he would cry uncontrollably. He felt as if bugs were crawling on his arms. Several times he heard voices urging him to kill himself and his family. Two or three times he "saw" his wife with her fingers cut off or with an axe in her forehead.

Though this appeared to be demonic, I did not discern much demonic activity. Since these behaviors can signify schizophrenia, I went to the nearest university library to review everything I could find on the subject.

I told Michael that schizophrenia was not my field of expertise. If I had not already begun counseling him, I might have referred him to someone more qualified. But we were well into the counseling process and the loss of our weekly sessions would have represented another unwanted stressor for Michael. Furthermore, he was fully aware that what he heard and saw were not real.

So I agreed to keep seeing him, and we established safeguards. He contacted a psychiatrist and got medication, which improved his condition a little. Later I communicated with the psychiatrist about the week-to-week changes I saw in Michael's symptoms. While I counseled Michael regarding personal issues, he and his family received counseling through the local mental health center regarding the stresses his illness placed upon them ("In abundance of counselors there is victory," Proverbs 11:14, NASB). We agreed that if at any time he began to think his "dream" was real, we would check him into an in-patient facility.

It turned out that Michael's childhood was indeed filled with double binds. He had been expected to meet impossible standards of courage and performance. He remembered crashing on his bike, gashing his leg almost to the bone. Rather than take him to the doctor, his father applied salt packs and scrubbed the open wound. He forbade Michael to cry, insisting it didn't hurt. Blinded by the pain, Michael tried desperately to fight back the tears. His father reprimanded him for the few whimpers he couldn't hold in.

Another time he worked for hours in the hot sun without a break, then asked for a glass of iced tea. His father called him a "lazy good-for-nothing."

With the constant castigation came guilt and an overblown sense of responsibility. Early in life he learned to blame himself for everything. Now that Michael was convalescing, on doctor's orders, with a bad back, he felt guilty that the woman in his life had to work.

I saw in Michael, among many other things, bitter root expectations that he must please others but that he could not; that guilt would follow him forever; that his pain would be more than he could bear; that he would be forced to feel it but not allowed to express it; that it was not all right to burden others with it.

Not once did I find any of Michael's psychotic symptoms to be a demonic manifestation. Actually there were many demons, such as those that exacerbated his self-defeat, disillusionment and self-abuse. But their intent with Michael was the same as with anyone—to shoot arrows through false armor. Furthermore, to be under demonic siege is one of the greatest of stressors, and for schizophrenics, stress tips the scale toward unreality.

In some cases certain symptoms, like hearing voices, are demons and not just the subconcious mind running amok. For these instances I know of no handy checklist to help you decide which is which. We all need keen spiritual discernment tempered by humility.

Whether Michael's experiences were truly due to double binds or whether the double bind hypothesis is false and they just happened to line up with it, even the experts cannot decide. The only thing for certain is that stress upsets the delicate chemical balance in schizophrenics. For Michael as well as for "normal" counselees, present stresses brought up unresolved issues from the past. Resolving these issues relieved the stress and enabled the medication to work better. Each session brought immediate improvement in symptoms.

Unfortunately, I moved away before healing was complete. But after three years Michael still reports a fair measure of improvement. Other counselors have used inner healing in similar situations and have reported good results.

Through Michael I learned much about limitations in helping the mentally ill. By the time his symptoms appeared, for example, I had already worked with him long enough to know how he would react to my forays into his inner world. Rapport had been established and he had come to perceive my interventions as stress-relieving, not stress-producing. I could thus proceed with a fair amount of confidence.

I have shared Michael's story partly to discourage anyone to try out meager skills on the mentally ill, no matter how good his or her intentions. My main purpose, though, has been to contrast my intervention with those who, as in the case of Misty's deliverance minister, afflict the afflicted.

I did not attempt to go beyond my depth. Rather, I made sure Michael had enough grasp on reality that I could do for him what I would do for any counselee. And I made sure that a psychiatrist was working with the more abnormal aspects of his illness. I did not pretend to know the kinds of stress schizophrenia puts on a family. I let Michael's family find more skilled help regarding those issues. If Michael had been truly insane, I would not have known how stressful it might be for him to "track" with me as we explored his complex inner world, and I would have referred him elsewhere.

It might sound as though I am being too cautious, or not depending on faith. Not at all! In no way do I disparage miracles. I have heard of people completely healed through others with little or no professional training. I do not wish to quench such moves of the Spirit. But God's anointing in select instances does not give us license to declare ourselves experts in all cases. God chooses when and where He does a miracle. When miracles do not happen, I urge an attitude of humility.

It is no sin to try mistakenly to cast out psychotic symptoms. We can easily be fooled by something that looks like what we have seen in the demonic realm. But once again there are those who will not admit their ignorance. Michael says he has met many other psychotics who want nothing to do with misguided church people. He himself has had to contend with more than he cares to recount.

"You don't need counseling," some told him. "And throw away your medication. Just get into the Word. Pray more." So he read the Word and prayed more, and his symptoms remained.

Some attempted to cast out the voices as if they were demons, with no change. "You must still have sin in your heart," they told him." Or, "You're not standing in faith." This was the medication they used to salve their own feelings of failure.

"Punished" for his inability to respond, Michael felt more stressed than ever and his psychotic symptoms worsened. He had been sacrificed on the altar of someone else's ego.

## Bipolar (Manic-Depressive) Disorder

Bipolar disorder is another illness that can appear to be demonic. Let me offer some descriptions from the third edition of the *Diagnostic and Statistical Manual of Mental Disorders*.

Symptoms of a manic episode can include an excessively "elevated, expansive, or irritable" mood; hyperactivity (often too much involvement in too many activities at once); "a nearly continuous flow of accelerated speech with abrupt changes from topic to topic"; "inflated self-esteem, decreased need for sleep, distractibility, and excessive involvement in activities which have a high potential for painful consequences, which is not recognized."

There is usually a greatly expanded social life, as the manic-depressive renews old acquaintances and calls friends at all hours. Friends might perceive interactions as "intrusive, demanding, and domineering," but the patient will not recognize them as such.

"Manic speech is loud and rapid, often filled with puns, plays on words, and amusing irrelevancies. It may become theatrical, with dramatic mannerisms and singing." There may be silly rhyming of sounds, called "clanging." "If the mood is more irritable than expansive, there may be complaints, hostile comments, and angry tirades."[11]

It is generally accepted that some individuals are genetically predisposed to bipolar disorder. But there is substantial evidence that bipolar disorder, unlike schizophrenia, is triggered by certain traumas in early childhood, most often severe losses, including separation from a parent or loved one, relocation, being weaned too rapidly, being forced to grow up too fast, or physical or emotional neglect.[12]

Some studies also suggest that some parents of manic-depressives are exceptionally demanding and hard to please.[13] These factors can foster an extremely pessimistic mindset. Without adequate support, the child is left unable to grieve, and suppresses both his grief and his pessimism. In adulthood, stresses can cause them to resurface, plunging him into the blackest depression.[14]

For these people, a manic episode is an escape from extreme emotional pain. They run too fast to notice they are hurting. They deny their feelings of despair, helplessness and shame by deluding themselves into thinking they are happy, competent, invincible.[15]

These are only exaggerations of some common inner healing and deliverance issues. Many "normal" persons have run from past hurts through denial, busyness or "putting on a happy face." The counselor needs to uncover the root issues that have prevented grief from surfacing. These can include fear that negative feelings are unacceptable; an inner vow not to share or even think about hurts; bitterness toward those who did not comfort; shame over that bitterness; the consequent denial; etc. If buried grief surfaces, the counselee will need comfort and healing prayer.

Demonization will sometimes occur, as is normal with issues such as fear, bitterness or denial. Occasionally, one of the aforementioned symptoms is actually a demonic manifestation. As with schizophrenia there is no handy list of differences; discernment and humility are called for.

Since symptoms can become extreme, however, and medication is often called for, the cautions I exercised with Michael also apply when working with bipolar disorder. We should make sure that, despite symptoms, the counselee maintains a good grasp on reality, so that we can proceed with him or her as we are accustomed. He ought also to be treated by professionals qualified to deal with the more "abnormal" aspects of the illness, especially the chemical imbalance.

Manic-depressives also often suffer, not surprisingly, the same religious abuse Michael spoke of. Cindy told me angrily that a woman counseled her in this manner: "We're all under pressure; just look on the bright side." And, "We can cast that out, and it will be gone and over with." After delivering Cindy of demons, she warned her that in order to keep her healing she must read her Bible and pray regularly.

Even though her depression worsened, Cindy obeyed, to no avail. Then the woman chastised her for not trying hard enough; that if she had read her Bible, prayed longer each day and stood firmly against Satan, these things would not have happened.

Cindy heard in the woman's words the impossible demands of her parents. She sank deeper than ever into despair, feeling she could not please God. In the pit of depression, she knew no way back into the light, with the possible exception of the next ominous "escape into joy." Unknowingly, the woman had shoved her closer toward her next manic episode.

## Don't Be Afraid of the "World's Knowledge"

As you have probably gathered I have read some "secular" books. Some might call me unspiritual. Others might accuse me of relying on psychology instead of the Bible. To the contrary, I accept nothing in the field of psychology that does not square with Scripture.

But I believe it is shallow and reductionist to say that *all* psychology is "worldly" or "of Satan." What is, in fact, satanic is the underlying philosophy that pervades much of the field—that human nature is basically good. We have no need, according to secular therapy, of a Savior. We need no death and rebirth, no transformation from the roots up. We are not corrupt, just dysfunctional. We need only be restored to our inherent goodness. There is no God. Or if there is, it is often identified as "the god within us." If it is seen as external, it is there not as savior, but as a kind of "cosmic resource person" available to help us help ourselves be good people.

This is indeed an evil philosophy.

But sometimes we need specific information the Bible cannot provide. It does not provide the clues that a child has been molested. It does not tell us the signs that suicide is imminent. It does not list the symptoms of schizophrenia. It does not tell what chemical is missing from the brain of a manic-depressive. It does not list the steps of the grieving process. It does not list the residual effects of incest on adult survivors.

This kind of knowledge is not anyone's philosophy. There is nothing moral or immoral about it. It is neutral—nothing more than facts gathered by simple observation. That non-Christians may have made those observations does not mean this knowledge is evil. God created the world; Satan did not. Let's not give Satan what belongs to God. We can gather data from unbelievers that they have gleaned by observing His world and interpret what we find according to biblical philosophy. We can take what is true and leave the rest.

## Is the Idea of Psychological Disorder Scriptural?

Some might refute this entire chapter by demanding scriptural precedents: "Where does the Bible ever mention schizophrenia as an illness? Where is multiple personality mentioned as a psychological phenomenon? Maybe both are demonic."

I believe these are the wrong questions. If anyone seeks a precedent, he or she had better be consistent. In the first place, most Christians do not require scriptural examples of alcoholism (or any addiction), anorexia, bulimia, phobias, hyperactivity or learning disabilities. Yet we accept these as psychological or genetic phenomena. Why, then, should we require scriptural precedents for these other categories?

Does the Bible ever specify, moreover, that psychotic symptoms are caused by demons? Almost never. Yet we cannot deny that the symptoms exist. So which explanation is more biblical? In all of Scripture, only the man with "Legion" appears to be mentally ill solely because of demons.

No, the Bible lends far more support to the idea that psychotic syptoms result from fractured thought processes exacerbated by demonization, rather than from demonization alone. More often than not, Scripture speaks of mental illness with no mention of demons.

In order to escape the wrath of King Achish, David "feigned insanity" (1 Samuel 21:13), which means literally (according to the *Hebrew and English Lexicon of the Old Testament*) that David "disguised his judgment." Why doesn't the passage say that David "pretended he had a demon"? Could it be that the Hebrews understood madness as having to do with a person's own thought processes? When Nebuchadnezzar went mad, he fell into a commonly recognizable psychotic symptom, a delusion: He believed he was an animal (Daniel 4:33). Once again, no demons are mentioned. Both these passages open up the possibility that demons are not always the culprit.

The reality of psychological disorders is not as hard to accept when we recognize that these maladies are exaggerations of normal traits. Under stress, for instance, we can all get a little "hyper." Should it be surprising that some people under extreme stress get hyper to the point of becoming manic?

Sometimes stress causes us to drift away from reality through daydreaming. We may forget where we are or what we were doing. Why should it surprise us that some people, unable to cope with stress, should take a permanent, schizophrenic vacation from reality?

We can all remember times we felt divided. Maybe while preparing to move to a new residence, part of us was excited about going while part of us wanted to stay. Or we look back on a painful event as unreal, as though it had happened to someone else. Is it so strange to think that some people, in moments of intense trauma, go a step further and actually become multiple?

To deny these possibilities is to minimize both the fallenness and fracturedness of human nature.

## A Case of Paranoid Disorder

In King Saul we have an an example of normal traits taken to an extreme. A demon came upon him, which David drove away through his music (1 Samuel 16:14–23). Saul became afraid David would steal his throne, so a demon induced him to throw spears at him (vv. 18:11; 19:10).

Saul's paranoia increased. For years he chased David with armies. Twice David passed up a chance to kill him (1 Samuel 24:1–7; 26:7–12). Each time Saul repented. But each time his paranoia returned.When Jonathan tried to talk sense to his father, Saul accused him of siding with David and threw a spear at him, too (20:30–33)!

Eventually Saul's judgment became so clouded with fear that his logic broke down. He was afraid of the Philistine army and longed for Samuel's support, but the prophet had died. So Saul went to the witch of Endor to bring Samuel up from the dead and hear an encouraging word. It did not even occur to him that the prophet would disapprove of his consulting a witch! In fact, Samuel prophesied that he would die in battle the following day.

Saul had developed all the classic symptoms of paranoid disorder (not the schizophrenic type). Listen to this textbook description:

> The paranoid, or delusional, individual feels singled out and taken advantage of, mistreated, plotted against, stolen from, spied upon, ignored, or otherwise mistreated by "enemies." . . . With time, more and more of the environment is integrated into [his] delusional system as each additional experience is misconstrued and interpreted in the light of [his] delusional ideas. . . . Although the evidence that paranoid persons advance to justify their claims may be tenuous and inconclusive, [he is] unwilling to accept any other possible explanation and [is] impervious to reason. . . . Argument and logic are futile. In fact, any questioning of his delusions only convinces him that his interrogator has sold out to his enemies.[16]

Some might argue that Saul's behavior was brought on by the demon that afflicted him. But he had exhibited the seeds of paranoia before the demon arrived. He had always been a fearful man. Afraid to be king, he had hidden among the baggage (1 Samuel 10:22). Before a battle against the Philistines, he saw his men scattering, gave in to fear and offered the burnt offerings himself, rather than wait for Samuel to do it, as he had been instructed (13:7–12).

Before a battle against the Amalekites, Saul kept some of the livestock and spared the king's life rather than destroy all of them, as Samuel had ordered (15:3–9). When Samuel confronted him, Saul was afraid to admit responsibility and blamed his soldiers, rationalizing that the livestock was saved for sacrifices (verse 21).

Saul's demon did not create his fear. It built upon his own fear, which he had neither recognized nor repented of. This is exactly what we have been saying about the work of demons among both "normal" and mentally disturbed persons. Demons do not create, for instance, anger, envy or lust. These are the "works of the flesh" (Galatians 5:20), which Satan works to his advantage.

## What About Medication?

Even if we admit that mental illnesses and disorders are more than just demonic, some may still take issue with my stand on medication. Am I giving in to the world's ways? Shouldn't we rely solely on inner healing and deliverance to cure?

It is a fact that many mentally ill persons have imbalances in their brain chemistry. But shouldn't we trust God to heal that imbalance? We will answer yes only if we expect every physical ailment to be healed miraculously.

Whereas we should accept and believe in miracles when they occur, the Bible offers a precedent for medical care:

> Is any one of you sick? He should call the elders of the church to pray over him and anoint him with oil in the name of the Lord. And the prayer offered in faith will make the sick person well; the Lord will raise him up. If he has sinned, he will be forgiven.
>
> James 5:14–15

At face value, this passage seems to have nothing to do with medical care. In our culture we think of anointing with oil in a symbolic sense. Some Christians, thinking they are following James' directive, put a drop of oil on the foreheads of people they are praying for, sometimes making a little cross in it with their fingertip.

While there is nothing wrong with this, it is not what James meant. He could have chosen any of several words for anoint. If he had meant that our anointing should have only spiritual significance, he would have used the Greek word *chrio*, which in the New Testament describes Jesus as the *Christos*, the "Anointed of God" (Luke 4:18; Acts 4:27), and, speaking metaphorically, "the oil of gladness" (Hebrews 1:9). *Enchrio* means "to rub in," and *epichrio* means "to rub on," but neither word is used in Scripture in connection with oil. *Murizo* means to anoint a body for burial (Mark 14:8).

James chose to use the word *aleipho*. It can mean any of the other kinds of anointing, but is the only word for "anoint" that can be used of a medical procedure.[17] The same word is used in Mark 6:13 in connection with the believers Jesus sent to minister to the sick, and in Luke 10:34 with the Good Samaritan who medicated the beaten man's wounds.

Nowhere in Scripture is anointing the sick spoken of symbolically. In Bible times medicine was a primitive science, and massaging the body with oil was considered an all-purpose cure for many ailments.[18] James was saying that while "the prayer offered in faith will make the sick person well," we also ought to use whatever medical procedures are available. Jesus Himself anointed (*epichrio*) a man's eyes with mud and spit as He prayed that his sight be restored (John 9:1–11). In his commentary on the Gospel of John, William Barclay states: "In the ancient world, spittle and especially the spittle of some distinguished person, was believed to possess certain curative qualities. . . . [Jesus] kindled expectation [of a cure] by doing what the patient would expect a doctor to do."[19]

We often hear stories of people told to flush their medications down the toilet and rely on faith. In a few cases God worked a miracle and the medications were no longer needed. Overall, though, misguided zealots have wreaked havoc with innocent lives as psychotic symptoms ran wild.

Do not tell someone to throw away his or her medication. Not only can it be harmful; it may be in direct disobedience to Scripture. Furthermore, it leaves you open to the charge of having practiced medicine without a license and to legal suits for which you will have no defense.

## Be the "Counselor of the Moment"

Given the cautions I have laid out, what can the untrained person do for the mentally ill or for people suffering personality disorders? I do not believe everyone is qualified to carry on weekly counseling sessions as a matter of course. This is true not only with mentally disturbed persons, but also with those with more "normal" problems, such as Jenny, Frank or April, whose stories are told in chapter 6. Such counseling can stir up issues that require training to deal with.

Ongoing "therapy" is a modern invention. But counseling "as the need arises" has been going on since before the time of Job, and can be done by persons as untrained (in the modern sense) as Job's friends.

What the average person can do is be (like Job's friend Elihu) the "counselor of the moment." Even those with no grasp of inner healing principles can lend support and a listening ear. We "professionals" often wish our more troubled counselees had greater support from the rank and file. I heard about a pastor who knew nothing of inner healing, for instance, who offered a multiple personality what he could. Though he could not counsel, he could evangelize. One by one, he "converted" her personalities and then baptized the woman. Another woman shopped for a schizophrenic friend when her symptoms were acting up. It relieved stress, which aided the counselor's efforts at restoring her.

Many can be helped through deliverance. As with any problem, some mental patients will need deliverance before they can deal with root issues. Some people are beyond our reach, however, locked in mental hospitals. It might seem to us they are doomed to hopelessness. We needn't despair. If the therapy lacks Holy Spirit power or even a sound biblical base, a hiatus from stress can bring raging psychotic symptoms into balance. If the patients are out of reach physically, or if they are so confused that deliverance might be stressful, we can deliver them from a distance, rather than in their presence.

There is precedent for this. Jesus drove a demon from afar out of the Syrophoenician woman's daughter, having never even met her (Mark 7:25–30)! Although the world has a poor track record for cures, supportive prayer and deliverance from a distance can relieve stress and make it more possible for them to return to us where we can nurture them face to face (albeit with an understanding of our own limitations).

Inner healing issues can often be resolved as they arise by relatively untrained church people. Gladys could have done that for Margie after Margie shared that she had been struck on the head and robbed the night before (chapter 7). This had brought back Margie's pain of having been raped a year prior. Gladys had felt prompted to ask Margie if her father had ever abused her. When Margie said yes, Gladys told her immediately that she had a bitter root expectation that men would abuse her. This only served to remind Margie of the time when, as a little girl, she had blamed herself for the abuse. Her shame returned, and Gladys' efforts were counterproductive.

Gladys didn't need a college degree. She just needed to use her natural listening skills. If she had let Margie pour out her heart, she would have heard shame in her words and seen it in her body language. She could have identified the real bitter root expectation: that Margie felt she was always the one to blame. She could have prayed with Margie to lay accountability where it belonged—with the abusers. She could have led her in prayers of forgiveness and restoration, and refreshed Margie's soul.

The mentally ill, in their saner periods, need prayer for the same issues as anyone else. They need the same kind of occasional counsel. (The altar after a worship service is an excellent place.) Again, I do not suggest that all Gladyses take on Margies as weekly counselees. They have only to meet them in their moments of need and apply the simple principles of listening, repentance and restoration that we call inner healing.

They may find that their simple ministrations will bring more wholeness than the best the world's philosophies can offer.

# 9

---

# When Deliverance and Inner Healing Are Inappropriate

At times in ministry, neither deliverance nor inner healing is appropriate and may do more harm than good. At other times inner healing may be called for but deliverance is not, or deliverance is necessary but not inner healing. Those of us who minister would do well to know which is needed when, especially in a situation when either or both might harm more than help.

Let's look at some of the situations in which neither deliverance nor inner healing may be appropriate.

## Deep Depression

There is a great difference between feeling depressed for a day or two and being in deep depression. (For a full exposition of depression, read chapter 7 in *Healing the Wounded Spirit.*) Here, let me distinguish the two by saying simply that whoever is despondent for a few days has hope; in a few more days, or even in a moment or two, he knows he will feel good again. If he just gets some exercise or good sleep or listens to music or prays—whatever normally rejuvenates him—his black mood will most likely lift and he will feel strong and well again.

People in deep depression know that tomorrow will not be better. They live day after day without hope. Each day will be as black as the day before. That is stark reality, not wrong attitudes or delusion.

The personal spirit of a depressed person has died to its capacity to function, like a gas range whose pilot light has gone out. The person can turn all the psychological knobs that used to motivate and energize his or her faculties and nothing happens—except another failure to function. People tell him or her to try harder, buck up, cheer up, think positively, have faith, read this book, try that diet, get more rest, etc., none of which helps, nor has he the motivation in any case. These well-intentioned suggestions reveal how little the suggester understands his condition, which immerses him further in loneliness and despair.

We cannot blame someone for the condition of depression, just as we do not condemn someone for catching a virus. Falling into depression is not a sign of a lack of faith; people of great faith can and do suffer depression. Nor is it an indication of weakness; strong, secure types fall into depression. Most important, relative to our subject, depression is not something demonic, nor is it to be confused with spirits of oppression.

Deep depression is marked by several distinctive symptoms. The eyes look flat and empty. Sullen anger may lurk behind the pupils, but there is little energy to express it. The shoulders may sag and the feet shuffle. Skin color may be pallid. The hair has lost its sheen.

Some people manage to look quite normal long into depression, so you must also watch their behavior and listen to what they say. Most people in deep depression know they are depressed and will tell you. If other indicators confirm, believe them. People's work habits change. They accomplish things more slowly. They get discouraged and want to quit, whereas before they were challenged by frustrations and difficulties. They pull back from social functions they used to enjoy. They complain of lack of sleep or that their sleep no longer refreshes. They lack the social resilience they used to exhibit; slights they used to throw off now get to them, or they spiral down from insults, unable to hold them in balance.

Depression is caused by a variety of factors, singly or in combination. The foremost cause is performance orientation. (For more information on this, review the section in chapter 3 and read chapter 3 of *The Transformation of the Inner Man.*) We are ruled by performance orientation when we accept the lie as children that we are not loved unless we can do enough to deserve it. Performance orientation is the psychological equivalent of the theological error of salvation by works. P.O. people are driven by fear: fear of rejection, of failure, of not measuring up, of being thought of badly, of thinking poorly of themselves, etc. They become an easy mark for religious spirits.

People can plummet from either end of performance orientation into the black sea of depression. From success, on the one hand, because success shows up the lie that one would be loved if only he did well. He did do well and still does not feel one bit more loved and secure. His inner being may say, therefore, "That's it, I quit, I'm tired of working so hard for nothing," and the person falls into depression. If a person fails to perform well, on the other hand, he feels bad about himself, performs less well, and so feels worse and performs worse, consequently spiraling into depression.

Loss of a loved one, divorce, amputation of a limb, retirement to a location far from friends and church family, being fired from work, being absent for too long from home, rejection by friends —any severe shock to our emotional system may trip us into depression. Does that seem like weakness? Strong people who will not take out their frustrations and hurts on others, who have practiced steadfastness in the face of adversity, are most often the ones whose energies give out. It is as though they have finally bankrupted their emotional reserve fund (usually in pouring out for others) and have nothing left in their spirit to sustain themselves.

The same strength, coupled with the desire not to hurt others, creates burnout, with many of the same symptoms. (We will look at burnout in the next major section of this chapter.) But depression is distinguished by lack of inner life. People in burnout may still have surges of life and desire; they are just too worn out to stick with what they want to do. People in depression lose even the desire. It hurts them that they cannot care anymore about what they used to feel passionate about. Caring has met failure to function so many times within the depression that their inner being has shut down feeling; it hurts too much.

Women can be afflicted by postpartum depression; here there is usually a physical chemical concomitant. Any depression, whatever the cause, may be accompanied by a physical chemical imbalance. It is somewhat of a chicken-and-egg question as to whether the chemical imbalance caused or was caused by the depression. Both must be treated—which is why any ministry to depressives should be in tandem with medical people.

## Treating Deep Depression

In all cases of deep depression remember this: No matter if demons have helped to push the depressive off the diving board, the condition itself is not demonic. Depression is a death within the personal spirit that requires patient resurrection ministry.

To treat depression as demonic and try to cast it off is cruel! Depressives are normally very conscientious. If you cast a spirit of oppression off a depressive, he or she may feel relieved momentarily. Then he will think he ought to be able to function normally, so he will try to pump up his hopes and try to be normal again, if only to please the one ministering to him.

But the oppressive spirit was only a surface thing, making use of his depression to sink him further, while the depression remains in full force. The person does not feel strong and free for very long, therefore, if at all. He may then conclude that he is truly lost. The devil surely has him; even God cannot help him. And his last state will be far worse than when you first tried to help him.

If you perceive the presence of a spirit of oppression, don't tell him. That is like saying to a hogtied man, "A steamroller is heading right at you. Move!" There is nothing he can do about it, and you are guaranteeing he will be loaded with fear! Bind and cast away the spirit of oppression silently. Keep oppressive spirits from attacking him so long as the condition persists.

We have all heard of foolish deliverance ministers and/or inner healing people who did a deliverance or bit of inner healing over a depressive, then told the person to throw his anti-depressant pills down the drain.

Never do that! That is practicing medicine without a license, for which you can be sued—held responsible legally for whatever happens to the doctor's patient. If you have been ministering to a depressive and he or she begins to come out of it, send him back to his doctor to describe how much better he feels. Most doctors will be only too glad to reduce his dosage. In the meantime, the same Lord who is healing him has the power to overcome any supposed deleterious effects from the drugs. Just continue to pray.

Inner healing is likewise inappropriate for those in deep depression. It requires inner spiritual strength to face sin and hold it to the cross long enough for it to die. A depressive lacks the strength to withstand the rigors of inner healing. It is not easy to go through the process of inner death. Emotional and motivational changes rocket through the person's center of control and demand balance and perspective. Depressives cannot maintain that; it eats up more energy than they can spare.

Before the depression hits full force, while the person is still sliding down, inner healing may deliver him or her from falling completely. And when the depressed one has recovered sufficiently, inner healing is necessary to get at whatever roots may have contributed to the depression, so that he or she does not fall back again.

Likewise, deliverance from besetting demons may be helpful before the depressive hits bottom, and soon after he returns to strength, but not during.

This means that ministry to depressives requires two kinds of perception: first, to know the level of depression the person presently suffers; and second, to recognize whether and to what degree a demon is presently oppressing the person and may be a causative factor, to be dealt with when the person is well enough.

Practice enables a person in ministry to detect depressives fairly easily. But to discern the presence of an oppressive spirit is not that easy. The usual ways of discerning apply: Some people "smell" demons or somehow "see" them. (Recall Mark's helpful discussion of discernment of spirits in chapter 7.) Since I am a burden-bearing type, I detect their presence by the fact that when I identify with the person, I feel oppressed myself. I feel the oppression the person suffers and know it is demonic. Everyone has his or her own "telltales" and needs to be aware of them.

Sometimes depressions lift unaccountably. When it happens as a result of ministry, it is usually long-term. To help accomplish this, enlist prayer partners to pray resurrection power into the person until he or she begins to come to life again. Don't get the wailers—the moaners and groaners and shouters. Even across space the depressive will feel their heavy emotions as a downer. Get bright, happy, positive people.

Minister to a depressive one on one, not in a group. He cannot stand their energy and is usually so conscientious he will try to accommodate all the people present, which is too much for him. If someone else does accompany you, tuck that person out of sight or far enough behind you that the depressive does not feel responsible to address him or her.

Do not pray long in any one session. Do not lay hands on the head, not even on the shoulders. Depressives do not possess the energy to sustain the weight of people's hands, and touch often jangles rather than comforts them. If you feel led to touch the person, lift his hand gently in yours, but do not lay yours on his. Pray vivid, affirmative prayers that celebrate that the Lord loves the person and is pouring His strength into his or her spirit. Since depressives are conscientious, they will most likely try to feel the Lord's presence and will be unable to. Say something immediately, therefore, like this:

"I know, Lord, that right now she [he] may be unable to feel Your power and may have trouble believing that anything is happening. That's all right. She doesn't have to feel or believe anything. I know it's happening anyway, and there will come a day when she begins to feel good again. At that point her own faith will work again, but for right now my faith is enough. She doesn't have to make it happen, and her inability to have faith right now won't hurt a thing. I know You will heal her."

Never say "if" in your prayers for depressive people. "*If* it be Thy will" will sink them again into despair.

Part quickly after the prayer, but not before saying, "I want to see you again." Make a specific date. Do not expect the person to come to you. If the prayer has not yet lifted her out of depression, she [or he] will probably not make the effort. You might even pick her up.

It is good, if possible, to get her away for prayer from her everyday environment; the new venue will do her good and the change of atmosphere may encourage faith. Do not fail to appear on that date. She will think, no matter what the reason, "I knew it. I'm rejected again, as I ought to be. I'm a wet blanket on anybody's party."

Persist in praying for her, with and apart from her, until she comes out of the depression. Then you can get at whatever roots left her vulnerable.

Christians can heal depressive people, only we *must* work in union with medical doctors. And we must minister sensitively, respecting where the depressive is at each level. *Well-meaning Christians full of zeal have harmed people* in depression, more often than not. If this writing prevents Christians at least from being insensitive and harming depressives, the effort to write the entire book will have been worth it.

## Burnout

Burnout is a condition brought on by continual depletion of energy without sufficient replacement. It happens to giving people who pour themselves out relentlessly for others. It is distinguished from simple tiredness by the fact that a good dose of sleep and proper dieting will not obviate it.

Burnout is not merely physical; it is also emotional and spiritual. It is entered by three successive stages over a long period. There is not sufficient space to fully describe the progressive symptoms of each stage and how to heal them. (They have been well delineated in my son Loren's book *Wounded Warriors, Surviving Seasons of Stress.*)

But here is an abbreviated version from his writings and teachings, so that the Lord's servants can be equipped at least rudimentarily to recognize the stages, in order to avoid wounding the already wounded and to help heal. Since I want you, our reader, to identify and check yourself against burnout, I will address these symptoms to you throughout. See how you fare as you read. Also, please note: *Both inner healing and deliverance are inappropriate for people in stages 2 and 3 unless administered very carefully.*

### Stage 1: Physical Symptoms

Stage 1 is marked by chronic fatigue. Rest no longer replenishes; you don't easily bounce back. Poor sleep at night is followed by heavy sleepiness all day. Catnaps no longer refresh; they make you feel drugged and heavy. Adrenaline rush still pumps excitement to accomplish, but the price is any one or more of the following: Your jaws occasionally lock and your teeth clench; you experience constant pain and muscle spasms across your shoulders; you have begun to have regular headaches and stomach trouble; you often find yourself tapping fingers nervously or jiggling a foot.

### Stage 1: Emotional Symptoms

Unnamed fears beleaguer your mind and anxiety runs as a constant undercurrent, causing you to strain to locate it so you can deal with it. You begin to take things personally that normally you would shrug off. You look aggressively for compliments, and if they are not forthcoming, manipulate conversations to wangle some. Twenty people may praise, but one criticism undoes you because you are losing emotional balance and perspective.

### Stage 1: Spiritual Symptoms

You can no longer tell the difference between anointing and adrenaline rush. You begin to question your worth and effectiveness. Problems no longer pose a healthy challenge; they bring only pain. The blessing of God has become connected now with doing everything right rather than with grace (though you know better). You see miracles as happening to others but not to you. Friends warn that you are on a downward slide but you cannot stop. Dry spots in your devotional times are becoming more frequent. Pressures cut relentlessly into prayer time. You seek highs in worship to overcome the slide.

### Stage 2: Physical Symptoms

All the above physical symptoms are increased. Sleep is now labored and dreams heavy; you toss and turn all night. You cannot turn your mind off. Instead of an adrenaline rush, you get sick waves, resulting in pain and shaking. You have become addicted to stress. You postpone preparation time to the last minute, hoping the pressure will produce the rush, which now comes only as nausea. You are hooked on Tums. You lack the drive you could still have mustered (at a price) in stage 1. You have no energy bank to draw on. Illnesses you used to throw off—like the latest round of the flu—get you down, and it takes a long time to recover.

### Stage 2: Emotional Symptoms

You have now nearly lost perspective. One family leaves the church, or one account leaves your business, and your mood is black. You expect failure. You feel powerless to control your feelings and reactions. You are afraid people will notice, so you avoid them—usually the very ones who could help you. All the other emotional symptoms of stage 2 have increased. And now, for the first time, your sex life suffers. Men have trouble getting and keeping erections; women don't want to be bothered.

### Stage 2: Spiritual Symptoms

You never get over the feeling you are ministering out of an empty bucket. You cannot trust people to do their jobs because you have lost perspective, so you begin to fail to delegate responsibilities. You would rather do them yourself than face the emotional consequences of being let down. So you increase your load just when you ought to be cutting back. You cannot trust yourself to act within the flow of the Holy Spirit, so you fall back on experience and logic, running more and more in the flesh. You have spiritual nightmares in which you are running in molasses.

You withdraw even more from the people around you who should be intimate and helpful. You have become blind to the good things that are still happening in your ministry. When the phone rings and people ask for help, you rage inside and feel like a hypocrite when you make yourself sound as though you are glad to talk with them. You may even rage at God, accompanied by fits of weeping and despair.

### Stage 3: Physical, Emotional and Spiritual Symptoms

Stage 3 is defined by one word: incapacity. Sleep is tormented. In your nightmares you not only wade in molasses, but discover, if warfare is called for, that the sword you have unsheathed, agonizingly slowly, is as limp as a wet noodle! You try to shout at the devil but drawl out sounds like a cassette tape playing at half-speed. Tapping and nervous jiggling have stopped; you do not have the energy.

Illnesses occur one on top of another. You cannot hold a chiropractic adjustment; your connective tissues have been eroded of strength. Headaches arrive daily. You urinate frequently and experience chronic indigestion. You dare not eat sugar; it results in almost immediate sickness. Your heart skips beats. Your breath is short.

Intimacy is so difficult as to be impossible. You cannot stand people in your face, so your spouse is no longer welcome to give you a kiss. You have no protection from negative thoughts. You no longer delegate responsibilities. You find yourself making up paranoid speeches, and paranoia looms so close it would almost be easier just to let go and be crazy than keep hanging on.

But you stop yourself from letting go and telling people off because you do not have the energy to live with the consequences. You are literally falling off the edge of your world.

### What to Do, What Not to Do

When the Lord's servants have been burning themselves out in stages 2 and 3, well-meaning but misguided Christians have all too often done the wrong things—*to* them rather than *for* them. Truly, God's people are destroyed for lack of knowledge (Hosea 4:6).

Once burnout has progressed to stage 2, there may be little to stop the slide. The person may have to ride it out to the bottom. But we can at least understand what *not* to do. Both inner healing and deliverance, as I said earlier, are inappropriate. Inner healing demands energy as the Lord calls inner structures to death. People in burnout are usually so conscientious they have done all the navel-gazing they can stand. Actually, death is happening to many things under the weight of the burnout—performance orientation, self-importance, control, self-martyrdom, self-righteousness, etc. But none of these can now be addressed through healing; the Lord is using the person's workaholic nature to crush him or her (Matthew 21:44).

Demons love to flock around a warrior in burnout, making use of his struggles to oppress him further. If you cast away demons, he may feel better only briefly; then the condition will reassert itself. People in burnout need intercessory warriors around them who will defend them without telling them about it.

People in second- and third-stage burnout need friends who will stand by them and not try to advise, reprove, heal or deliver. In stage 2 they can still respond to an afternoon of non-religious hilarity. Those in stage 2 also need people to protect them from the "devil telephone." He or she may be sitting ten feet from the phone, but it is all right for you to say, "He's not available," because emotionally and spiritually he really isn't.

It is O.K. to be an interceptor. At meetings head off the leeches and loquacious ramblers who will only drain the person's energies. Get into his or her face and remind him of all the good things happening in his ministry. Do not tell him how good things are going to become. He will feel responsible to make them happen, then deprecate himself if results are not immediate.

Joke with him. Surreptitiously take some of the load he has been carrying. Get lots of bright, happy people to hold his arms up in prayer. Guard his Sabbath days, even from himself. Do not upbraid or scold if he vents anger by blowing off steam, especially at you, his loved one, or if he merely sits and stares.

In stage 3 he is falling off of his world. Go after him. Give him frequent snatches of affection, not frontally but with light touches and words of encouragement. Do all I listed for those in stage 2 but redouble the prayer watches. You may have to put the person on an extended sabbatical, but do so carefully because extended time without responsibilities may work in reverse, plummeting him from burnout into the black hole of depression.

People in burnout have to learn to do some things for themselves: eat lightly; avoid sugar; rest; maintain a professionally prescribed program of exercise; protect Sabbath days devoutly; pursue healthful hobbies that distract from worries; and, most important, learn to talk with intimates, sharing honestly and openly. If any analogy fits people in burnout, it is that they are workaholics whose only route to recovery is akin to that of the chemically dependent: *They must hit bottom.*

In stage 1, helpers can do everything common sense tells us to do for someone who needs deliverance or inner healing. Only do not be too disappointed if your ministrations fail to stop the slide. If the Lord is dealing with workaholism and nothing else has helped yet, it may be the Lord's plan to let the person go all the way to the bottom. But we need to mount vigils of prayer protection for him, lest forces of darkness take advantage and he crack with a nervous breakdown or fall prey to some sexual or other temptation while he is down.

It takes years to fall into burnout. Nor are there quick fixes. It takes a minimum of three years before stage 3 people can again rely on stamina. Until then their energies will be skating on thin ice; they can fall through to re-collapse at any moment. They will have to discipline themselves, like recovering alcoholics, to keep working their program.

One final consideration: In most businesses, and unfortunately in many churches, the moment a leader begins to show weakness, the sharks begin to circle. All of us have seen people get into a feeding frenzy of gossip and slander. When a leader is undergoing burnout, therefore, we who love him must do three things.

First, we must protect him from people—e.g., tell "friends" who inquire as little as possible. Most of them will turn whatever we say into gossip, which he will sense. We must pray that their energies will be deflected from affecting him. And we must protect him from well-meaning deliverance and inner healing ministries.

Second, we must protect him (without telling him you are doing it) from demons that will try to act through "Job's comforters."

Finally, we must not let ourselves get down. Remain bright and positive, without flaunting that before him. Be an emotional anchor he can rely on when the rest of his world is falling apart. Whether you are his friend or his spouse, he needs to be able to rest in your love, knowing that no matter how much of a stinker he is becoming, your love does not waver and you will neither withdraw nor become upset and judge him. Stand therefore, and having done all, stand (see Ephesians 6:13).

## Molestation and Incest

I will not take space here to try to teach how to minister to people who have been sexually abused or taken in incest. That would require an entire book (see Paula's book, for example, *Healing Victims of Sexual Abuse*). My concern, rather, is to show when either deliverance or inner healing is inappropriate.

Those molested as children, usually by authority figures they trusted, often exhibit behaviors that appear to be demonic. As children they may suddenly become fearful in the night. Unwise deliverance ministers may see rightly that a demon is present and wrongly command it away, as though that solves the problem. The problem is, some fear *should* be there. Normally children quickly suppress memory of the violation, unless it continues over several months or years. Even then, when it terminates, they may suppress memory of it. Their fear is normal, whether or not the incidents have been suppressed.

To cast away a demon of fear may bring partial relief, but the original need to fear will remain. The continuing fear will then be increased. Parents (or the non-offending parent) must be taught to bathe the child in comforting prayer, with and apart from the child. "Perfect love casts out fear" (1 John 4:18).

A molested child may begin to exhibit symptoms of lust—pornography, voyeurism, bothering other children sexually, and, later, promiscuity. It is easy to regard the problem as a demon of lust. There may indeed be a demon, but that is not the problem. The unclean spirit must eventually be cast away, but not before extensive healing enables the person to stand and resist its return. We do not want to invite seven worse ones.

Wounded children have often been horribly re-wounded by an immature church shouting over them at demons, then expecting them to change overnight. They have often fled the Body of Christ and the faith, concluding that they cannot trust anyone but themselves—which inevitably leads them into further harm and trouble.

Sexually wounded children may become inordinately compliant. But that is not from an obedient heart; it is from fear. When they begin to individuate, long-suppressed angers may turn their feelings into rebelliously destructive actions, especially in teen years, since authority has fractured their trust.

Again, it is easy to regard the problem as a spirit of rebellion. But although a demon may be exacerbating the problem, demons are not the cause, nor will it help to cast away a spirit of rebelliousness. When the victim is prepared to forgive, that forgiveness will remove the ground of the demon's attachment. It may also require a word of command, but ripeness will make the deliverance easy. Patient listening and healing of the heart must precede deliverance, or further harm will be done to an already gaping wound.

## Angers

Sometimes long-suppressed angers need to emerge. They may not always come out appropriately. In fact, most often they do not. But to say to a person undergoing that form of catharsis, "Stop it! Get yourself under control," is to telegraph that you do not understand. Worse yet, you may be interrupting and postponing what would otherwise take perhaps months or years to surface and be healed. The person needs to be free to express the anger, then helped to know where to direct the anger so as to find forgiveness and healing.

We deal most frequently with what is called "misdirected anger." Seldom does anger come up cleanly, directed only where it should be. Even if it is directed, for example, at a husband who forgot a date and left his wife standing on a cold street corner, that justifiable and proper anger often hooks up other angers, both at the husband and at others, such as the father figure who molested her in childhood. It behooves those who minister, therefore, to refrain from jumping to conclusions, even if causes seem obvious and simple.

Sometimes in ministry to those expressing anger, only a little understanding is enough, or a listening and sympathetic ear. On other occasions, the present stirring of emotions is a signal not to be missed that leads to an inner heart chock-full of memories that need to be healed. On still other occasions, healing may not take place at all because a blocking demon is using anger to mask its presence.

I plead here for wisdom and sensitivity, so that we do what the Holy Spirit wants us to do, and what the person wants or will allow.

Great harm has been done by those who jump too quickly either to deliver or to apply inner healing. Let us remember that time is our friend and haste is our enemy. If we must err, let us err on the side of doing too little, not doing too much too soon. The Holy Spirit will guide those who wait for Him.

## Multiple Personality Disorder

Multiple personality disorder—which Mark explored at some length in chapter 8—used to be quite rare. Now it is increasing alarmingly, as a society turned from God to a depraved mentality (Romans 1:24–32) results in more traumatic childhoods.

Multiple personalities occur, as we have already seen, when childhood traumas cause the person to develop distinct personalities to cope with the pain. Each personality in the person's inner being, deeply wounded and fractured, takes on a life of its own and may have no cognizance of the others. Usually there is a "host personality" that acts as the doorkeeper to allow the various personalities to hold center stage for their allotted time.

Uninformed deliverance people may see that a manifestation is not the normal personality of the person—such as happened with Misty in chapter 7—and conclude that a demon has entered. But it is not a demon; it is part of the person's own flesh. Thus, an immature deliverance ministry may be ripping out part of the person's fleshly constitution, which actually needs to be received and redeemed.

One woman, who usually appeared quite prim and proper but sometimes acted like a vamp, ran afoul of an immature deliverance ministry. On being asked afterward what happened, she wept and said, "She has died. She has died." Part of the woman herself had been slain. It would take years of healing before that part of her, represented by the vamp, could be resurrected and brought to healing.

Many good books are now being written on the subject of multiple personality disorder. I suggest that you become acquainted with several before trying to minister to MPD people. Lay counselors should refer them to professionals as soon as they discover that they are multiple. Great harm can be done by hasty, overconfident believers who think that, because they are Christians, they can tackle anything.

Please remember two admonitions of the apostle Paul: "Do not be wise in your own estimation" (Romans 12:16) and "I say to every man among you not to think more highly of himself than he ought to think; but to think so as to have sound judgment, as God has allotted to each a measure of faith" (Romans 12:3).

## Alcohol and Drugs

Alcohol and drugs create addictions in the flesh. Behind these addictive substances lie great strongholds and principalities of dominance and control. It is tempting to charge against the strongholds and local demons that blind and bind our friends, but unless we are ordered by the Lord of the battle, it may be like Don Quixote tilting at the windmills of his day!

Dealing with alcoholics and substance addicts requires a combination of deliverance and inner healing, but each in its appropriate time and way. It is unwise to apply either inner healing or deliverance so long as the addict is still in denial.

Denial has several stages. In the most extreme, the chemically addicted person is unwilling to admit he or she has a problem. In the next stage, he begins to admit he has some difficulty, but he still thinks he can handle it. But he is not ready to admit he is out of control, much less that he is helpless. In the final stage he must "put the bottle on the table," meaning he admits he is an addict.

Before he comes to full surrender of his pride and false notions of self-sufficiency, any ministrations of inner healing or deliverance will become part of his denial system. "See there, I've been to get help. It's all taken care of. Now get off my back." Before any inner healing or deliverance is attempted, he must commit to sobriety, manifested by concrete steps, such as becoming involved in a good 12-step program.

I suggest taking several hours to visit with local substance abuse people. Attend an AA session or two. Learn who the professionals are in your area and pick their brains. They are almost always surprised and delighted when someone is willing to listen to their wisdom on the subject. Learn from them what an intervention is and how it is done.

In the process, your zeal to do what God has *not* called you to do by way of deliverance and healing may be checked and humbled. Work with informed people in your area. Then, if deliverance and/or inner healing is indeed called for, your actions have a much better chance of being appropriate and helpful and getting at the root causes of addiction.

## Other Ministry Situations

I could continue to list many other occasions in ministry: the demons and strongholds behind abortion and the needs there for inner healing; flight mechanisms and withdrawals; separations and divorces; family feuding; greeds and jealousies where we work; abandoned babies; children given up for adoption; etc. All of these situations and more can have demonic activity behind them and need inner healing to redeem causative roots.

But the primary need is the same as behind all ministry: sensitivity and patience in listening to the Holy Spirit and to the one being ministered to, so as to act in obedience to the Lord, in concert with others, and in individual humility.

No one never stumbles in ministry. We all learn by trial and error, no matter how much we try to listen to the Lord and to the wisdom of those who have gone before. There is nothing shameful about making honest mistakes. Our Lord has taken that into account and overshadows all we do for Him. He is able to turn our dirty water into the best wine for the feast (John 2:1–11).

The reprehensible thing in ministry is when our arrogance prevents us from learning from trial and error or from the admonitions of our brothers and sisters in the faith. When our pride, masked as a need to obey the calling of the Holy Spirit *right now*, causes us to act rashly—and who hasn't done this?—we need to humble ourselves and say, "Bring me to death in my fleshly zeal, Lord. Set me free from pride, to listen to You and to others. Make me sensitive to the people to whom I minister. Make me appropriate."

# Deliverance and Healing from Types and Functions of Demons

# 10

## Delivering Places

Several years ago an Assembly of God pastor and his wife came to our region and called together law enforcement officers and pastors. They said they had it on good authority that satanist groups were planning to establish their headquarters in the Rathdrum prairie of Idaho, near Coeur D'Alene.

The pastor's wife, before her conversion, had been a satanist "missionary" sent to disrupt Christian churches. She would become involved in a congregation, listen to her "voices," which would tell her the weaknesses of various members, then plant seeds of distrust and slander until fighting had destroyed the unity and effectiveness of that church. Then she would move on to another.

Through the contacts she still maintained, she had learned the plans of the Satan-worshipers. They do not establish their headquarters in a region merely because it is remote, isolated or beautiful, she explained, but because they feel secure where there is an already established deposit of evil in the land. The pastor then reminded the officers and pastors that satanist groups had previously been active in the Rathdrum prairie until faithful prayer warriors had banded together in intercession and driven them out.

But the pastor's wife said, "You did not know to cleanse the land of the evil deposit. That's why they're coming back. We'd better pray while there is still time to prevent their return."

Some of the pastors got up and walked out. Such talk was too far beyond the limits of their theologies. But others heard and entered into prayer—and the satanists never returned.

We never learned whether a spiritual deposit had somehow "stained" the area, whether demons had actually inhabited the area, or both. We merely asked the Lord to cleanse the land, wash it in His blood and burn away by His fire whatever devices or objects might still give demons and satanists access to operate.

## Defilement of Lands and Places

We do not know how spiritual deposits are left in a land, nor what they may actually be. New advances in photography have enabled researchers to photograph fields of energy that remain in a given place after a person has been there, especially when that person has been under stress. Scientists tell us that simple green plants receive sensory impressions, and stones actually "record" events that happen nearby—which recalls Genesis 4:10: "The voice of your brother's blood is crying to Me from the ground." Recall, too, that the land of Israel became "defiled" by the sins of the nations that had inhabited it (Leviticus 18:24–25). In an age when messages and music are impressed onto records, tapes and compact discs, it should not surprise us to realize that a place can be affected so powerfully that people actually feel or sense it.

How many Christians have walked into a motel room and thought instantly, "This place has a bad atmosphere; there'll be no sleep here unless I ask the Lord to cleanse it"?

A missionary returning from the Far East informed me that it had become common for a Chinese family going on a trip to ask a Christian family to come and live in their home while they were away, especially if there had been a death in the family. They knew that when they returned, their home would again possess a clean, wholesome atmosphere because of the prayers of the Christians.

A couple came to me for counseling who had enjoyed many years of happy marriage. They had experienced normal disagreements but had worked them out. Now, suddenly, they were fighting constantly and unable to reach understanding and reconciliation in Christ. Checking into their personal histories, I discovered that both came from affectionate families. They were basically whole people. Furthermore, the content, intensity and frequency of their quarrels did not match who they were or how they normally reacted.

Then the Holy Spirit prompted me to ask about their residence. It turned out they had purchased and moved into their house only recently. When I asked about its history, they reported a surprising tidbit they had learned: that the marriages of the previous five couples who had lived there had all ended in rancorous divorce! Thus I knew that there was a deposit in the building itself, no doubt strengthened and used by demons assigned for that very purpose!

We asked the Lord, who is not confined to our limits in time, to walk through the history of the house, cleansing all defilements and deposits of evil. We prayed that all resident demons be cast away and that it be washed clean from all deposits of rancor and disagreement. If we did not pray for the history of the house, we knew, worse demons could return, just as they can to unredeemed character structures within a person. The couple subsequently lived happily and at peace in that home.

How do inner healing and deliverance interrelate in these examples? Inner healing, as we have said, is a misnomer. It is really sanctification, the application of the cross and blood and resurrection life of Jesus to whatever in history has not yet been redeemed. People, animals, plants and places all have histories—events that leave their marks. "Unhealed" imprints or evil deposits serve as points of access and control for demonic powers to do Satan's work.

To cast away a demon from a person without leading him or her into repentance and healing does not remove Satan's dwelling place in the character of the person. Just so, it would not have sufficed merely to cast away the demons of strife and rancor from that couple's house without healing the deposit of history.

Whether in a person, animal, place or thing, inner healing and deliverance must work together, for if we try to heal history without casting away the demonic, we may find ourselves blocked and accomplishing little healing. If we merely cast away demons, on the other hand, the unhealed house may serve to "reinvite" them and provide a dwelling. (Bedouins will not camp in the ruins of Babylon to this day, interestingly, for this very reason; see Revelation 18:2, which describes Babylon as "a dwelling place of demons.")

We do not know, nor do we need to know, if our Lord indeed traverses history to heal throughout time or if He simply heals history's effects. (If He does not transcend time, then the effects of the cross ended when the day of crucifixion ended and we are still gripped by our sins!) I leave it up to Him whether, in answering our prayers, He actually reaches across our supposed boundaries of time or merely heals in the present. It suffices that when we pray about history and ask Him to cleanse, He does.

It is interesting that although the Lord makes clear in Matthew 12:43–45 that He is speaking of an unclean spirit going out of a *man*, He says that the demon "passes through waterless *places*, seeking rest, and does not find it." Then the demon says, "I will return to my *house* from which I came. . . ." Demons seek places to rest in and houses to inhabit. Though I am sure they prefer to be encased within flesh, why not also resting places that are also actual houses to live in?

## Inhabited Houses and Places

"There are more things in heaven and earth, Horatio, than are dreamt of in your philosophy," said Hamlet to his friend in Shakespeare's play.

In the late 1950s, while Paula and I served the First Congregational Church of Streator, Illinois, I belonged to a group of young men connected with the YMCA. Once the Y's Men planned a banquet to which all the men and their wives were invited. It was to be held at a large cabin the group had purchased recently (at a good price) about ten miles out of town.

When Paula and I arrived, we were instantly apprehensive. Something was wrong with the atmosphere of the place. But we found ourselves seated on opposite sides of the room and were unable to communicate, because of the number of guests, until our hosts dropped us at home at the end of the evening. Then we compared notes and found we had had the same reactions as the evening had progressed.

After the meal, the planners had decided for humor's sake to guide the speaker, by notes written on hidden bits of paper, to one end of the room and up some stairs to a high balcony, from which he would address the group. Paula and I had continued to feel "wrongness" during the entire meal and special apprehension as the speaker mounted the stairs and began to speak.

He told us later he had intended to give an affirmative and encouraging talk, and had prepared such a message. But he found himself launching into a diatribe against the alleged failings of everyone there. The banquet ended on a sour note.

At home, when Paula and I asked the Lord what had gone wrong, He gave us a vision that we both saw and described to one another: a tall, emaciated man bound in ropes and chains, lying on the floor a little way down the hall behind the balcony. He emanated such hatred that it had defiled the speaker into making that vituperative speech.

We asked the Lord who this bound man was. He was the original owner of the building, the Lord told us, a state senator during the 1920s, an exceptionally wicked man who had held sexual orgies and wild drinking parties there. The Lord also told us he had committed suicide in one of the four side rooms off that hall behind the balcony.

Suddenly, in our simultaneous vision, Paula and I saw fire engulfing the building. The Lord told us the cabin had served as one of Satan's "fueling stations" for activities on earth and that He was going to destroy the building and purify the land. Seeing in our vision that the flames were drawing near where the senator lay, we asked what we were to do about him. The Lord said, "Nothing. You leave him to Me."

Over the next few days, we asked everyone we could about the history of the place. It had indeed been owned by a state senator during Prohibition and had been used for wild parties and sexual debaucheries. The senator had indeed committed suicide in one of those upstairs rooms. No one had wanted anything to do with the place, which was why the Y's Men had been able to buy it so cheaply.

We advised the Y's Men to sell it, though we could not tell them why. They listened to us anyway and sold it six months later to the Girl Scouts for a summer camp. Within weeks after the Girl Scouts purchased it, the place burned to the ground. But insurance covered the loss and the Girl Scouts built new buildings on what, as we later heard, became a wonderful campground for the girls. The Lord Jesus had cleansed and redeemed it and turned it to good use in His Kingdom!

To this date Paula and I do not know what we saw in the form of that tall, emaciated man. We may have seen a familiar spirit, Satan's "angel" assigned to a person or family, who copies the appearance and mimics the person's voice and personality. Or we may have seen the spirit of the person, a ghost who afflicted anyone who came near.

Some portions of the Church are firmly convinced that when a person dies, he or she is cast immediately into hell or received into heaven. Other segments believe that a person's spirit may for some reason not be received into heavenly habitations or may become an earthbound spirit (literally, a ghost) who wanders about.

I do not intend to get involved in this debate. I minister to all parts of the Body of Christ. But following are corollary thoughts on earthbound spirits that may shed some light (or raise some new questions)!

### *Mysteries in the Bible About the Departed*

Scripture contains some references to the departed that reinforce the mystery:

> At that moment the curtain of the temple was torn in two from top to bottom. The earth shook and the rocks split. The tombs broke open and the bodies of many holy people who had died were raised to life. They came out of the tombs, and after Jesus' resurrection they went into the holy city and appeared to many people.
>
> Matthew 27:51–53, NIV

Where had these spirits been? The passage says only that "the bodies . . . were raised to life." How can a body live and move without the spirit? And what became of these holy people afterward? Did they go back to rest or up to heaven? The Bible does not tell us. But here is a clear instance in which the spirits of the departed were evidently not yet confined to either Hades or Sheol or to heaven from which there could be no return to earth.

Peter also speaks of the departed and where they resided:

> Christ . . . [was] put to death in the flesh, but made alive in the spirit; in which also He went and made proclamation to *the spirits now in prison*, who once were disobedient, when the patience of God kept waiting in the days of Noah, during the construction of the ark, in which a few, that is, eight persons, were brought safely through the water.
>
> 1 Peter 3:18–20, italics mine

> The gospel has for this purpose been preached *even to those who are dead*, that though they are judged in the flesh as men, they may live in the spirit according to the will of God.
>
> 1 Peter 4:6, italics mine

What is meant by "the spirits now in prison" and "those who are dead"? Much of the Church agrees that, in the justice of God, the Lord Jesus went to preach to the spirits who lived before the flood. Some think He preached to them only so that their condemnation might be just, but 1 Peter 4:6 makes it undeniable that He went to them that they, too, might "live in the spirit according to the will of God." Where were these people? Apparently, by the mercy of God, He transferred those who believed to better quarters in heaven.

Another fascinating question from Scripture arises from the account of the witch of Endor, who at the bidding of Saul called up the deceased prophet Samuel:

> When the woman saw Samuel, she cried out with a loud voice; and the woman spoke to Saul, saying, "Why have you deceived me? For you are Saul." And the king said to her, "Do not be afraid; but what do you see?" And the woman said to Saul, "I see a divine being coming up out of the earth." And he said to her, "What is his form?" And she said, "An old man is coming up, and he is wrapped with a robe." And Saul knew that it was Samuel, and he bowed with his face to the ground and did homage. Then Samuel said to Saul, "Why have you disturbed me by bringing me up?"
>
> 1 Samuel 28:12–15a

We will look at spiritualism (and this story) in more detail in chapter 15. For now, let me say that even if modern-day theologians are correct that today's spiritualists most often contact familiars rather than the departed, it is unmistakable in this instance that the witch of Endor actually called Samuel up from his rest. She saw him as one who looked like "a divine being," but as "coming up out of the earth," not "down from heaven," nor as a pre-Christian person from Sheol or Hades or hell. He simply came "up from the earth." Where had he been?

From the story of the poor man Lazarus in Luke 16:19–31, many scholars infer that there is a chasm fixed between the place of the departed and the earth, so that the dead cannot come to earth. But if such a chasm exists, obviously Samuel could traverse it when he came to Saul!

Truly there are enough mysteries and enigmas unanswered in Scripture to keep us humble and unbiased.

### Ghosts or Familiars Afflicting the Living

Many times I have been called upon to cast the ghosts or familiar spirits of departed people out of living persons, usually relatives of the departed. In my congregation in Illinois was a woman who had come from Canada and married a farmer. One day as we walked through her fields, I was witnessing to her about receiving the Lord Jesus as her Lord and Savior.

Suddenly out of this tiny woman came a heavy masculine voice that said, "Can I, too, be saved?" I did a double take, realizing a demon or ghost or familiar (something certainly not her) was talking to me through her. But I continued to preach the simple Gospel to her, aware that whatever had spoken through her was listening.

By the time we returned to the privacy of her house, I had collected my wits and was prepared to pray for salvation with her and deliver her from that thing. Then the Lord told me that, as a child, she had held a special place in her heart for her stepfather, a Mormon, and that she had been unhappy for a number of years in her marriage. I checked these words of knowledge with her and found them to be accurate.

Then it seemed the Holy Spirit was telling me that when her stepfather died, his spirit had come to help her, but he had instead become tied to her and could not go on.

This was absolutely beyond my theology! I thought, *Am I listening to a spirit of deception?*

To this day I do not know. Many may be ready to write me off for not knowing, believing I ought to have chucked the whole thing as obviously illusory. Perhaps it was a familiar in her, and a spirit of deception was trying to entrap me into believing false doctrines. I relate my own experience vulnerably here, because I have spoken to many servants of the Lord who have experienced similarly confusing incidents and been reluctant to share them with others for fear of being rejected as a heretic.

Let's walk in the light, dear children of God, and unburden ourselves to one another. We may not be able to come up with definitive answers—and perhaps we shouldn't, since the Lord hasn't yet revealed all truth to us. But at least we can end the loneliness and some of the fear Satan uses to drain our energies.

And I implore those who hear such a story, please do not jump to conclusions and scold your brother or sister for falling into sin by being involved in experiences beyond his or her ken! Christians above all others need to be free to reveal themselves to kindred gentle hearts who will not accuse and frighten them further.

> A new commandment I give to you, that you love one another, even as I have loved you, that you also love one another. By this all men will know that you are My disciples, if you have love for one another.
>
> John 13:34–35

My counsel is that, as you listen, pray silently that if anything demonic is involved in what your friend is sharing, you and he or she will be protected. Keep your fears to yourself and help your friend talk things out. You do not have to have answers. But your friend's heart and mind may be hurting and fearful about the experience, and your respectful listening can minister important and needed healing.

Let's return to that farm in Illinois. The farmer's wife, I learned, had been bothered for years by recurrent thoughts that she had to return to Canada. Thoughts would come into her mind that she was "out of place" here. It had been particularly confusing because she had wanted to get out of her bad marriage and "go home." She had also endured occasional bouts of extreme sadness and lostness, while her thoughts dwelled on death. When those feelings and thoughts persisted for days or weeks, she would sink into depression.

But the Lord had long since healed her marriage. And now she felt at home on her farm in Illinois and had no overt longing to head north. Yet the thoughts kept coming.

As I saw it, whatever that spirit was knew it belonged in Canada, and its feelings came up within her as though they were her own. So, in addition to praying with her to receive Jesus Christ as her Lord and Savior, I asked the Lord to send His angels to carry away that spirit (whatever it was) to where it should go. And I asked the Lord Jesus to heal this woman's childhood.

Because she had never been able to let go of her stepfather—the only one who had shown her compassion and tenderness during a tempestuous childhood—I prayed that she would be able to grieve for him, then release him psychologically. I asked the Lord to accompany her through the years of her life and enable her to cherish it for all He had taught her through what she had suffered.

Had the thoughts and feelings in her indeed been from that spirit? Or were they partly her own because she did not yet know Jesus as her Savior? Could they also have come from the fact that, although she and her husband had worked their way through to a good marriage, her heart remained full of unhealed hurts and memories of her childhood in Canada? Probably all of the above. In any case, after our session in prayer, she never again suffered feelings of nostalgia or thoughts that she had to return to Canada.

Who or what had talked to me in her voice? And was it the Holy Spirit I heard, or a deceiving spirit, saying that her stepfather's spirit had become tied to hers and could not go on? Is it possible that departed loved ones can actually be hindered from going directly into their habitations? Had this woman's unwillingness to release her stepfather in some way entrapped him?

I know some readers will send me their interpretations of Scripture, sure that their understandings of the Bible are absolute, one way or the other. I only wish the Lord had made His Scriptures more unequivocal. And I plead with the Body of Christ not to be too sure. In this chapter I am purposely sharing mysteries beyond my own understanding because I believe we need to be humble and undogmatic about many things not central to salvation.

This woman's story, in any case, is another example of how deliverance and inner healing belong together. If her inner being had been allowed to retain its hurts and scars, would those not have served to reinvite whatever it was I cast from her? If I had not cast it away, how much of her healing might have been blocked or lost?

Remember that Jesus said that some seeds fall beside the road and then "the devil comes and takes away the word from their heart, so that they may not believe and be saved" (Luke 8:12). The word *salvation* comes from a root word that means "to be made whole." So it follows that the devil takes away the Word from our hearts to prevent our healing as well as our conversion. Healing and fullness of life in Christ may not be possible in many instances without both inner healing and deliverance.

### *Prayers for Deliverance*

I do not, as I said, know what Paula and I saw in the form of the tall, emaciated man at the Y's Men banquet, nor if what we have seen in exorcising many houses and churches were ghosts of the departed or familiars masked as the departed. Let each come to his or her own conclusions.

But it is not necessary to know in order to be effective as a prayer warrior. For purposes of deliverance, it often does not matter which the reality is. Prayers for deliverance are effective by faith in our Lord and do not vindicate any particular theology. When Paula and I see such a thing today, we deal with it simply by binding it in Jesus' name and casting it into the hands of the Lord's angels.

A Christian departed would not harm the living, of course, even if he or she were not taken immediately to heaven. But who can tell what harm the wicked—or at least their familiars—are able to perpetrate after their demise? These are mysteries of which no one knows the full truth. I only call us to think and pray. Meanwhile, it would do no harm, when someone dies who has not come to the Lord and who has been a harmful person, to ask the Lord to send His angels to carry such a one to wherever He intends him or her to be. We can also pray for the healing of that person's history among the family members.

Some in deliverance ministry see demons or spirits and shout such words as "I cast you into the pits of hell, you servant of Satan." I believe it is neither wise nor scriptural to pronounce judgment, nor is it yet the time—just as it is unscriptural (as we have already discussed) to revile demons. Listen to Jude's words: "And angels who did not keep their own domain, but abandoned their proper abode, He has kept in eternal bonds under darkness for the judgment of the great day" (verse 6). Our Lord has apparently not yet cast even recognizably false angels into the lake of fire, but holds them captive awaiting the Judgment Day.

We have no business, therefore, deciding where demons should be cast before that great day. When Jesus encountered a legion of demons possessing and tormenting the Gadarene man, remember, He did not cast them into the pit of hell but allowed them—for whatever reasons within His wisdom and mercy—to flee into a herd of swine, who rushed into the sea and were drowned. Whether the entity we oppose is a demon or a ghost, the Lord can direct His angels to take it wherever He knows best.

I do not know just how spirits or ghosts can influence those nearby, nor how a place can act as a "fueling" or "coaling station," as was the case with the cabin owned by the Y's Men.

As much as I can understand, however, a coaling station is a kind of beachhead that grants energy to demonic spirits, a place of rest, perhaps a hiding place where they can feel secure from the Lord's angels for a while. A coaling station is apparently a place held by powers of darkness where they can regain energy for warfare, akin to a base for military officers in human warfare, and where they can scheme their next attacks on the Lord's Kingdom.

## Rightly Handling Christian Sensitivities

After a while, the Lord so fine-tuned Paula's and my sensitivities regarding places that we could walk onto a property or into a church building and sense immediately what kind of spirit was res-ident in it. We could tell whether the leadership of the place was in unity and if there had been a "bad history" that had never been healed.

In the early days of such sensitivity, we would sense some awful history and consequent deposit of evil and think, "It's going to be tough to minister here. What an evil presence!" And since that was where our faith was, that is what we reaped! The ministry there truly became tough and dry.

Then the Holy Spirit gave us Psalm 84:5–7:

> How blessed is the man whose strength is in Thee;
> In whose heart are the highways to Zion!
> Passing through the valley of Baca, they make it a spring,
> The early rain also covers it with blessings.
> They go from strength to strength,
> Every one of them appears before God in Zion.

Paula and I sensed the Lord telling us that we carry our own atmosphere within us, and because He is in us, we are more than conquerors. We felt then that we are simply to believe that what-ever we experience in a place, He will overcome it and transform it to good. We repented that our faith had celebrated the supposed power of evil rather than the Lord's victory.

Since then we may well sense what has happened in a place and what kind of deposit faces us. But either we pay it no mind, know-ing the Lord will overcome it, or we do a little warfare and healing and then forget all about it, knowing our wonderful Lord will turn that desert into a place of springs!

We have thus had to learn balance and positive faith with regard to sensing.

## Delivering Properties

A friend of mine, a real estate promoter, asked for help. He was developing a piece of property along a high ridge, which looked ideal for family dwellings. But though he had used every scientific method to find water, the wells he drilled came up dry. He began to wonder if something spiritual could be blocking. So he drove me onto the land.

The Holy Spirit revealed that the ridge had been a special meeting place for Native American spiritual dances and celebrations. The Indians had been angry that it was taken from them in the last century, and there remained a curse on the land.

We prayed in repentance and asked the Lord to accomplish forgiveness. Then we took authority and broke the curse on the land. Subsequent attempts to find water proved abundantly successful.

Another real estate promoter wanted to develop a ridge that promised even better views, but every negotiation with owners and ecologists broke down in rancor and bitterness. He also asked me to come and see the land. The Lord revealed first that white men had tricked the Indians out of the land and that two brothers had subsequently fought over it. If memory serves me correctly, one had murdered the other. I am sure, at least, that murder and betrayal lay in the property's history.

Subsequent checking proved we had heard and discerned rightly. Again I prayed for healing.

As yet, the real estate promoter, owners and ecologists have not come to an agreement. In any event, the land still feels bad to me when I come near it. I have not felt called to continue the warfare necessary to cleanse it. Perhaps that is someone else's task—which is another lesson in deliverance and inner healing ministry. We should fight only those battles the Lord calls us to.

## Psychometry

Satan copies everything the Lord does. To be able to sense what is in an area and discover its history by listening to the Holy Spirit are skills enabled by several of His gifts. But some people can discover the history of things and places without the aid of the Holy Spirit, sometimes simply by holding an object or walking onto a property. That skill is called psychometry. It is, of course, occult and as such forbidden.

A Christian who has been so gifted must be careful that others do not seduce him, consciously or unconsciously, into operating by his or her own carnal sensitivity, trying to respond to the importunities of men rather than being humble to listen only to the Holy Spirit. That is why, although victory was not won in regard to that second piece of property, I pursued it no further. To press beyond the Lord's calling would have opened me to demonic "help."

There is a fine line between "sight in the Lord" and psychometry: That line is obedience buttressed by reticence.

## Charge In or Hold Back?

Paula and I were speaking in another country. Our hosts took us up to an elevated, panoramic location. The Lord opened my eyes and I saw human sacrifices that had occurred hundreds of years before being performed on a nearby mountain.

Our hosts, I learned, were well aware of the history of the area. It amazed them that I described exactly what had happened on the mountain and on the hill on which we stood. That history had left a deposit that was still defiling the present inhabitants. I cannot recall what all the effects were, but I do remember that sexual sins were rampant in the area, plus a high crime rate and many murders.

A high incidence of such sins may stem from other causes as well, of course, but would any spiritually aware Christian deny that such former activities can enable demonic powers to "push people's buttons," until healing of history and deliverance have cleansed the land?

When the Lord opens His servants' eyes to see the past, or see the demons in a place or object (more about objects in a minute), He wants His servants to do something about what He shows them. The greater responsibility, therefore, lies in finding out His will.

Sometimes it is a call to intercession. At other times the Lord is taking us into immediate warfare. Sometimes the Lord's servants are to speak about what they see to just the right people. At other times they are called to pray in silence and anonymity. "From everyone who has been given much shall much be required" (Luke 12:48). So if the Lord has gifted you in this area, let humility rather than pride be your clothing.

On that day Paula and I joined with our hosts in prayer. The Lord led us to pray for the cleansing of the area by the blood of forgiveness and cast away whatever demons were still making use of that unhealed history.

I think of another case of defilement of a place. When a woman named Adele came to Elijah House for help, the Holy Spirit gave me a mental picture of a house. I described it to Adele as having a veranda across the front and a yard enclosed by a picket fence. It had a front door in the middle and large windows on either side. In the yard, on both sides of the sidewalk, were two large shade trees.

I saw the Lord Jesus walk into the house and disappear up a central staircase. A few moments later He came back down the stairs carrying by the scruff of his neck a smallish man wearing red long underwear, suspenders and hobnail boots. His head was balding and his face ruddy, with beady eyes and a small pug nose.

I knew this man had been the continuing cause of trouble in Adele's family and that the Lord Jesus was carrying him away; and I described all this aloud to an astonished Adele as I was seeing it.

She exclaimed that the place was her family's homestead where she had grown up, and that it looked exactly as I had described it. The man had been her grandfather, now long deceased, who had been abusive to everyone in the family. He had dressed exactly as I had seen him. He had also molested her.

The vision served several purposes. First, its accuracy was a sign to her that the Lord was truly present and acting on her behalf. Second, it revealed what we needed to know in order to pray for her healing. Third, I suppose the Lord revealed this knowledge in this way because He knew that her grandfather's ghost (or the familiar of him) needed to be removed, or healing could not be complete for her and for her family.

In His wisdom, God knew that more was required than Adele's personal healing. Somehow that house and its occupant were defiling and afflicting the entire family.

## Artifacts as Points of Contact

A Christian psychiatrist friend, Lee Griffin, and his wife, Cynthia, purchased a house on top of a mountain near Spokane. We lived at the time in Wallace, Idaho, about eighty miles away. One night soon after they moved in, Lee called me, frantic, at 2 A.M.

"Cynthia just ran down the hall screaming and leaped into my arms. Demons are after us. Help!"

"Lee, if I didn't know you're a psychiatrist," I mumbled, "I'd say you needed one!"

Nevertheless, there was nothing for me to do but roll out of bed and drive over there. The Holy Spirit caused me to look at a long shelf high on the dining room wall. There sat a collection of idols and figurines from Africa. The Griffins had recently returned from a missionary stay in Ethiopia and, it turned out, brought with them souvenirs and gifts natives had given them. Unknown to them, these had come from witch doctors and occult uses and were serving as open invitations to the powers of darkness.

"I'm not coming over here again," I said, "unless you burn all these statues and fetishes."

They did, and the Griffins had no more demonic invasions.

Idols and articles used in occult practices serve as points of contact and access for demonic powers. In Corinth, Paul preached so effectively and worked such miracles that "many of those who practiced magic brought their books together and began burning them in the sight of all; and they counted up the price of them and found it fifty thousand pieces of silver" (Acts 19:19).

Loren and Georgia Murphy have sailed throughout the South Pacific, transporting missionaries and goods from one station to another. They told me the following story, which I quote, with their permission, from their November/December 1987 newsletter:

Two days after arriving in Port Vila, a high government official invited Raynold [skipper of the Haggai], the crews of American Flyer [Loren and Georgia's ship] and Haggai [a sister missionary ship] to his home for dinner and consultation. He and his family have been subject to strange sickness and oppression for the past few years, and he had been seeking the Lord for answers, as his household was Christian.

On arriving at his home it was apparent that there were idols everywhere. When asked about all the "artifacts," he explained that he was the director of culture and heritage for Vanuata. We shared with him what the Bible says about idols in our homes, such as in Deuteronomy 7:25–26: "The images of their gods you are to burn in the fire. Do not covet the silver and gold on them, and do not take it for yourselves, or you will be ensnared by it, for it is detestable to the Lord your God. Do not bring a detestable thing into your house or you, like it, will be set apart for destruction. Utterly abhor and detest it, for it is set apart for destruction" (NIV).

He took the Scriptures to heart and gathered up every idol from every room and building there. We built a great fire and burned them. As the flames leaped to the sky, he exclaimed he could feel a heaviness lifting from him, and later, as prayer had been given for forgiveness, even the atmosphere of the home changed from one of heaviness to one of joy and release. Praise the Lord!

The next day the official called Raynold and thanked him for bringing us, and that their home is completely changed. There is no more oppression, but joy and peace. "Blessed . . . are those who hear the word of God and obey it" (Luke 11:28).

Loren and Georgia Murphy may have been modest in their newsletter. They told Paula and me personally that the governor's wife had been afflicted with a debilitating disease in her arms, but that the next day the governor had called to exclaim that his wife had been totally healed!

## Inhabited Churches

Churches can be inhabited by local demons and ruling spirits. Near a small town where Paula and I served, a Pentecostal church was suffering a repeated pattern: The wife of every pastor who came to serve there died suddenly, some by disease, one by tragic accident.

When we prayed, the Holy Spirit revealed that a history of vituperation, jealousy and attack upon pastors' wives had allowed a ruling demon to inhabit the church building itself, thus to rule the people's hearts. We prayed for that history to be healed, repenting of Christians' jealousies and malicious tongues. We exorcised the church and then cleansed the place. That pattern ended.

Another congregation called on me to come and see what the Lord might reveal about their church. It was a round, modernistic building, beautiful in design and accouterments. When I walked into the sanctuary, the Lord opened my eyes. Although I had never met any of the church members, He showed me what many looked like and where they usually sat. Then He showed me how demonic forces moved on them and caused them to act in ways they would never normally allow.

I do not know why, but the Lord did not reveal the demonic presences to me by sight. I only felt their presence and knew how they influenced the unwary members. I knew there was a ruling spirit of rancor, suspicion and criticism, and what members the demons could influence most easily. To this day I do not know if that church got free or not. The Holy Spirit called me only to see and report to the praying people what I saw.

Again let me emphasize that our Lord Jesus wants only obedience to His call, not ambition or the thrill of battle or the pride of being known as a warrior for Christ.

## Holy Water

I have been led by the Holy Spirit many times to use holy water for the cleansing of buildings, especially churches. Some branches of the Church use holy water regularly; others do not. I do not know that I comprehend it, but I do know its power.

Holy water is an ordinary substance, plain water over which prayers of cleansing and consecration have been offered. (Some Christians add a pinch of salt.) But God uses ordinary substances as "points of contact." Look at the Scripture references to anointing with oil (Psalm 133 and James 5:14 are two examples) in order that consecration or healing come to us. Aprons or handkerchiefs Paul handled caused the sick to recover and evil spirits to leave (Acts 19:12).

Tom Stipe, pastor of the Wheatridge Vineyard in Denver, invited me to visit his newly purchased home. He had not yet felt comfortable there, especially in certain rooms. As we walked through the house, the Lord revealed certain things to me about its previous occupants and the history of the place. We took water, prayed over it and went through all the rooms sprinkling the entire place.

This was a new experience for Tom. But we reveled in joy as we found the atmosphere of the house perceptibly lightened as we went from room to room.

Some years ago I learned that what Tom and I carried out solely by the guidance of the Holy Spirit has long been part of the tradition of the Church. We were to speak to a gathering of 3,000 Roman Catholic charismatics in Sacramento in a large secular auditorium that had been used for all manner of unholy purposes. It reeked of uncleanness!

One of the bishops present read the prayers for exorcism, took a container of holy water and went from door to door through the auditorium, sprinkling each liberally and anointing each with oil in the sign of the cross. We could feel the atmosphere change as he proceeded, until the entire room sparkled with the presence of the Lord and His holiness.

Having spoken in many churches where the uncleanness was oppressive, I have often wished we could drop our prejudices and fears and learn from one another's truths.

Since Satan copies everything, as we have said, and since he uses objects as points of contact between himself and his victims, objects must also be delivered sometimes from evil spirits.

## Cleansing from Immediate Warfare and Defilement

Sometimes places must be cleansed not from long inhabitation but from present ministry and warfare.

A man came to our home on a Saturday morning. Paula and I had been counseling his wife, trying to convince her to return to him. But he was furious at us and sat on the end of our couch for three hours, berating us and threatening to sue us for alienation of affection. Before he left, the Holy Spirit mollified him and we were able to minister to him in prayer.

We never thought of the possibility that anything demonic had been dislodged, else we would immediately have cleansed our home by prayer. But shortly thereafter I carried our daughter Andrea, then three years old, past the couch. She screamed in fear and pointed at the spot where he had been sitting. "That's bad! That's bad!"

Thinking she sensed only an emanation of his presence, we comforted her—and didn't think to pray and discern whether anything demonic might be occupying our house.

Late that night our eldest son Loren, then about twenty, came home and discovered his little sister paralyzed and gagging, being suffocated by a demon! He burst into our bedroom with Andrea in his arms, sobbing with fury and love and anger and shouting, "No demon's going to get my little sister!"

We cast the demon off Andrea but could get no sense of peace that we had banished it from our home. The next day we went to a brother pastor, who joined his faith with ours and cast that thing away entirely.

I add that latter detail to say by personal testimony that no one should allow himself or herself to be proud or private in these matters. By then we had become noted for our competence as exorcists—but we knew enough to ask for help. It is by God's design, after all, that we are members of an army.

A similar instance occurred one evening when I was ministering to the last counselee of the day. She said she thought she had a demon. I had not discerned anything and knew her to be somewhat dramatic. Nevertheless, to humor her, I wearily said words of exorcism. There were no signs of a demon leaving. But the woman said she felt better and left.

If I had believed she had been demonized, I would have carefully cleansed my office and our home. (My counseling office at the time was down the hall from our living room.) I did not.

That night after supper, our then son-in-law Ron brought our grandson Jason, about two-and-a-half, for a visit. They began to play together. Ron lay down on the living room floor. Jason ran down the hall toward my office, turned around and came racing back, giggling, and threw himself on his daddy's tummy. He did this several times.

Then Jason ran down the hall and stopped, screamed in fear, and came flying back shouting, "Bad! Bad!" The Lord opened Ron's eyes and he saw a demon standing in my office door. We bound it, handed it into the care of the Lord's angels and comforted Jason.

Another important lesson can be learned from these experiences. What we adults cannot see or what the Lord has to open our eyes to see, children often see naturally. Andrea and Jason both saw with unaided eyes what we were too blind spiritually to perceive.

## Bedrooms and Children's Imaginations

Children sometimes cry out in the night, "Daddy, Mommy, there's a man in my room." Or, "There's a big dog." Many parents call back, "It's just your imagination. Go back to sleep."

Even when there are no demons present, this is a mistake. Disbelief, ridicule or sarcastic scoffing tell a child that his or her imagination is not to be respected. This can hamper or destroy proper use of the imaginative faculties later on.

If a demon *is* present, such a response from parents leaves the child defenseless. Missionaries from African posts have told us it is not uncommon there for children and even adults to be choked to death by what they call the "black wraith." Paula and I have been jumped on in the night by demonic powers, paralyzed so instantly that we could not move a muscle! Knowing what to do, we said in silent prayer, "Jesus is my Lord, stronger than any demonic force." Eventually we could speak words of command aloud and force the demon off.

But what of a child who does not yet know how to pray?

Parents can go to their child's room and say, "Yes, I know, honey, but Jesus is here, too, and He's stronger than any old bad man. We'll just ask Him to take that thing away, and we'll ask Him to send His strong angels to watch over you all night."

It is also wisdom to remain for a while by the child's bedside, quietly praying affirming prayers of the Lord's faithfulness and ever-present care and love until the child falls soundly to sleep.

If nothing was in fact in the room, the parents' loving response at least demonstrates that the child's imagination is something valuable and will be respected.

I have wondered if, whatever the physical cause for crib death, there might also occasionally be something demonic involved. We know, at least, that Satan wants to destroy children, especially those destined to be the Lord's powerful servants. Witness what happened when Moses and the Lord Jesus were born! In Egypt all the firstborn children of the Israelites were killed; and in Bethlehem Satan sought to kill all the children two years old and under before one of them could crush his head.

## Danger at Work and at Home

Sometimes demonic forces can linger about construction sites, seeking to cause harm by accidents and breakages. One summer Loren was earning money for his college education by working for our friends the Griffins. Lee and Cynthia had obtained some property high above the Spokane River, with access to the river. They were in the process of building both the house and the dock.

In a dream one night I saw Loren swinging by slender yellow lines down from a high and dangerous place. As Loren was about to leave for work the next morning, I called to him and asked which site he would be working at that day. He said he would be down at the dock. Relieved, I told him I had had a premonition, and to be careful.

Later that day, Cynthia came with her two teenage girls to inspect the house. She had been a trained ballet dancer. Her balance and coordination were excellent. But as she squatted by the edge of the cliff to look at the foundation, a powerful force hit her in the back and knocked her off the side! She fell nearly fifty feet and landed on a narrow ledge about halfway down. No one could know then that she had broken three vertebrae in her back.

Loren was a weight-lifter and had always been blessed with the balance and agility of a cat. He went up the cliff to Cynthia. The girls, at his direction, tied together some long, strong yellow electric extension cords, looped one end around a tree and threw the other down to Loren. He tied the cord about his waist, picked up Cynthia very carefully, and with the girls holding the line taut, walked with her held out in his arms down the face of the cliff.

Because of my warning, he had parked our station wagon down below rather than up above as was his custom. He laid her gingerly in the wagon and drove as cautiously as possible to the hospital. The doctors said later that if he had slipped and jostled her at all, her spinal cord could have been sliced and she would have been paralyzed or even killed. Within three weeks the Lord totally healed Cynthia, and she bears no continuing damages from her injuries.

Needless to say, we went after that demon and cast it away from the premises into the Lord's hands!

One wonders how many "accidents" may not be humanly caused at all! It behooves all of us involved in ministry to pray regularly that our homes and workplaces be cleansed from all possible defiling and attacking spirits. It is a simple matter to pray as Paula and I often do, "Lord, whatever spirits have seen us or attached themselves to us or our home today, we ask You to send Your angels to carry them away. Cleanse us and our home, Lord Jesus. Thank You, Lord."

## Delivering Cities, Regions and Nations

Cities, regions, nations and their lands can be inhabited by demons, principalities and "world rulers." Our next book, *The Healing of the Nations*, will teach fully about how to cast away, cleanse and heal in such situations. The subject is too large even to be sketched here. In the meantime, though, several authors have written helpful books on the subject. I would recommend especially John Dawson's *Taking Our Cities for God*.

## Authority for Every Christian

Every Christian has authority over all the powers of darkness. The least Christian, when ordered and empowered by our Lord Jesus Christ, can defeat hordes of demons and overcome principalities!

Be encouraged, Church. I believe the Lord allowed demons to jump on Paula and me many times that we might learn in the depths of our minds and hearts that He is indeed stronger than any demonic forces, and that we have nothing to fear as we abide in Him.

I close this chapter by quoting Psalm 149:5–9 (italics mine). When it mentions people, kings and nobles, let's take that in this context to mean demons, world rulers and principalities.

> Let the godly ones exult in glory;
> Let them sing for joy on their beds.
> Let the high praises of God be in their mouth,
> And a two-edged sword in their hand,
> To execute vengeance on the nations,

And punishment on the peoples;
To bind their kings with chains,
And their nobles with fetters of iron;
To execute on them the judgment written;
*This is an honor for all His godly ones.*
Praise the Lord!

# 11

## Delivering Animals and Objects

Usually Christians do not think about demons inhabiting animals. We deliver *people*. But the Scripture tells us at least one instance when demons did enter animals: when Jesus allowed the legion of demons to go into the herd of swine, which plunged into the sea and died. We are not told why the demons asked to enter the pigs. Apparently it is a comfort for demons to live within the shelter of a body, human or animal.

While I was pastoring a small church in Kansas, I called on one of the farmers of my parish. I found him in his barn, worrying over one of his best cows. A thunderstorm had passed through the area the night before. The cow had been in the field when lightning struck close by. Though she was not actually hit, it had so terrorized her that she refused or was unable to get up. (If a cow does not stand up, it will die.) The farmer had tugged and pulled, pushed and lifted, twisted her tail, cajoled and scolded, all to no avail. He had even used his tractor blade to lift and carry her out of the elements into the barn, but there she remained, immobile.

The farmer went to do some chores and left me with the cow. By the prompting of the Holy Spirit, I squatted in front of her, looked her steadfastly in the eyes and prayed aloud. I asked the

Lord to heal her memories of the storm's terror and cast away a spirit of fear. Then I went to help the farmer with the chores.

About a half hour later we returned to find the cow standing up chewing her cud contentedly. The farmer slapped his hand to his forehead and exclaimed, "Holy cow!"

That cow remained normal, producing a healthy calf every spring. And from then on the farmer called her Holy Cow.

Another of my parishioners in that Kansas church was a retired woman with a beagle for her constant companion and friend. The dog was friendly and approachable by any adult, even a stranger. But if a child came near, she was instantly hostile and became so frightened she would urinate on the floor, especially if the child ran by or simply moved quickly.

I inquired about the dog's history. She had been one of a litter owned by a family with many children. The children had been allowed to run about unsupervised and had been vicious to the animals on the property. They had often teased and kicked the puppy. As soon as the puppy was weaned, my parishioner took her into her home and lavished love on her. She had become loving and usually calm—except when children approached. Her unhealed memories had given access to a demon of fear.

With the woman's permission, I took the dog onto my lap and asked the Lord Jesus to enter into her history and heal her fear of children. Then I cast away a spirit of fear.

Shortly thereafter I brought Communion to this parishioner, accompanied by our son John, then about four years old. Johnny knew nothing of the nature of the dog, and perhaps I had forgotten to tell him. In any case, he ran right up to the dog and hugged and played with her, and the dog loved it! No hysterical barking, no growling, no wetting the floor, just a normal dog who loved children from then on.

It would not have sufficed to cast away a spirit of fear from the cow or the dog. Their memories would have given worse demons access to return. Nor would it probably have been enough just to heal their memories. Demons of fear could possibly have remained and enlarged their hold through other unhealed areas (as Mark has outlined in his treatment of the "burrowing" habits of demonic beings in chapter 5). When the main causes of inhabitation were healed and the demons cast out, there was insufficient access in any yet unhealed areas for the demons to return.

Animals know and experience far more than we give them credit for. At times inner healing and deliverance are both needed and should work together.

## Animals' Unique Characters and Personalities

I suppose most of us at one time or another have known some animals that were definitely evil, and others that were positively "saintly."

As a boy I had two cows. Queeny was so wicked I wanted to butcher her, but Spring was my beloved friend. Had I only known what I know now, perhaps Queeny could have been transformed. How I celebrated when my parents finally sold her!

On my grandfather's ranch in Oklahoma, I rode the same horse my mother had ridden to school every day as a girl. "Old Joe" was as gentle and wise as a saint. Every evening I rode him out to the upper pasture to cull out the tame cattle from the wild cattle and bring them home for milking. Old Joe knew the way and did all the work; I just rode along and held on for dear life. Grandpa rode a great black stallion no one else could ride or even get near. We gave that horse lots of leeway!

I share these remembrances to make the point that each animal has its own distinct personality and is to be treated with the same respect one would grant a person. Each animal possesses its own personal history and consequent character traits, which can be blessed vehicles for the Holy Spirit or inhabited by demonic powers.

I remember visiting as an adult on a farm in Kansas. The family asked if I would like to go horseback riding. Their teenage daughter offered to go along. Since it had been years since I had ridden a horse, she saddled the old tame mare for me while she rode bareback on the mare's colt, a young stallion. Then she led the way across the pasture.

Somehow I knew exactly what that mare was thinking. Animals establish pecking orders and protocol. She was becoming increasingly angry that her young son was allowed to have her place as leader of the expedition. I knew she was biding her time, waiting for an opportunity. She plodded along docilely, trying to lull me into unawareness—until just the right moment.

At an incline, she suddenly bolted ahead of the colt and lashed out with a vicious kick at his head. Then she surged forward, swerved suddenly to the left, and stopped abruptly, trying to throw me off.

No one can tell me animals cannot think and scheme! She had planned out her entire campaign. Had I been a novice or less sensitive to animals, it would have worked. She would have put her young colt in his place and dislodged me, all in one quick, clever maneuver!

I do not want to debate whether animals have souls. (I do not believe they do.) My point is this: Because animals have memories and can definitely (in their own way) think, they can be inhabited and used by demonic powers, or by the holy. Remember, the Lord opened the mouth of Balaam's donkey and she spoke to the prophet.

> When the donkey saw the angel of the Lord, she lay down under Balaam; so Balaam was angry and struck the donkey with his stick.
>
> And the Lord opened the mouth of the donkey, and she said to Balaam, "What have I done to you, that you have struck me these three times?"
>
> Then Balaam said to the donkey, "Because you have made a mockery of me! If there had been a sword in my hand, I would have killed you by now."
>
> And the donkey said to Balaam, "Am I not your donkey on which you have ridden all your life to this day? Have I ever been accustomed to do so to you?" And he said, "No."
>
> Then the Lord opened the eyes of Balaam, and he saw the angel of the Lord standing in the way with his drawn sword in his hand; and he bowed all the way to the ground.
>
> And the angel of the Lord said to him, "Why have you struck your donkey these three times? Behold, I have come out as an adversary, because your way was contrary to me.
>
> "But the donkey saw me and turned aside from me these three times. If she had not turned aside from me, I would surely have killed you just now, and let her live."
>
> Numbers 22:27–33

Several things are noteworthy. Observe first that the donkey remembered her entire history with Balaam and his with her, and reminded him of it. Second, she had a strong sense of justice and called Balaam to repentance because of his injustice to her. Third, she possessed a capacity (no doubt aided by the Holy Spirit) to see the angel of God and the sense to have proper and holy fear. (Remember that the four living beasts in Revelation 4–6 fall down before the throne of God and worship Him along with the elders and the company of heaven.) Fourth, she could count, and she persisted in refusing to go forward into danger though struck three times. Fifth, she could reason with Balaam and made a better case for herself than many of us could when under pressure! Sixth, she had wisdom and used it to save her master from destruction.

This is a special case, of course, in which the Holy Spirit enabled a donkey to perform in ways far beyond what dumb beasts normally can. But notice, *God's Word says only that God opened her mouth, not that He reasoned or spoke through her!* Apparently God lifted for a moment the curse that has rested upon nature ever since Adam's fall, and allowed the donkey to reason and act as He created all animals to do before the Fall (see Romans 8:20–21).

Whether or not this speculation contains much truth, it is true that animals have memories, a sense of justice and a capacity to think. Thus, they can be inhabited and used by powers of darkness.

## Respect for Animals

The same principles hold true for the deliverance and healing of animals as for people. We must respect their free wills. We can meet an animal's spirit and read its character much as we can with humans, and must therefore respect each animal's unique nature. Fundamentalists and legalists can argue all they want that an animal cannot have free will and its own distinct character. Those of us who have grown up among farm animals know that an animal has both a will and a personality all its own!

Memories need to be healed in animals as well as in people. Demons must be cast away, but not without removing their access by healing the memories. Animals, like people, need love and affection if they are to receive and maintain their healing. Likewise, animals need to be allowed to express their gratitude and love for those who deliver them from trouble.

## Animals in Heaven?

Even if animals do not possess a soul, I wonder whether there are animals in heaven and, if so, what that means. If there are not animals in heaven, how will Jesus come riding out of heaven on a white horse (Revelation 6:2)? And how will the "living creatures" be crying, "Holy, holy, holy," one with the face of a man but the others like a lion, a calf and a flying eagle (Revelation 4:7–8)?

Such thoughts are beyond the purview of our subject here, but I raise them because if Christians are to be effective in this field, some will first have to allow truth to batter down the walls of their biases! We just do not know what lies beyond the few necessary truths the Lord has given us for the salvation of our souls. It behooves us, therefore, to pray for an open and humble mind. No one possesses an all-inclusive theology—and if we did, the Lord would have to smash it in order to use us in such areas as these!

## Animals Used as Familiars

Let's not abandon the subject before mentioning that animals, especially cats, can be used as familiars for warlocks and witches. This kind of familiar is different from the familiar of a person or family. A familiar used by a witch or warlock is an animal possessed by the spirit of or controlled by the mind and sorcery of a warlock or witch. Such familiars are used as messengers or spies. Somehow the controller can actually see and hear through the eyes and ears of the familiar, reaching across space by occult means and using a local animal to "spy" on intended victims or enemies.

Let me recount an extremely unusual example. Paula and I were to take a team to a speaking and healing engagement at St. Mary's Priory in Victoria on Vancouver Island, Canada. The team held an advance prayer meeting at Johnnie Bisaro's home in Kellogg, Idaho, in a large basement room with several chairs and a couch lining the walls.

As we interceded about the upcoming meeting, the Holy Spirit led us to read the Scripture passage about when Paul was opposed by a magician named Elymas on the island of Salamis, now known as Malta (Acts 13:4–12). The Lord let us know that we would be going up against a warlock and a coven of witches on our mission, so we started praying against that warlock and his coven.

A cat suddenly burst out from under the couch, yowling and screeching, and shot up the wall, clawing frantically as though it would climb to the ceiling! It dropped on Dawn Mattmiller's back, frightening her half out of her wits, then shot up the walls several times more. At last we caught it while it hissed and growled at us. We took it gingerly by the scruff of the neck and the fur on its back and carried it out of the house.

Johnnie said she had never seen the cat before that day, when she had noticed it skulking about the house and had been unable to catch it. She had no idea how it had gotten inside, much less down to the basement.

We knew we had been visited by a familiar, and prayed much more fervently!

Sure enough, the moment we arrived at the Priory in Victoria, a group of Christian women approached us. "We're so glad you've come," they said. "A boy in a hospital here is dying of a rare blood disease the doctors can't diagnose, and we know there's a warlock and his coven on a nearby island who are hating him to death."

Before we could enter into prayer, word came that the boy had died. That plunged us into a battle that lasted for several months. Eventually the warlock was injured in a car crash, his coven stripped of power, then disbanded.

Some Christians testify of knowing of various birds used by warlocks and witches, especially ravens. Many are convinced that snakes are always under the power of demons. I doubt this, but I can see how they could occasionally be used as instruments of demonic powers.

Lest we walk around fearful that every strange dog or cat may be someone's familiar, let us remember that such occurrences are very rare. Most animals are simply the innocent pets they seem to be. It requires discernment in the Holy Spirit to know when an animal is actually being so used. After thirty-plus years of ministry, the above is the only clear-cut case I have experienced of an animal being used as a familiar.

If an animal is suspected of being a familiar, Christians can get together, listen to the Lord, then simply deliver any such animal from the control of the warlock or witch. We are more than conquerors.

## Objects Inhabited by Demonic Powers

Objects also can be inhabited by demonic powers. In late 1984 Paula and I were racing against our editor's deadline to finish the book *Healing the Wounded Spirit*. Because we own a one-week time-share in a lovely condo on a beautiful lake north of our home, we took our brand-new electronic typewriter up there. Our friend Bonnie Crouch, a professional secretary and excellent typist, came to help us and brought her new electric typewriter.

We were unprepared for what happened! As we were trying to type up the final copy of the chapters on occult involvement, spiritualism and exorcism, neither typewriter would work properly! We examined them and found nothing at all the matter with them. They were new, undamaged and should have operated perfectly. Yet they would break down and refuse to type. Or they wouldn't start at all. Or they would not print what was typed.

Finally it dawned on us that this was not mere happenstance. The devil didn't want these chapters in print. So, feeling foolish but desperate enough to try anything, we laid hands on the typewriters and exorcised them! Immediately both typewriters ran flawlessly. After that, every time they balked, we exorcised them again.

When those chapters were done, both machines worked without a hitch, and we finished typing the rest of the book in time for our deadline.

Later on Paula and I obtained two new computers, and were once again up against a deadline, each of us on a different book. Again we had carted our computers to the condo to escape interruptions and the telephone. Wouldn't you know, both brand-new computers refused to work correctly! While I worked on a chapter revealing the deceits of the flesh and Satan's entrapments of unwary Christians into fornication and adultery, my printer actually spat out two pages of curses at me! It filled both pages with those marks cartoonists use when their characters are cussing—!* !*/ !*.

It wouldn't quit even when I entered the command Stop Printing. Finally I had to unplug it!

This time, however, we were experienced. We exorcised the computers and had no more trouble.

Others tell of cars that would not run right until exorcised, and washing machines, even printing presses and huge machines in factories. Satan annoys any way he can.

## Gifts that Need to Be Destroyed

Years ago I taught in a conference on inner healing in the Northeast. After the conference, the leader of the seminar invited me to stay overnight. While we were enjoying an autumn fireside chat, the doorbell rang. I answered the door. A man who had attended the meeting stood there, holding some objects in his hand.

"I just thought I ought to bring you these as a gift," he said.

Surprised, I said, "Thank you," and accepted them, whereupon he turned around and left without another word.

The gift turned out to be cufflinks fashioned like miniature Buddhas. When we asked the Lord what He wanted us to do with them, He said, *Burn them.*

We both understood that, whereas the man may have thought he only wanted to give me a gift, subconsciously he was asking me to destroy his idols. So we laid them on the logs next to the blaze. I know how brightly plastics and metals burn, but these glowed with uncommon intensity. We felt our spirits lifting in exultation as the flames consumed those idols.

I did not even connect this at the time with God's command in the Old Testament to burn such things—the passage quoted in Loren and Georgia Murphy's newsletter report, for instance, cited in the previous chapter. (See also Deuteronomy 7:5 and 12:3.) Let me quote it again:

> The images of their gods you are to burn in the fire. Do not covet the silver and gold on them, and do not take it for yourselves, or you will be ensnared by it, for it is detestable to the Lord your God. Do not bring a detestable thing into your house or you, like it, will be set apart for destruction. Utterly abhor and detest it, for it is set apart for destruction.
>
> Deuteronomy 7:25–26, NIV

Since the experience with the cufflinks, I have often asked the Lord what He wanted me do with a number of such gifts. The answer is always *Burn them*. I have counseled others to do the same. People often give the Lord's servants gifts that are really "devoted objects" or idols, sometimes purposefully intending to snare, most times with the best of intentions. It is ironic that the word gift in German means "poison"! Satan means such gifts to be poison and a point of contact for demonic invasion. Our obedience turns them into defeat.

Many Christians could share far more dramatic experiences in delivering animals and things than we, but perhaps these few stories will suffice. Our purpose is not to exhaust the subject but to open up possibilities to those who suspect that such realities exist but are reluctant, lest they be regarded as weird. We need to walk close to the Lord so He can reveal when animals or objects are being invaded or used by demonic powers.

It is a simple matter to set animals and things free from demonization. But we need to remember that neither inner healing nor deliverance should stand alone. Both are required.

## Balance and Wisdom

I can just see some immature Christians becoming exasperated with their cars and trying to exorcise what a simple mechanical adjustment would fix! We must be particularly careful in regard to demons so that unbelievers do not view us as superstitious fools and we besmirch the cause of Christ in their eyes.

Careful listening to the Lord ought to precede any attempts at exorcism, especially when unbelievers might gain an opportunity to blaspheme the Lord's works.

It is a joy to know, on the other hand, in truth and in fact, that demons are indeed subject to us! We don't have to fear anything. The Lord in us is stronger than anything in the world—or out of it!

# 12

## Demonic Specialists

Like human beings, demons have individual natures and personalities. And like human beings, whose persistence at particular tasks over time may affect and even reshape our character, so it is with demons. Long practice at certain tasks has not only made them adept, but shaped their personalities and characters.

Demons specialize. Some are especially cruel and destructive. Some can appear as angels of light (2 Corinthians 11:14). Some can even appear benevolent. Many times I have labored to dissuade women seduced by incubus spirits they thought were their best friends! (More on incubus spirits in a moment.)

We need to be armed with understanding and wisdom. Others might put together a more comprehensive list of the types and tasks of demons, but in this chapter I will present those I think are most pertinent to equip us as the Lord's warriors. To do justice to this subject would require an entire book with a chapter for each type of demon. Such a treatment would include several story examples for each type, advice on how to discern, and more teaching as to how to oust invading demons. Lacking space, I have elected to present the basics and trust the reader to think things through and seek the Lord's wisdom for additional details.

## Seductive Spirits

A seductive spirit is one that specializes in temptation. A seductive demon has long-developed techniques for involving people in whatever weaknesses present an opportunity.

There are many types of seductive spirits. Some specialize in tempting men into power-grabbing and self-exaltation. Some act in sexual areas. Some work mentally, as in 1 Timothy 4:1: "In later times some will fall away from the faith, paying attention to deceitful spirits and doctrines of demons." Some cause divisiveness in relationships or tempt into rancor, gossip or slander. Some tempt financially.

I suppose there are as many types of seductive spirits as there are ways to sin.

## Mental Demons

The mind is where I believe war is waged daily, hourly, for the control of mankind! The first sin was mental—eating the fruit of the tree of the *knowledge* of good and evil. Jesus was crucified on Golgotha, translated "The Place of the Skull," the residence of the mind. Satan and his hosts concentrate more on influencing and controlling how people think than on any other aspect of life.

This warfare is so important that the entire next chapter is devoted to exposing how demons work through individual mental strongholds, and how principalities and world rulers work through corporate strongholds.

## Power-Grabbing and Self-Exalting Spirits

How often in history have noble, magnanimous men started political projects with good motives, working for the benefit and release of downtrodden people, only to become seduced into becoming tyrants themselves? It has happened over and over, especially in Central and South America and Africa.

Napoleon succumbed to this temptation and allowed himself to be declared emperor. Satan himself acted as a seductive spirit when he tried to tempt Jesus in this very thing: "The devil took Him to a very high mountain, and showed Him all the kingdoms of the world, and their glory; and he said to Him, 'All these things will I give You, if You fall down and worship me'" (Matthew 4:8–9).

The temptation to grab power does not lure only those in high places. Fathers can fall to the same temptation in the management of their families; foremen at work; employers with employees; teachers with students—wherever authority must be expressed. Jesus taught us that the person who wants to be the greatest must be as the least, and the person who would rule over others must be the servant of all.

The task of seductive spirits is to cause us to forget those words, to expand whatever areas of pride and hunger for power remain uncrucified in our hearts until we become oppressive, and to use whatever as yet unhealed false or hurtful role-modeling from our early family life gives them leave to cause us to domineer and control others.

This temptation wreaks havoc in the Church when internationally known television evangelists elevate themselves above their calling, trying to act as pastors, teachers and prophetic disciplinarians over the rest of the Body of Christ, or establishing ministries, universities or great overseas missionary works in their own name. (To his everlasting credit, Billy Graham has never succumbed to such a temptation.)

What can we do when we see the onslaught of seductive spirits enticing leaders in any capacity into self-aggrandizement? Here again, understanding the relationship between deliverance and inner healing is important. It will not do merely to discern a spirit of megalomania or self-exaltation and cast it away. It will only return and make the last state of that leader and his or her works worse than before. There must be confession until the childhood roots relative to authority, and all subconscious needs to domineer and control, have been recognized and crucified and new ways built in.

Demons may block recognition, repentance and confession unless first bound and silenced.

Every leader worth his or her salt needs to grant a strong, select few the forum and authority to deal with him openly and honestly. He must fellowship with them constantly, enabling them to be so intimate with his entire life as to be able to discern accurately when a spirit is trying to get to him.

It is "lonely at the top." No man or woman is so strong personally as to be safe. A major part of Paula's and my ministry for thirty years has been to minister healing to leaders, including many of the most visible servants in the Lord's army. I have seen many leaders fall, and know of no fallen leader to whom loved ones and friends had clear license to speak warnings or were offered enough exposure to be accurate! Each one was isolated and unable to receive help from the Body of Christ, although countless loved ones stood by wringing their hands, wanting desperately to save him from himself.

This has been such a grief to us that I wish I could take hold of every leader at risk in the Body of Christ, shake him by the shoulders and shout, "Wake up! Surround yourself with strong people who can reprove and correct you, daily if necessary. Give them authority over you. Listen to them. Obey them. Your stony heart and your pride are leaving you vulnerable to demons. Open yourself to friends. Trust them. Cherish no secrets; let your friends know what troubles you. Spend the time necessary in fellowship for them to really know you."

Unless someone has counseled literally hundreds of fallen leaders, he or she cannot know how desperately these words need to be heard and how few leaders hear them!

Many leaders have the good sense to collect intercessors about them who pray daily for their protection. But *isolation undoes those prayers*. Just as you cannot cast away a demon from a person who wants to keep it, you cannot protect a leader successfully whose ways constantly invite seductive demons to control his or her life.

Pray for the leaders you know that God will give them humble, listening hearts. Take authority to bat away the demons until the leaders' thoughts and actions no longer give them access. We must win the battle for leadership today. Satan's plan is the same as always: "Strike the shepherd and scatter the sheep."

## Demons of Greed

Who has not watched a loved one fall to the temptation of greed? It is not always for money or possessions or power. We can covet other things, like praise. Satan scours the earth looking for anyone to worship him—which is what he wanted when he offered Jesus the kingdoms of the world.

We are not much different than he. We lust after people to honor us, to give us accolades, to crown us with praises. The system of the world is based on this lust: Witness our banquets and celebrations for Emmys, Oscars, Heisman trophies, Davis Cups, Olympic gold medals, World Series championships. You name it, anything and everything we do is encompassed by our human need and, yes, greed for honor and reward.

This nearly universal human weakness gives demons a playfield in our hearts. For that reason Jesus offered this counsel:

> When you are invited by someone to a wedding feast, do not take the place of honor, lest someone more distinguished than you may have been invited by him, and he who invited you both shall come and say to you, "Give place to this man," and then in disgrace you proceed to occupy the last place.
>
> But when you are invited, go and recline at the last place, so that when the one who has invited you comes, he may say to you, "Friend, move up higher"; then you will have honor in the sight of all who are at the table with you.
>
> For every one who exalts himself shall be humbled, and he who humbles himself shall be exalted.
>
> Luke 14:8–11

Jesus was not speaking of mere table graces or teaching us to be clever guests. He was striking at the root need in all of us to be honored and praised. All of us must haul to the cross our longings for the plaudits of others, else we will not be free from Satan's specialists in greed.

Who has not seen wealthy people dissatisfied with all they have and striving to earn more? They have been gripped by greed, along with its stepchildren, envy and jealousy. How often have we ground our teeth when a friend or co-worker got a hefty raise or won a contest or was honored in some way? We told ourselves we were happy for him or her, and maybe we were, but another side of us may have been full of envy and jealousy.

The antidote? Allow brothers and sisters in Christ to point out what they see in us. Let the Holy Spirit convict us. Ask God for a humble mind and heart that can not only receive rebuke but seek it avidly in order to be whole.

How can we discern whether the greed we see in operation is not just unredeemed flesh but is demonically empowered? A first sign is when it begins to go out of control, when the demands and actions of greed can no longer be halted. Sometimes even that can be explained by some tragic flaw in the flesh, so we need the Holy Spirit's discernment. But when we see inordinate needs driving a person, we are alerted to seek the Lord's wisdom and gifts.

Again, deliverance is a matter of both overcoming the flesh and casting away the demonic. Strangely, the roots of excessive greed for money and power seldom have to do with money or the lack of it. Most often they have to do with feelings of not being chosen and cherished in infant and pre-school years, and with the lack of affection and appropriate affirmation for accomplishments in early school years. Thus, the adult is still trying subconsciously to do or accumulate enough to satisfy the needs of his or her inner child for parental acceptance and approval. Demons have taken hold of those subconscious needs and driven the person out of balance.

Merely shouting at a demon of greed will bring at best only temporary relief. There must be two kinds of discernment: of spiritual entities and of human nature. To see all as demonic is myopic. To see all as defects in the old nature may be blind and equally ineffective.

## Sexual Demons

Sexual seduction is, next to mental seduction, Satan's highest priority. He knows that our bodies are the temple of the Holy Spirit (1 Corinthians 3:16) and wants above all to destroy that temple. He knows sexual sin is the only sin within our body (1 Corinthians 6:18) and that whoever commits adultery destroys his or her own soul (Proverbs 6:32). Surely a *rhema* meaning of Revelation 12:15 is that Satan is spewing out of his mouth a veritable Niagara of sexual smut every day through every possible medium—movies,

TV, novels, magazines, etc.—to try to sweep away the woman who is the Church.

How tragically successful his campaign has been! When I first entered the pastorate, it was commonplace for a woman to come to her wedding day with her virginity intact. Today that is the exception. In church after church, couples live together without benefit of marriage vows, thinking themselves good Christians. We need not labor the point; the specter of AIDS haunts our world primarily because of rampant sexual sin.

### *Incubus and Succuba Demons*

Within the class of sexual tempters are several specific demons. First there are incubus and succuba spirits. An incubus poses as the Lord or as a benign and loving spirit in order to seduce women sexually.

An incubus may come to a Christian woman and tell her that it is her right and joy as the bride of Christ to please Him by making love to Him physically! The demon then manifests itself to her so fully, disguised as a beautiful and desirable man, that it actually can make her feel its touch. It can arouse her and take her completely through to climax. She thinks she has enjoyed intercourse with the Lord Himself!

With the less gullible, the incubus may realize it cannot fool a woman into thinking it is the Lord, so it claims to be her guardian angel with whom it is, of course, all right to enjoy the ministrations of his love. After all, God has sent him, and God has only the best of intentions for her. She has been so lonely. He will always be the one friend she can count on. His love will never fail her. He will always be there for her, understanding her when no one else can or wants to. She begins to look forward to these times of privacy in which his delicious touch is such a comfort to her. She may even be so deluded as to thank God fervently for sending her guardian angel to love her.

Sometimes Paula and I have had to argue, scold and plead with an incubus victim for hours to convince her that its true intentions were to take her to hell if it could! We could not cast it away and keep it away so long as she longed for its "love." When her eyes were finally opened, she would cringe in revulsion, rage at the deception and repent. Then we could pronounce forgiveness, cleanse her spirit and soul in the water and blood of Jesus, and set her free.

Whenever couples enter into sexual union, Paul tells us they become one flesh (1 Corinthians 6:16). God has built us for covenant, a spirit-to-spirit bonding through sexual intimacy. God has so created a woman that her spirit fastens onto the first man who enters her and she never forgets that union. From then on, though her mind may forget him, her spirit seeks to find and fulfill him, to comfort him and bear his children. If she sleeps with first one and then another, she is horribly scattered and confused, her spirit drawn here and there.

A man is likewise built to bond to the first woman he enters, to care for her, protect her and provide for her all his days. His spirit also cannot forget each successive union.

Some think that the scriptural concept of "one flesh" means simply "one in spirit or attitude." I disagree. That interpretation seems to stem from a platonic and possibly Docetic view of human nature. (Platonism idealized the spiritual rather than physical world, while Docetism claimed that Christ only appeared to have a human body.) No, God makes couples who unite sexually one *flesh*.

Whenever we hear a confession of fornication or adultery, therefore, we need not only to pronounce forgiveness for the penitent one, but also to take up our authority in the Lord Jesus Christ and loose their spirits from one another (Matthew 18:18 and 16:19). We speak directly to the person's spirit and command it to forget the union(s). Then we address the person's soul, telling the mind to release responsibility for the other and the emotions to let go and forget.

The mind is not to forget the sin; the remembrance will yield gratitude, humility and the ability to minister to others. But the spirit and emotions will be free to unite in sexual wholeness and bond properly with the spouse.

The same kind of bonding happens with incubus spirits. The demon uses that attachment and sense of belonging to further secure its hold on a woman. So the healer must not only convince the woman to reject the demon; he must also use his authority to break the attachment and set her free to bond properly where and when she should.

It is also necessary to ferret out the causes in childhood that left the woman lonely and vulnerable. The most common childhood wounding behind adultery with incubus spirits is undealt-with feelings of rejection, usually by the father, sometimes well-hidden and repressed.

A succuba is a demon posing as a lovely woman. I have ministered to men who have awakened in the middle of the night to find themselves already aroused and erect, stimulated almost to the point of ejaculation by a spirit they might also "see" in the dim light as a beautiful woman, touching them lovingly. These demons cannot pose as the Lord, of course, who is the husband. Perhaps this is why they often come to a man in his sleep, bypassing his mind so they can arouse him until he cannot or does not want to stop.

Afterward he may so come to enjoy "her" visits that, though his mind and conscience nag at him that something is wrong, he does not want to deny "her," or he cannot muster the willpower. The succuba uses the natural bonding of his spirit to strengthen its hold.

The man, too, must come to detest this thing that has defiled him. Confession, repentance and forgiveness must be followed by deliverance prayers and breaking the false bonding. Again, root causes should be found and brought to the cross. The most common cause is rejection by or frustration with mother figures in childhood, feelings of not being chosen and touched by the mother. Sometimes lack of breastfeeding or being weaned too soon may be part of a man's vulnerability to succubae.

We have ministered deliverance repeatedly to a bachelor whose unsatisfied sexual needs constantly reopen the door to succubae. Though we have tracked his entire history to heal everything we can see, he seems unable to receive the gift of celibacy. To date we have been unable to find the key to enable him to close his doors irrevocably.

This is to say, although it is often easy to cast succubae away, the greater responsibility and more difficult task may be to find how to prevent their returning.

## *Unclean Spirits, Sexual Abuse, Molestation and Incest*

As our society turns from God and toward "degrading passions" and "a depraved mind" (Romans 1:26, 28), molestation and incest are just two examples (as bad as they are) of sexual sins that are on the rise at an alarming rate. The result: broken homes, dysfunctional families, parents driven by powerful subconscious urges, children fractured by their parents' actions, etc.

There is nothing more harmful than sexual abuse or incest on a child by a parent (see Paula's book *Healing Victims of Sexual Abuse*). These two sexual sins fracture children's trust of authority, destroy self-esteem, trash their glory, defile them and admit spirits of uncleanness. Such children often become promiscuous in teenage and adult years, and usually cannot enjoy (unless they are carefully and tenderly healed) the true blessedness and joy of Christian marital sex.

Spirits of uncleanness not only tempt parents and others to molest and commit incest; they actually enter the victim through those activities. Paula and I have often found it necessary to deliver adults from spirits of uncleanness that entered and began to defile and subdue them when they were molested or taken incestuously as children. From then on they may have had to fight lustful feelings, especially pornographic imaginings, tendencies to addiction to masturbation, lust of the eyes for pornography, voyeurism, burlesque shows, "adult" and X-rated movies, etc.

Unclean spirits urge men to ask or demand more from their wives than wholesome cherishing allows. They often use a common deception that some Christians have taught—that whatever happens in the marriage bed is holy. If that were true, Paul would not have written:

> For this is the will of God, your sanctification; that is, that you abstain from sexual immorality; that each of you know how to possess his own vessel in sanctification and honor, *not in lustful passion*, like the Gentiles who do not know God.
>
> 1 Thessalonians 4:3–5, italics mine

Let no one be deceived: A man can commit lust with his own wife! Demons of uncleanness prompt him to demand anal sex or oral sex. So also fellatio (in which the wife assists his masturbation by placing her mouth over his penis). Whatever enhances the meeting, bonding and cherishing of a married couple for one another is holy and clean. *Whatever uses the other solely for self-gratification is, by definition, lust.*

Demons push the normal desires for fulfillment in sexual union into unclean desires for degrading acts. When passions and sexual titillations grow beyond feelings of holy cherishing and meeting, no longer does a man "possess his own vessel in sanctification and honor." He is acting in lustful passion.

There should be a joyous sharing of touch and excitement. The marital act should be overshadowed by a sense of holiness, of wholesome refreshment and fulfillment. Degrading passions destroy that sense—even though in the heat of the moment the couple is excited by the stimulation of it—and leave them feeling let down.

Unclean spirits try to expand whatever homosexual and lesbian tendencies may have been created by early woundings. They hook into the strongholds of homosexuality (discussed in the next chapter) and invite principalities of delusion to help them justify and secure their hold upon their "gay" victims.

I counseled a woman who felt defiled every time her husband made love to her. They had seven children. Her attitudes toward sex were wholesome. I could find in her childhood neither molestation nor sufficient woundings to account for her negative feelings. Then she discovered that her husband was a "closet queen." He had taken young boys regularly to their summer cabin for homosexual orgies. No wonder she felt unclean!

Unclean spirits use hidden hatred of women to cause men to become promiscuous or to commit rape. No man who seeks illicit unions is a lover of women, no matter what he thinks. He hates women and loves to defile them. His emotions are ruled by spirits of uncleanness. "For there is no good tree which produces bad fruit; nor, on the other hand, a bad tree which produces good fruit" (Luke 6:43). Love, being good, cannot produce evil. Fornication and adultery are evil. Love cannot produce fornication and adultery. Evil produces evil. Hate and demons of lust, and nothing else, produce illicit sex.

The same is true for women. Only hatred of men, not love, produces promiscuity. Demons use women's need for romance, and their desire to feel chosen and beautiful, to make them vulnerable to lecherous men.

Demons and principalities of uncleanness today (as we will see in the next chapter) are having a heyday as "world rulers of this present darkness" manipulate the media to croon Satan's siren song of sex and destruction over a gullible world.

How shall we set free the entrapped? First, become aware. Minister the fullness of healing. Bind and cast away. Find out what fractured and wounded in childhood, especially sexually, giving the demons access. Heal the heart through the grace and cross of Christ.

But don't stop there. Resurrection ministry is in order. Pray wholesome life into the person. If molestation or incest created the vulnerability, cherish the child rejected by being used uncleanly. Help to rebuild the inner heart and character. This means long-term counseling and may require becoming as a father or mother in Christ so that the other can drink wholesomeness from Him through you as His instrument for healing.

## Controlling and Domineering Spirits

In the early '70s the "shepherding and discipling" movement began with some of the most solid, best-known teachers in the charismatic renewal. Its intentions: to resurrect true corporateness within the Body of Christ; to mature God's people into the fullness of the nature of Christ; to instill proper respect for authority in the hearts and minds of a rebellious and immature people. But it degenerated into a damaging cult of control and domination. Why?

Because deluding domineering and controlling spirits overshadowed it and brought it down.

In 1975 I sensed the Lord directing me for a time into a group connected with shepherding and discipling. I obeyed reluctantly. While involved in it and committed to a "shepherd," Paula and I came to St. Louis where Francis MacNutt, then a Roman Catholic priest, resided in Merton House. Francis invited us out to dinner. We asked him what he thought of shepherding and discipling.

"When we Catholics and the Protestants got together," he replied, "we drank from each other's strengths but also, unfortunately, from each other's weaknesses. The shepherding and discipling movement is moving under the same three strongholds we Catholics just left: domination and control from the top down; the belief that only the priests know what is going on, and are thus the only ones who can make the right decisions for people's lives; and the arrogation of all interpretation of the Bible to the priesthood."

The principalities that had held strongholds of domination over corporate structures now moved that control over men who thought they were restoring order and discipline under authority. Local demons poured into unhealed areas in those men's hearts: known and unknown anger against parental authority, unmet needs to be fathered, hunger to belong and be accepted, etc. Unhealed scars in relation to controlling mothers were used to reduce women to the position of chattel, under the guise of the catchword *submission*. Whoever objected or offered words of wisdom or restraint was accused of being rebellious. Whoever threatened to leave was told he or she would miss the Kingdom. Fear ruled.

One time I went to teach among friends (the teaching had nothing to do with shepherding and discipling). But as I expounded, I felt a wave of power—not of the Holy Spirit—that flowed from above me out over the congregation. Meanwhile, those who had always heard me eagerly sat with wide eyes, recoiling in fear. "And a stranger they simply will not follow, but will flee from him, because they do not know the voice of strangers" (John 10:5). The presence of the overshadowing principalities and demons of domination and control made me, their long-trusted teacher and friend, a "stranger."

After that I sensed the Lord releasing me from the shepherding and discipling group. One afternoon I spent several hours trying to convince a friend, one of my spiritual brothers under the same shepherd, that he, too, should come out. Finally he agreed. We prayed him clean from those demons. But on the way home he began to fear he would miss the Kingdom of God, and subsequently plunged back into several more years of misery before finally leaving for good.

Thank God, nearly all who were caught up in that deception have by now struggled free, and most of its leaders have seen their errors and repented. I will teach in the next chapter what I did not know that afternoon with my friend—what strongholds are, how they can move to recapture their victims, and how to deliver people from them.

## Jezebel Spirits

Another spirit, sometimes classed as a sexual spirit of seduction but one I prefer to call a spirit of domination and control, is the well-known spirit called *Jezebel*.

Jezebel spirits create division and rancor among friends. They stir up envy and jealousy, gossiping and slander. Since they tempt many into illicit sexual affairs, which are visible and dramatic, some Christians think of Jezebel spirits as primarily sexual. But their name is derived from King Ahab's wife, whose ways were domineering and controlling. "Surely there was no one like Ahab who sold himself to do evil in the sight of the Lord, *because Jezebel his wife incited him*" (1 Kings 21:25).

It is ironic that landlocked Israel could prosper only when allied to the seafaring Phoenicians of Tyre and Sidon (who in turn needed the caravan routes that came through Israel). But whenever Israel was linked to Phoenicia, their false gods corrupted her. Israel had thought to cement her tenuous relationship to Tyre and Sidon through the marriage of the Phoenician princess Jezebel to King Ahab. But Jezebel brought with her devotion to false gods and her ability to influence and control others.

Jezebel spirits operate through women to seduce church leaders into quarreling and jealousy. They operate through idolatry. Whenever women give themselves unconsciously to the false gods of success, acclaim, ambition, self-exaltation, adulation and power, these demonic specialists turn their motives into driving forces that destroy balance, perspective, common sense and fellowship in Christ. When men unknowingly serve such false gods, Jezebel spirits cause women to manipulate men into the strivings that cause rancor and division.

The spirits' goal is not only to destroy individuals but, through them, to divide and bring down thriving churches.

Rescue and freedom cannot be obtained merely by discerning Jezebel spirits and rebuking them away. If inner forces in people's hearts are not addressed, the same or other spirits will soon return. Repentance is called for.

If Christians do not regard each ministry, gift and position in the church as their Isaac and put all on the altar, the Lord will have neither their works nor them. They will become servants of their own ministry rather than of the Lord Jesus Christ. Pride and flesh, not the Holy Spirit, will rule their service. It will not be long before Jezebel spirits discover the "fertile ground" and go to work.

I suggest fervently that each reader pause this very moment and say the following prayer:

"Lord, I lay on Your altar every gift, every talent, every position of honor and service to which You have called me. Let me be dead to each one. I know You will give them back, but henceforth they will be Yours and not mine. Let me be ruled by the self-sacrificial love of the Holy Spirit and not by the strivings of my own flesh. Forgive me for serving the false gods of my own strivings. Bring me into rest. Thank You, Jesus. I believe You are accomplishing the death of ambition within me. Amen."

That prayer will need to be repeated often, and all the more with higher callings and greater giftings.

It goes without saying that it is also important to ferret out whatever quirks in our nature from childhood formations grant such spirits access. Only our continual death on the cross with Jesus (as in Galatians 2:20 and 5:24) can set us free from the baleful influence of demonic powers, especially Jezebels.

## Shrike Spirits

A shrike is a bird that impales its victims on a thorn and tears them apart muscle by muscle. In human form, a shrike is a hyper-performance-oriented person who has learned in childhood to derive a sense of well-being and power by outdoing siblings and even adults in the family. A Christian shrike is a self-righteous striver who cannot allow anyone to appear more righteous than himself or herself. Such people garner all the righteousness of the family or group to themselves and unconsciously defile everyone nearby so that they find themselves stumbling, making mistakes and even falling into sin.

Readers can easily check this out. Is there someone in whose presence you cannot be your best self? Try as you will, near that person you goof up what you could normally handle anywhere else. It puzzles you because you find yourself continually doing stupid things before you can stop yourself. In his or her presence you feel embarrassed, insecure and somehow "wrong," whereas you are normally quite competent.

Shrike spirits lay hold of human shrikes to cause them to gather "armies" around themselves, ostensibly to help people—their bumbling pastor, for example—but actually to undermine respect for authority and create suspicion and divisiveness. In the family or church, only the shrike seems to have the righteousness and stability to save everybody else from themselves! Until the game is discovered, everyone wonders how they could have survived without the shrike's presence and counsel. Shrikes shatter the confidence and strength of their victims in the very act of seeming to help them. Thus, they "tear them apart, muscle by muscle."

Is there someone who has offered to help you, but you feel less and less capable each time you are with your "helper"? Paula and I knew a man who would sit beside his daughter to help her at the piano. In a few minutes she would sidle off, downcast and dejected, while he sat there playing a concert! He would try to be helpful in the kitchen but would soon so berate his wife for alleged mistakes that she felt like an inept child in her own kitchen (though in fact she was so skilled she could rank as a gourmet chef).

He himself, a highly trained engineer, lost job after job. In each new position he would quickly learn the tasks in the office, then set out to advise and help everyone else. His unconscious shrikism soon made them feel put down and ignorant. Finally the boss would discern that he was the cause of the increasing dissension and mistakes in the office and would have to fire him. I attended a meeting at which he interrupted his present boss's speech three times to give him "helpful" criticism and correction! (Needless to say, he soon lost that job!) He had no idea that what drove him was not purely his desire to be helpful but an unconscious need to put others down and exalt himself.

Shrikes are wounded children in grownup bodies who desperately need acceptance, approval and compliments—but they do the very things that drive people away. So they try harder, only to accelerate the process of defilement and inevitable rejection. This condition serves as fertile ground for demons to plow and sow.

Our son Loren was driven nearly to distraction trying to build up a church in which five shrikes (two men and three women) were all working hard to "help" him! They ripped apart the fabric of unity in the church, tore kinship groups asunder, created jealousies and dissensions and, most importantly, kept convincing church members that Loren, poor fellow, didn't know what he was doing and needed their help. He was just too young and immature; "we have to pray for him."

It was not merely their own natural shrikism at work. Demons controlled their thoughts and tongues and moved on everyone who became defiled, convinced by their attitudes and words.

Hebrews 3:12 makes clear that Christians may have an unbelieving heart that can lead them from life unto death. Paul affirms in Romans 2:28–29 that only the circumcised in heart are the true circumcision.

But *Christian shrikes cannot believe in their heart that they are saved and loved without having to earn it*. In this sense they are unbelievers and scoffers. How scoffers? They resist healing: "I'm all right; it's all these other sinful people who need help." They are, in reality, scoffing at those who would help them.

In the end Loren managed with effort and sacrifice to snatch two out of the fire (Jude 23). When one of the two was being ministered to, the group confronted her again and again, driving the Word of God into her mind and heart. Finally she saw what she had been doing, repented and fell to the floor, writhing in convulsions while the demon of shrikism tore its way out of her.

Gentle but firm, persistent confrontation and deliverance are the only way shrikes can be set free. Friends who have experienced what the shrike creates must testify repeatedly and clearly to the truth of this effect until finally the shrike cannot help but see it.

It is a painful process because the demon will continually smoke-screen its presence by turning things back on the failings of those who are confronting.

If, after friends make repeated attempts to save and heal, shrikes will not hear and repent, pastors and leaders must have the fortitude to put them out of the church. Scripture says, "Drive out the scoffer, and contention will go out, even strife and dishonor will cease" (Proverbs 22:10). But church expulsion is the last thing their demons want, because it quenches their effectiveness within the local body. So they try to convince everyone, through the shrike, how unchristian and unloving this pastor and church are if they cannot love them enough to let them stay.

I teach this carefully because, when discernment is clear and confirmed and shrikes will not be healed, leaders must act decisively with a clear conscience. (The other three shrikes in Loren's church were eventually put out, resulting in great peace.) Otherwise, the church will be unsettled continually by disrespect for authority and destruction of unity.

I have ministered to many broken pastors who could not understand what happened to their thriving, healthy congregations. The demons had used these pastors' kindly, longsuffering natures to keep their "servants" in the church. In this regard, Christian leaders must put their natural kindness and compassion onto the altar, lest they remain longsuffering when the Holy Spirit prompts sternness and decisiveness.

We are at war, and this kind of warfare often calls for decisions that seem unchristian. Shrike demons will remind everyone in leadership that Jesus said to leave the ninety-nine and save the one lost sheep. "What? You won't do that? How can you call yourself a follower of Jesus Christ?" Translation: "Let me manipulate you, for after all, if you won't do that, I'm a better Christian than you."

We must not fall for the demonic deceptions attempted through these poor, hurting people. We do not help by letting them destroy another church.

I suggest that you, the reader, test what I teach here by checking out the history of the shrikes you have known in previous churches or in your current church. I think you will find a consistent pattern of devastation.

One final comment: Christians who become shrikes sometimes seem to be inhabited. I said earlier that, in my opinion, born-again Christians filled with the Spirit of God cannot be possessed or even entered; yet I have seen hardened shrikes not only demonized from without, but definitely entered and controlled. How shall we understand this?

As I pondered this question, the Lord reminded me that He could not do many mighty works in Nazareth because of their unbelief (Matthew 13:58). Since shrikes are actually unbelievers in heart, Jesus' presence in them is "encysted" and made ineffective. (See chapter 2 to recall how a demon can be encysted.) The Holy Spirit is thus not released and is quenched within the shrike, until repentance enables His power to cast out the demon of shrikism.

These speculations make sense to me and, I hope, to you as well. Spiritual reality seems determined not to be boxed in by our tidy mental definitions, no matter how hard we struggle to comprehend things far beyond us.

## Afflicting Spirits

There are many types of afflicting spirits. We shall speak only of a few of the most prominent.

### *Warrior Demons*

These afflicting spirits hurl missiles, "the flaming missiles of the evil one" (Ephesians 6:16). Most Christians have probably felt at one time or another—for a spiritual, not physiological, reason—as though someone has suddenly jabbed them with a pin in the thigh or arm or buttocks, right through layers of clothing, causing a few moments of intense pain. Some Christians have experienced being "jumped on" in the night, usually while asleep, instantly paralyzed and unable to move a muscle.

I suppose the devil, knowing he cannot overcome us, tries to frighten us or wear us down by attrition. But we learn more deeply than before that the Lord in us is stronger than "he that is in the world," and that He will defeat demons every time they attack.

Following the spiritual warfare on Vancouver Island against the warlock and his coven of witches mentioned in the last chapter, I began to feel drained. In a month or so, people I knew with prophetic gifts were telling me I needed more protection around me.

One night in an audience where I spoke friends sat with tears streaming down their faces. Afterward I asked, "Was what I said so bad it made you cry?"

"No, John," they responded. "We could see in the Spirit that you are being hit again and again, moment by moment, day after day."

Truly I did feel like a punch-drunk boxer, black and blue all over.

Later, after I spoke at a Christian camp, a friend who is gifted as a masseuse saw the hurt and ache in my body. "Maybe it would help," she said, "if you let me give you a rubdown." Leery of that but willing to try anything, I made sure someone else was present. Then we spread a blanket on the grass and she began to massage my back.

Again and again she came to the same spot midway down my spinal column on the right side. She seemed puzzled. Finally I asked, "What is it? You seem disturbed about something."

She replied, "I don't know, John. I've never encountered anything like this. There's something evil here."

We sent for a woman at the camp, Marilyn, who had a keen gift of discernment. When she arrived the masseuse said, "There's something in John's back. I don't know what it is. I want you to take it away." She told Marilyn nothing more than that and gave her no indication as to exactly where it was.

Marilyn prayed quietly for a few minutes, then grabbed forcefully that very spot in my back, jerking something out and away from me and letting out a scream in the process. Instantly I felt relief from pressure and pain.

"What was it?" we asked.

"It was a spear," she said when she had regained her composure, "an evil thing of Satan, sticking right there in John's back."

Lest that seem impossible, consider this Scripture in another light: "In addition to all, taking up the shield of faith with which you will be able to extinguish all the flaming missiles of the evil one" (Ephesians 6:16). Perhaps one reason the Lord let me experience what I did was so we could know beyond doubt that this Scripture is sometimes to be taken literally. Those darts are real. No one can tell me otherwise. I felt the sickness of it in me. I felt it when Marilyn pulled it out of me, and I knew the relief and the health that flooded into me again.

Warrior demons do not necessarily inhabit. Nor do I know that they can be avoided. Any servant of the Lord whose ministry begins to dislodge demonic forces can expect to be attacked occasionally by Satan's warriors. After some years of experience and growth in the Lord, however, I also know that such attacks become less and less frequent and may eventually stop altogether.

It causes demons great pain to come close to one who abides deeply in Jesus. The light and power of the Lord flow all about His redeemed. His blood continually washes clean. His angels encamp about His own to deliver them (Psalm 34:7). Eventually Satan's hosts no longer risk attacking; it brings increasing anguish and diminishing returns. This is what the apostle John meant when he wrote to young men "because you are strong, and the word of God abides in you, and *you have overcome the evil one*" (1 John 2:14, italics mine).

### *Tormenting Spirits*

Then there are afflicting spirits that specialize in torment. In *Healing the Wounded Spirit*, Paula and I wrote an entire chapter about imprisoned spirits. A spiritually imprisoned person has been locked away from life in his or her personal spirit. Demons have surrounded the person's spirit and imprisoned it so that the victim goes through the motions of life unable to experience the fullness of emotions and meanings. Tormenting demons gather frequently about imprisoned spirits. Their victims feel wounded inside as if bruised and worn out, though nothing obvious is bothering them. They begin to wonder if they are suffering from paranoia, since they fail to find any explanation for their feelings of being watched and bothered when no human agency can be detected.

Tormenting spirits also bother people who are not imprisoned. Their usual method: to find some unhealed area in the person's deep mind and heart and prey on that weakness. A woman might have had normal anxiety as a child, for example, because her father was alcoholic and unpredictably explosive. Now she finds herself suffering panic attacks. (This happens more often to women.) Tormenting demons play her fears like a violin. People afraid of snakes, spiders, even dogs or cats, may be terrorized in the night by horrible dreams in which those animals are about to get them.

This kind of demon is like a bully on a playground. If it can find something that wounds or terrorizes, it delights in agonizing its victim with it. If it can get a person out of control emotionally, screaming in fear or anger, so much the better.

A tormenting spirit is dealt with by finding what caused the fear or traumatized area in the heart, then applying the comfort and healing power of the Lord Jesus Christ. Many panic attacks have stopped altogether when a counselee simply forgave her father for coming home late at night, shouting drunkenly and banging on doors and people. In such cases one could almost give thanks for the demons, because their pesterings forced the person to face what he or she had been unwilling or unable to acknowledge.

Satan is a fool who overplays his hand. That tips off the counselor, then the counselee, as to what needs to be healed.

### Spirits of Infirmity

The most common afflicting spirit is a spirit of infirmity. These are demons that have learned how to enter the physical body to affect health and proper functioning of joints, nerves, muscles, organs and glands. Jesus delivered a woman who had been so afflicted by a spirit of infirmity that she could not straighten her back for eighteen years (Luke 13:10–17).

There is often a direct relation between sin and sickness. Jesus indicated this when He said,

> "Which is easier, to say to the paralytic, 'Your sins are forgiven'; or to say, 'Arise, and take up your pallet and walk'? But in order that you may know that the Son of Man has authority on earth to forgive sins," He said to the paralytic, "I say to you, rise, take up your pallet and go home."
>
> Mark 2:9–12

The sick person did not necessarily commit a particular sin that caused the illness. We are affiliated with all mankind. The sins of some bring sickness and death on innocent people. (Witness those afflicted with AIDS through blood transfusions or infected health care workers. Homosexual and heterosexual sins have caused the disease to run rampant in our society.) Sin is the cause—but not necessarily the sin of the person afflicted. Sickness can also be incurred through inheritance by generational sin patterns.

The Church has always distinguished two kind of sins—sins of omission and sins of commission. The latter occur whenever we do something forbidden, the former whenever we fail to do what we should. Within each of these, the Church distinguishes two further types—intentional and unintentional sins. A person may decide not to do something he should or to do something wrong. Or he may unintentionally act in error, through ignorance or accident, thereby failing to do right.

God looks on us with compassion. Jesus said that those who do wrong intentionally will receive a severe beating and those who do not know, a light beating (Luke 12:47–48). But demons have no compassion, nor do they make distinctions. They take each infraction of law as an opportunity, even as a legal contract, to afflict. Wherever they discover unforgiven sins, they move against the body to wreak havoc.

Some illnesses, on the other hand, are the result of our own personal sins. A man may fail to pray and rest in the Lord, so that his trust is not in the Lord's providence. This is a sin of omission. His body now bears the result of his sin. He may get ulcers, headaches, high blood pressure, whatever area of weakness admits illness. Demons may not yet be involved; they are not omnipresent. But if a demon discovers an opening, he can move into that existing condition to expand it into something life-threatening, or at least more painful than it should have been.

Suppose a woman has been molested in childhood or raped when she is grown. She has reason to be angry. Anger itself is not sinful. But letting the sun go down on anger gives the devil a foothold (Ephesians 4:26–27). In His grace the Lord may allow the sun to "stand still" within us, as it were, until He can heal our hearts enough that we can forgive. Time, like all things, is the Lord's, to whom one day is as a millennium. And if it takes some time for the rape or molestation victim to forgive her violators, the Lord understands that.

But if she, through intention or mere omission, chooses to let too many suns set without releasing her anger through prayer, she opens herself to demonic attack and, worse yet, the inexorable law of God: If we do not forgive others their sins against us, neither will we be forgiven our sins (Matthew 6:15). Resentment unrepented of can fester in spirit, soul and body and create illness, emotional torture and stunted spiritual growth.

The following is a quote from *The Reader's Digest Medical Encyclopedia* (italics mine, in this and the succeeding quotations):

Bones are the source of vital constituents of blood. They are the storehouse from which the calcium in blood plasma is obtained. The pores and cavities . . . are filled with red marrow. And marrow consists largely of blood corpuscles in all stages of development. About 5 million mature red blood cells . . . are produced and released every second. The blood platelets, clot formation, and *white cells which protect the body against infection are also formed in the red marrow.* The shafts . . . of the long bones of the arms and legs are hollow and filled with yellow marrow, a fatty substance whose function is not known.

Now let us look at what only a few of many Scriptures say about bones:

There is no soundness in my flesh because of Thine indignation; *there is no health in my bones because of my sin.*

Psalm 38:3

A tranquil heart is life to the body, *but passion is rottenness to the bones* [referring not to healthy sexual passion but to strong negative emotions].

Proverbs 14:30

A cheerful heart is good medicine, but *a crushed spirit dries up the bones.*

Proverbs 17:22, NIV

Trust in the Lord with all your heart, and do not lean on your own understanding. In all your ways acknowledge Him, and He will make your paths straight. Do not be wise in your own eyes; fear the Lord and turn away from evil. *It will be healing to your body, and refreshment to your bones.*

Proverbs 3:5–8

Can anyone fail to see the psychosomatic connection? Five million red blood cells are produced in the marrow every second, and sin and wrongful emotions dry up the bones! Bones produce the white blood cells that are the warriors of our immune system, and "there is no health in my bones because of my sin"! No wonder AIDS threatens to kill millions, destroy our medical facilities and bring down our entire economy under the weight of caring for multiplying numbers of victims!

One would think we would put two and two together and come up with four. It has never been known that a husband and wife making love honorably, nothing else intervening, causes debilitating illness. Marital sex never causes disease. But whenever illicit sex is entered into, there soon follow syphilis, gonorrhea, herpes (and now a type of herpes that has been declared incurable), AIDS and who knows what else. Sin literally dries up the bones and destroys our immune system!

All this creates a playground for demons of infirmity. Do we begin to see how the flood out of Satan's mouth (Revelation 12:15) is intended "to sweep away the woman"? The more he can involve Christians in sin, the more he destroys God's temple of the human body.

It may not be sufficient, therefore, to pray for healing for the sick. If the illness is induced psychosomatically, and the sins and the sin nature are not forgiven and stopped on the cross, the same or another scourge is likely to return. If those demons that have found opportunity to augment the illness through the sins and sin nature are not cast away, how long is the person apt to remain well?

Perhaps that is why James said so carefully:

Is anyone among you sick? Let him call for the elders of the church, and let them pray over him, anointing him with oil in the name of the Lord; and the prayer offered in faith will restore the one who is sick, and the Lord will raise him up, *and if he has committed sins, they will be forgiven him.* Therefore, *confess your sins to one another,* and pray for one another, *so that you may be healed.*

James 5:14–16a, italics mine

**Epileptic Demons.** There are a few specific spirits of infirmity of which I think the Lord's servants need to be aware, including demons that increase epileptic seizures. It may be a "chicken-and-egg" question whether demons cause epilepsy or merely take advantage of an already existing physical condition. Perhaps in some instances the physical comes first, whereas in other instances demons are the main or even the sole cause.

Epileptic demons are tough to dislodge and the condition hard to heal. Recall that the disciples failed to overcome the demon of epilepsy in a young boy. According to some late manuscripts Jesus explained, when asked, that "this kind does not go out except by prayer and fasting" (Matthew 17:21).

What limited success Paula and I have had in delivering epileptics has come by persistently tracking every childhood wounding we could discover and gently bringing each reactive structure in the old nature to the cross. Every session of inner healing was followed by prayers for deep comfort and resurrection of the person God intended when He created that child.

In the beginning with each person we do no deliverance prayers whatsoever. Then, as the person grows in strength and knowledge, we offer some direct prayers for deliverance. It has required long, patient months of counsel and prayer (although perhaps others have found ways to deliver epileptics more quickly).

**Death Wish Demons.** The most dangerous spirits of infirmity I have encountered are those that specialize in death wishes. These push depressive people into thoughts of suicide. They take hold of natural, deeply hidden death wishes to bring about terminal illnesses.

Not every terminal illness has behind it a death wish, but we have found that certain diseases are likely to host demonic spirits of death. Of all those who suffer from multiple sclerosis or muscular dystrophy, not everyone harbors a death wish and consequent demonic spirits of death. But those to whom I have ministered have acknowledged hidden death wishes since early childhood, even if no demon has yet found the wish as a lodging place.

Death wishes and their consequent spirits do not succumb just by being recognized. Much deep inner healing, usually of prenatal wounds, must precede the dispatching of the demon. (For those to whom the possibility of prenatal wounding is new, the first four chapters of *Healing the Wounded Spirit* and a two-tape video series from our counseling schools can be ordered from Elijah House.) Suffice it to say, when people first encounter life in the womb, they often react in their spirits (which God gave them at creation) to the pollution of our society and to the nausea of Adamic sin, and may want to flee. That is the sin of rebellion and the beginning of a possibly potent death wish, which may soon host a death-dealing spirit.

Death wishes, even if they do not result in illness or suicide, are dangerous in other ways, as pointed out by the Parable of the Talents. Jesus said that the master would take away the one talent the lazy slave had buried and give it to the slave who had invested ten talents (in another account, five). "For to everyone who has shall more be given, and he shall have an abundance; but from the one who does not have, even what he does have shall be taken away" (Matthew 25:29).

That seems manifestly unfair, but what did the one have to whom more was given? Trust. He was willing to risk his talents, and so gained more. What did the one not have from whom even what he thought he had was taken away? Trust. He was afraid and could not trust, so he buried his talent.

*I have found it an absolute principle that those who bury their talents in fear and distrust will lose even what they think they have.* Whenever people (either from within the womb or later in life) shrink from the risks of life, they lose what they have—job, friends, spouse, skills, wholesome desires, even health.

If we want to deliver people from death wishes, therefore, we must find out when and against what they reacted. Was there trauma in the parents' lives during that time *in utero*? Were they unwanted or illegitimate children? Had their parents wanted the opposite sex? Were they natural burden-bearers for whom life quickly became too sad and oppressive? What happened to turn them off from life?

Whatever clues we find, we should always remember that the primal cause is spiritual rebellion. Deep within, the person has refused the life God has offered. He needs to be brought to repentance and then forgiveness. Then those character structures that shut the gates to life can be brought to death on the cross, and the demons of death successfully be sent away.

Finally, resurrection is in order. These people must be wooed to life. I express the love of God for them in every holy way I can, and then ask them to say prayers every day like this: "I do not choose death, Lord. I choose life. I choose to be present to life. I will risk its hurts and not flee. I reject that death wish and all spirits connected with it. I choose to be whole."

Remember when the Lord Jesus asked the man, "Wilt thou be made whole?" (John 5:6, KJV). We must ask these people the same question, because they need to be urged to voice their decision to live life to the fullest, loudly and clearly, again and again.

**Vampiric Spirits.** Another afflicting spirit of infirmity is what I call a vampire spirit. This is one that fastens itself on the chest or back of its victim, and every once in a while drains the person of energy. It is as though it sucks the person's blood.

I doubt that a blood count would reveal significant losses; this demon somehow draws off its victim's "life force." The person may be feeling quite well, and within a minute or two depleted of energy and ready to lie down or go to bed. The condition does not always appear when expected, such as after he or she expends a great amount of energy. It can happen any time of the day, at the peak of one's vitality or the valley of normal tiredness, causing nearly unbearable feelings of fatigue. The person aches all over, as if he or she had the flu, though without a temperature.

A telling mark of such a demon, then, is its capriciousness; there seems to be no rhyme or reason to its attacks. More sensitive Christians may feel as though something unclean has touched them. Others feel it as a weight on the chest or back (usually on the chest).

Vampiric spirits attach most often onto naturally empathetic, burden-bearing Christians. (More on burden-bearing can be found in *Healing the Wounded Spirit* or in a teaching video from our basic school on Christian counseling.) Suffice it to say, the Lord commands us to bear burdens for one another. Paul calls this "fulfilling the law of Christ" (Galatians 6:2), which is, of course, to love one another as He has loved us (John 13:34).

Bearing burdens is accomplished by sharing with our Lord as He draws the hurt and death out of others into Himself (see 2 Corinthians 4:10–12; Philippians 3:10–11). *We* are not to bear the burdens; it is the Lord who is the burden-bearer in and through us. The Lord knows the stopping places. Galatians 6:5 says each person must bear his own load. The Lord bears only enough of whatever is weighing on a person so that it does not overwhelm him and prevent him from thinking and praying clearly.

In this sense, burden-bearing is a primary way of preparing the heart of the other. It lifts off enough trauma, and so begins to touch the heart with love, that the other is enabled to do his or her own thinking and praying and come to personal repentance and confession for healing.

Burden-bearers become accustomed to feeling suddenly weighed down as they share with the Lord some burden He is lifting off of someone's heart and mind. When we bear burdens rightly in the Lord, it is joyous and light even if it is a burden of sorrow. "My yoke is easy and my burden is light" (Matthew 11:30, NIV).

But sometimes the Lord's burden-bearers fail to discern that the sudden burden they feel is neither joyous nor light. An afflicting vampiric demon has taken advantage of their familiarity with burdens to slip in and attach itself.

True burdens lift after a while. The vampire knows this, so it stops draining its victim shortly after attaching itself, so that the Christian will not suspect what is going on, even if he senses something wrong. Later on the vampiric spirit resumes periodic draining of its victim's energy and strength.

"My people are destroyed for lack of knowledge" (Hosea 4:6a). Very few teach about burden-bearing and fewer yet know what a vampire spirit is. Many Christians are left, therefore, without the protection of wisdom and knowledge (Ecclesiastes 7:12).

Feelings of being drained can also come from physical sources like hypoglycemia. The symptoms are nearly identical, except that hypoglycemic tiredness is more predictable in its appearances, when for a variety of reasons the body is low on glucose, or blood sugar. Periodic tiredness can be attributed to so many physical factors that the gift of discernment is necessary to know if a vampiric spirit has in fact laid hold.

Vampiric spirits are to be cast away by the word of authority. But there is also a need to pray for healing balm to flow over the area where the demon attached itself physically. At Elijah House we pray for healing, then for all doors that have been open to demonic entrance to be closed.

Although in a sense vampiric spirits are demonizing from within, I do not believe that merely being attached to the body is the same as a demon's being ensconced within the heart and soul. Not only are some Christians demonized by vampiric spirits, but because these attach most often to burden-bearers, Spirit-filled Christians are more likely to be invaded by vampiric spirits than nominal or non-Christians.

If a vampiric spirit is to be prevented from returning, further prayer may be necessary. Burden-bearers must learn to pray the prayer of Hebrews 4:12, which is to separate properly the functions of soul and spirit. We can be likened to a car motor, which has separate places for gasoline, water and oil. These must remain separated, for if gas or oil or water run together, the car won't run or the engine may explode.

Likewise with us there are times for thoughts to control things, other times for emotions to take center stage, and still other times for us to experience distinctly in our spirit (as in devotions or worship).

But Satan has so scrambled us through Adamic sin that the mind and feelings often war against each other. Feelings run amok, or the mind shuts down emotions. If burden-bearers have not prayed for proper separation of their soul and spirit, when the Lord lays a burden on their spirit (which is where we bear burdens), the mind and emotions are overinvolved. Spiritual burden-bearing then becomes fleshly and tiresome, because our mind and heart are engaged in the labor of it, feeling and thinking too much of what ought to be borne mainly or only in the spirit.

A supreme burden-bearer myself, I was often so exhausted I could hardly put one foot in front of the other. Burdens meant to be shared with Jesus in my spirit were bogging me down in every other part of my being. Then I learned to pray for the separation of the faculties of my soul and spirit. Now the Lord can lay a heavy, sorrowful burden on my spirit, but I can preach a sermon happily or play a game with my grandchildren. Though my spirit may be sharing the Lord's grief over some lost soul, my mind and heart are unaffected and I can go joyfully about my business.

All this is to say that if a burden-bearer has not prayed for the separation of the functions of his soul and spirit, he finds it hard to discern when tiredness is not the light load of the Lord but the heavy invasion of a vampiric spirit. Whenever I discern and cast away such a spirit in someone, I check to see whether the person comprehends Hebrews 4:12 and has said prayers for proper separation.

The prayer is simple. I suggest that if you have never said such a prayer, you do so now. Even if you do not fully understand it yet, the prayer cannot hurt and it may bring great release and freedom to your overtired nature.

"Lord Jesus, let Your sword of truth cleave through me, to the separation of the functions of my soul and my spirit. Calm my mind. Quiet my emotions. Speak peace to my spirit. Set me in order inside. End the warfare between my mind and my feelings. So separate my soul and my spirit that You can give my mind a problem to think on and stir my feelings while my spirit is at rest; or lay a burden on my spirit, and my heart and mind will be undisturbed. I don't have to be torn up everywhere at once anymore. Thank You, Jesus."

You may need to repeat this prayer periodically. God heard it the first time, but you may need to repeat it so that your own inner being can agree to it progressively as you come into the Sabbath rest promised in Hebrews 4:9–11.

**Soporific Spirits** The final type of spirits of infirmity I want to teach about are "soporific spirits." A soporific spirit induces people to fall heavily into sleep at the wrong times and in the wrong places. Have you seen a brother or sister suddenly conk out during an exciting service or sermon? If that happens only once or twice, maybe he or she was just overworked or tense and fell naturally into a good, restful sleep.

But if it keeps happening to the same person, suspect a demon. Such a quick doze will not refresh. The person awakens feeling heavy and drugged. Satan is a hypnotist. It is as though he has cast a spell over the person, lest he or she hear the truth and be set free.

Soporific spirits do not confine their activity to services, teachings and sermons. Soporific spirits may augment our natural tiredness when we are driving, to try to plunge us into an accident. Or they will waste our preparation time for needy projects by suddenly plummeting us into slumber or such heaviness that we cannot function properly, and may give it up altogether. I have even ministered to a couple whose sex life was severely hampered. Whenever they engaged in foreplay, he would suddenly become overwhelmed with fatigue, lose his erection and crash into deep slumber!

The condition of narcolepsy may most often be demonic in origin. It is marked by sudden and uncontrollable deep sleep for brief periods. Each of the soporific conditions listed above is related to doing or listening to something, whereas narcolepsy comes on its victims at any time, unrelated to fatigue or anything else.

Casting away soporific spirits requires the gift of perception, because sleepiness can result from natural causes like exhaustion or letdown. Many mothers complain, as mine did, that every time their sons come home from college, all they want to do is sleep. That is not demonic; it is only letdown in a safe place conducive to rest and much-needed recuperation. So let not foolish Christians jump to conclusions and chase demons just when wounded warriors need desperately to crash!

One help in discerning the presence of a soporific spirit is that, if you are the one ministering, you may suddenly begin to feel unaccountably sleepy.

A short time ago Paula and I were interviewing a couple prior to praying for the wife. Suddenly I found myself fighting to stay awake. My eyes became so heavy and red that the woman said, "John, you're too tired. Why don't we stop for awhile and start up again later?" But I knew by the suddenness of it, and by its unaccountability (I had enjoyed plenty of sleep and was not tired), that a soporific spirit in her was using my empathetic identification with her to make me think *I* was sleepy so that I would postpone ministering to her. When I explained that and we prayed, casting away the soporific spirit, I was again refreshed and wide awake.

Soporific spirits seldom can be simply commanded away. Usually there is some point of access. Highly performance-oriented people may need desperately to let down, for example, but are so conscientious they will not allow themselves to rest. They resist the desire of their inner being to stage a sit-down strike. A soporific spirit sees its opportunity and joins with the inner wish for rest in order to take hold of the person. Or a person may have conscious and subconscious desires to quit an oppressive job. He has recognized and fought down the conscious desire to quit, but the demon squirms into the door of his unrecognized needs and immerses him in heaviness and sleepiness. (Sleepiness is often a flight mechanism from some undesired situation.)

Healing is best accomplished by finding out what gave the soporific demon its opportunity, removing that by forgiveness, and applying the cross to the structures of flight, or whatever in the sin nature is the open door.

## In Summary

People ask constantly if there can be a "demon of *such and such.*" It seems to be ingrained that there is a finite list of demonic types and, if we can just codify and label them, we will be able to stay out of harm's way. Nothing could be further from the truth! The vital thing to remember is that, where sin flings wide the gates, there can be a demon of *anything.*

In dealing with all the types of demons discussed in this chapter, I hope it has become even clearer that demons require a house of character in which to operate. We must not only deliver, therefore; we must dismantle whatever character structures grant the demons opportunity. Whether we do inner healing first or deliverance may be important only in some cases. Consequently, the servant of the Lord must always listen carefully to the Lord and to the counselee.

Valid healing efforts always involve meeting the other with the Lord's respect and patience. We reopen wounds in those already hurting if we merely practice our latest ministry toys at their expense. Time is our friend, haste our enemy. People need love "with skin on it." Many under attack cannot for a time find that love directly from the Lord. So for that period, we may be the skin.

Our wonderful Lord will deliver when we command in His name and with His leading. We are victorious over whatever types of demons we may encounter. Only let us be sensitive to Him and to those to whom we minister.

# 13

# Strongholds, Individual and Corporate

The foremost effort of Satan is to capture the minds of men and women, and thus their souls. The mind is the citadel of the soul. Under the anointing of the Holy Spirit, it rules our heart and directs our life. Satan knows if he can get hold of the way we think, he can expand his rule into every other area of our life!

Not only is our conscious mind his target. "For as he thinketh *in his heart,* so is he" (Proverbs 23:7, KJV, italics mine). Satan wants to captivate the deep mind, to control our motives and thoughts below the level of consciousness. He concentrates his demonic forces, therefore, on the battle for the control of people's minds more than any other endeavor.

Paul spoke of this warfare in a familiar passage that is really about the mind and not about demons.

> For though we walk in the flesh, we do not war according to the flesh, for the weapons of our warfare are not of the flesh, but divinely powerful for the destruction of fortresses [other versions say *strongholds*]. We are destroying speculations and every lofty thing raised up against the knowledge of God, and we are taking every thought captive to the obedience of Christ.
>
> 2 Corinthians 10:3–5

Paul is teaching here about warfare against "strongholds," "speculations," "thing[s] raised up against the *knowledge* of God," "taking every *thought* captive." Paul expounds elsewhere (Ephesians 6:10*ff.*) about warfare against demons; but here the subject is our thoughts and the warfare for our minds.

In ancient days citizens built fortresses, walled cities with access to their own water supply and plenty of storage space for food. When an enemy approached, all the people came together into the protection of the fortress. The enemy would bring up siege engines and dig trenches around the city. They would use catapults to hurl boulders against the walls, probing for a weak spot that might crumble so they could rush in to plunder the city. They would also hurl fire-bombs over the walls, hoping to start blazes that would divert enough defenders from the walls that the fortress could not repel the attack.

Paul used his readers' knowledge of siege warfare to say he would lob the Word of God, the power of God, over the walls of their hearts to start unquenchable fires. He would hurl boulders of truth against their defenses (despite the weakness of his personal presentation) until the Word of God broke through. God's Word, Paul was saying, is not limited by the weakness of the one presenting it. It is divinely powerful to topple human speculations and destroy strongholds of thought! Through God's holy and powerful Word, we take the thoughts of men and women captive to the obedience of Christ.

In this chapter I will describe mental strongholds, individual and corporate, and how demons and principalities use these strongholds to control individuals and groups and nations. As we see the power that demons have to control our thoughts, let us remember from the outset that our weapons—which include the sword of the Spirit, the love of God, the blood of Jesus, the shield of faith, and prayer and repentance—are far more powerful than anything the enemy has. We can destroy every stronghold we encounter, for we battle not with our own strength, but with the weapons of God, eternal and invincible.

## Individual Mental Strongholds

An individual mental stronghold is a way of thinking and feeling that has developed a life of its own within us. We were created in the image of God, with free will. Whatever we create within us likewise has a life and will of its own. If we develop a habit of temper, for example (or jealousy or alcoholism), that habit forms a life of its own within us and does not want to die.

Even if we decide not to lose our temper anymore, we discover to our chagrin that one simple decision does not kill it. The next time the "right" circumstance arises, the habit may take us over and we find our anger (or jealousy or drunkenness) still in control.

An individual stronghold is more than a habit, then: It is a center of fleshly control within us that uses habits to maintain its control over us. *Individual mental strongholds are the fortresses of thought and emotion ringed about the "nation" of selfishness that is at the core of us all.*

The function of a stronghold is to put up smokescreens to keep things like sermons, teaching and counseling from piercing our inner man with truths that could bring repentance and freedom. A stronghold guards the untruths that keep us in bondage to self and the flesh. Its task is not merely to fend off outsiders, but to prevent our spirit and renewed mind from seeing our own deceptions. Strongholds give us tunnel vision, preventing us from seeing what common sense would tell us is wrong. Strongholds create inner captivity to deception and misery.

Each stronghold marshals thoughts and fleshly habits about a central core of lies. A young girl's experiences with her parents may have created a strong sense of worthlessness, for example, especially if she was molested sexually. The lies that become the walls of the stronghold might sound something like this: "I'm guilty. I'm a slut—always have been and always will be. I'm good for nothing but to be used by men. I'm ugly. [She may actually be beautiful, but these words describe the emotional content of her feelings about herself.] Nobody would like me if they knew what I'm really like. Nobody really knows me; nobody really cares for me; nobody wants me for *me*."

When blessed happenings or truths threaten one of those walls of deception, the center of control within the stronghold quickly reinforces the weak spot with more lies and false feelings, trying to counter that bit of truth lest it break the walls and set the person free. How often we have heard someone touched by a moment of truth blurt out, "Yeah, but what about . . .?"

And out comes the string of lies that make up the rest of the wall: "But nobody else likes me. I can't be like that; I'm too weak. I'm worthless. I can't change now; it's impossible." *The function of an individual mental stronghold is to keep the person from thinking effectively, or feeling repentant, or praying in ways that would defeat it as one of the fortresses of the ruling center of flesh within the person.*

A stronghold is like a boil on the brain. It has a sick core, surrounded by the pus of twisted feelings and thoughts. It sends pain and sickness throughout the body of personality and character. The poultice of the Lord's persistent love is needed to draw it to a head, and the pressure of truth and forgiveness to pull out the core. When the ruling center of the stronghold has been broken or extracted, then its lies can be dismantled one by one on the cross of Christ. So the "pus" is expelled and healing comes to the body.

Hebrews 2:15 says the Lord Jesus became like us in order to "deliver those who through fear of death were subject to slavery all their lives." It is not physical death Christians fear. That would be a hallelujah; we would get to go home to the Father! What we fear is being out of control, as though the Holy Spirit could not or would not corral our unruly passions. Fear is the primary weapon of strongholds. We fear letting go and trusting the goodness of God.

Perfect love casts out fear (1 John 4:18). Love begins the battle against strongholds. Love enables us to see truth. Love is the siege engine that hurls truth over the walls of self-deception. Love causes us to repent. Love enables us to persist, to slog through the storms of deceptions and lies as we struggle to break free.

It is easy to see how demons use strongholds. They nestle in and marshal other demons to help them establish and maintain control. The stronghold itself already functions to block truth, so it is a perfect home for blocking spirits. The stronghold is already a fleshly center for control of the person's thoughts and feelings (and therefore actions), so it provides a home for controlling spirits.

The stronghold gathers fleshly motives and feelings about itself, which become landing fields for demons that specialize in hate, fear, envy, lust, slander, etc. A mental stronghold is the fleshly equivalent of, or home for, a demonic strong man. Strongholds seldom exist long before demons find nesting places in their structures.

To set people free, it is not enough to bind the strong man and cast him away. We may be prevented from plundering his house until the power of the stronghold has been broken. And again, it is persistent applications of love and truth that finally break down a mental stronghold.

You can discern when a stronghold finally loses its hold. Suddenly the person begins to brighten. His mind begins to catch the truths you tell him, the first time. He starts to see things accurately for himself. He helps you discover truths within him rather than smokescreening and blocking. He sets about plundering the stronghold of the strong man. Hope shines again in his face. His faith is rekindled.

He may block you all over again when you begin to tackle the next stronghold, but in this area he has found freedom. And, much as a flanking maneuver in human warfare enables an army to roll up its enemy from one end to the other, it becomes progressively easier to disrupt and overcome the remaining strongholds.

## Key Truths to Set Free

I was counseling a woman who had built up a stronghold of judgments against men. Freda was distancing her loving husband from her, unable to see his worth, smokescreening so that she could not see the origin of her problems—which was with her father in childhood.

The Lord's love flowed over me into her and caused me to feel her deep, agonizing loneliness. With warmth and compassion I spoke to her inner child: "Freda, I feel how very, very lonely you are inside." She broke, and sobbed and sobbed. That loneliness and consequent bitterness was the strong man's stronghold by which it cobwebbed all other feelings and thoughts.

Now Freda began helping us dismantle her stronghold, remembering details of her life, forgiving the people involved, choosing to remain "out there," risking her heart openly with her husband.

A man came to Elijah House who kept having trouble with bosses. Either Erik would outwork everyone else without the boss seeing it, or he would be blamed (he thought) for the failings of others. He perceived every helpful suggestion as criticism and attack. If anyone was to be laid off, "it's going to be me." (No matter that he had more seniority.)

It did not take us long to see that Erik's father had never affirmed him and had been hypercritical. But to get *Erik* to see it was another matter. His stronghold of rebellion and anger made him want to see the problem as his boss' fault alone. "Look at the facts!" he would exclaim.

Erik did not want to see cause and effect. His stronghold kept tossing us what in counseling parlance are called "golden apples"— little gems of revelation that are really a sidetrack. (In Greek mythology Cassandra won a footrace against a man faster than she by tossing out golden apples, which he stopped to pick up, and thus lost the race.) If the counselor stops to trace those irrelevant little gems, the strong man of the stronghold "wins the race" and remains in place undetected.

So Erik kept directing our attention to detail after detail on his job. When that failed to distract us, he related disappointments with teachers in high school, athletic coaches who had overlooked him, leaders in various clubs who would not listen to his advice. Any story or remembrance would do, so long as it kept us and him from looking at the real cause—his resentment against his father. The stronghold, energized by a strong man, was doing everything it could to prevent our breaking through.

The key truth to set Erik free was the acknowledgment of fear— fear of rejection, fear of not measuring up. The key action to reach his heart: simple acceptance and affirmation. Once he felt unconditionally loved—that he would not be upbraided, that we thought him a great guy for all he had been through—his heart began to open like a frosted bud in spring sunlight.

Sometimes one must bind the strong man and the stronghold before anything can penetrate. Most often Paula and I do that silently while listening to the person. After the person has begun to see and desire freedom, then the strong man and stronghold can be addressed aloud, directly if necessary.

That was the route we had to follow in Erik's case. While showing him love by our understanding and compassion, we bound his stronghold silently and the strong man that used it to hold him captive. Eventually he was set free, and the last we heard he had held the same job for more than ten years.

## Counterattacks

Strongholds and strong men counterattack. So we must not abandon the battle before time and good experiences have had sufficient "room" to settle the healing. People being set free from strongholds need people around them. But sometimes family members possess the very strongholds that would throw the person back into his own. The redeemed family of Christ needs to surround the person with a fortress of love and prayer.

In the movie *One Flew Over the Cuckoo's Nest*, Jack Nicholson played an inmate in a mental institution whose inner freedom began to set others free. The movie climaxed in a wonderful night when the inmates of the ward enjoyed a celebration. One severely inhibited lad burst through his inner bondage and encountered life. The encounter was immoral, which I in no way endorse. But the film was making the point that he chose to risk living. The next morning the head psychiatric nurse (in one of the most poignant scenes of the movie) tormented the young man by asking, "What would your mother think if she knew?" One could almost see the walls of resignation and defeat closing about the boy as she reinstalled his strong man of withdrawal and shame.

Family members, especially the unredeemed, often do that to those we are attempting to set free. It is usually unintentional, but even more cogent because of the hidden nature of the family's negative structures. We must be careful, then, to guard the aftermath of healing. Delivered people need wholesome, celebrative, nonaccusatory friends who accept them in all their failings and love them anyway.

Sometimes even church families can come under the control of a strong man. This puts the counselor on the spot who can see that the counselee's negative, condemnatory church family will destroy his newfound freedom. At Elijah House, since we work for unity in the Body of Christ, we are reluctant to advise anyone to leave his or her church. But sometimes it is necessary to suggest that a counselee refrain from attending a particular church for a while. Later, when he is strong enough, he can not only return but perhaps even help to set his church free.

## Corporate Strongholds

Individual mental strongholds may also be attached to corporate strongholds, in which case they may be much more difficult to dislodge. *A corporate stronghold is a way of thinking, feeling and acting that is built into the common mentality we all share.* Just as individual strongholds are built from lies accepted in childhood, so corporate strongholds are built from deceptions and ways of thinking long practiced in a particular culture. The walls of the stronghold are composed of philosophies, traditions, corporate loyalties, religious rites and taboos, cultural norms and values, etc.

Paul wrote:

> See to it that no one takes you captive through philosophy and empty deception, according to the tradition of men, according to the elementary principles of the world, rather than according to Christ.
>
> Colossians 2:8

If philosophy is "empty," one might ask, how can it take someone captive? The answer is that philosophies and traditions are not inert words on a page or innocuous ways of doing things. Whatever we create, within or between us, bears life in itself. Philosophies and traditions can become corporate strongholds, in which case they are *real and powerful forces that can take hold of people's minds and actually control them.*

View a corporate stronghold like the giant squid that attacked Captain Nemo's *Nautilus* in Jules Verne's *20,000 Leagues Under the Sea*, waiting for people to swim near so it can wrap its tentacles about them. Whenever people begin to think in certain ways, principalities can maneuver appropriate corporate strongholds into position to clamp about them and actually rob them of the freedom to think.

While individual strongholds serve as lodgings for local ruling demons, corporate strongholds offer a home to what Paul referred to:

> Put on the full armor of God, that you may be able to stand firm
> against the schemes of the devil. For our struggle is not against flesh
> and blood, but against the *rulers*, against the *powers*, against the
> *world forces of this darkness*, against the *spiritual forces of
> wickedness* in the heavenly places.
>
> Ephesians 6:11–12, italics mine

Corporate strongholds are wielded by principalities, rulers,
demonic archangels that use them to imprison the minds and control the thoughts of entire peoples—nations, cities, denominations,
local churches, political parties, even philanthropic groups. If you
have ever asked, "How could principalities become world rulers
of this present darkness?", the foremost answer lies here—by
means of corporate strongholds.

The function of a corporate stronghold is to imprison the minds
of a people or group, to take away their freedom to think anything—including cold, hard facts and logic—contrary to the mindset of the stronghold. It hypnotizes whomever its spell overshadows, so that they cannot see portions of the Word of God (or even
secular truths) that might set them free from its delusive grip.

> But their minds were hardened; for until this very day at the reading
> of the old covenant the same veil remains unlifted, because it is
> removed in Christ. But to this day whenever Moses is read, *a veil
> lies over their heart;* but whenever a man turns to the Lord, the veil
> is taken away.
>
> 2 Corinthians 3:14–16, italics mine

That veil, to me, is a corporate stronghold of unbelief, put into
place by the discrediting and ultimate rejection of Jesus by the
Jewish people. Satan's highest archangels are enlisted in the struggle to keep the veil in place, lest the Jews see the truth and find
their true Messiah in the Lord Jesus Christ.

> Even if our gospel is veiled, it is veiled to those who are perishing, in
> whose case *the god of this world has blinded the minds of the
> unbelieving,* that they might not see the light of the gospel of the
> glory of Christ.
>
> 2 Corinthians 4:3–4, italics mine

How do world rulers of darkness deceive people so as to control them? Primarily through the power of corporate strongholds.

### An Example from Recent History

Before the second World War, Adolf Hitler began to preach the doctrine of the Aryan "super race." This gospel of Aryan superiority enabled world rulers of this present darkness to move that corporate stronghold over the German mentality. Whoever among the German nation was not grounded in the Word and in the love of the Lord Jesus was overcome by that stronghold until he or she actually believed he was superior. World rulers of this darkness enlisted hordes of local demons to blind the German people to anything that would reinstall humility, compassion and common sense.

Racial superiority was and is an ancient, well-fortified corporate stronghold, built long before the Jews and Samaritans thought themselves racially better than the other and both disdained the even "less acceptable" mixed breeds of Galilee.

Hitler began to declare the alleged right of Germany to establish the Third Reich and conquer whoever stood in the way of this glorious vision of mankind at the apex of civilization. This teaching laminated two great strongholds—the great Utopian dream of elevating mankind to the heights (as old as the Tower of Babel) and the long-practiced stronghold of aggression, which has activated and controlled men from the earliest days of warfare through the Khans, Alexander the Great, Caesar, the Huns, the Moors, Charlemagne, the Crusades, Napoleon, the Kaiser, etc. Powers of darkness moved the powerful stronghold of aggression over the German mentality. Whoever could not stand firm in Christ found himself goose-stepping off to war, or applauding those who did.

Then Hitler began to activate ancient prejudices to destroy the Jewish nation—a stronghold as ancient as Satan's hatred of the Jews for being the nation through whom the Savior of the world defeated him at the cross. Throughout history Satan has built and nurtured that stronghold of hatred, causing Jewish people to be persecuted, rejected and slaughtered in nation after nation, century after century, to this day.

Although Hitler's propaganda originated in the pit of hell, many German people were so mesmerized by this stronghold that they actually thought they were doing God a favor by killing Jews. After all, the Jews had put His Son to death on the cross! Hitler wrote in *Mein Kampf*, "Today I believe I am acting in accordance with the Almighty Creator: by defending myself against the JEW, I am fighting for the work of the Lord."

Sid Roth, a messianic Christian scholar, documents for us in his excellent book *Time is Running Short* the shameful history of the Church in this regard. Look in the quotes that follow for the corporate strongholds of racial superiority and hatred.

Martin Luther added fuel to the fire by saying that the Jews should not merely be slaves, but slaves of slaves, that they might not even come into contact with Christians. In his "Schem Hamphoras," he said the Jews were ritual murderers, poisoners of wells; he called for all Talmuds and synagogues to be destroyed.

In his "Von den Juden und Ihren Luegen" (1543), Luther writes: "What then shall we Christians do with this damned, rejected race of Jews? Since they live among us and we know about their lying and blasphemy and cursing, we cannot tolerate them if we do not wish to share in their lies, curses, and blasphemy. . . . We must prayerfully and reverentially practice a merciful severity."

Before we diminish the importance of these views of Martin Luther on the Jewish people, listen to the *Encyclopedia Judaica*, commenting on Luther's statements: "Short of the Auschwitz oven and extermination, the whole Nazi Holocaust is pre-outlined here."

And lest we consider Lutheranism and the German nation solely at fault, listen to Sid Roth's recital of what others throughout Christian history have said and done:

**Justin Martyr** (d. A.D. 167) was one of the first to accuse the Jews of inciting to kill Christians.

**Origen** (d. A.D. 254) accused Jews of plotting in their meetings to murder Christians.

**Eusebius** (c. A.D. 300) alleged that each year at the holiday of Purim, Jews engaged in the ceremonial killing of Christian children.

**St. Hilary of Poitier** (d. A.D. 367) said that Jews were a perverse people, forever accursed by God.

**St. Ephraim** (d. A.D. 373) wrote many of the early Church hymns, some of which maligned Jews, even to the point of calling synagogues "whore-houses."

**St. John Chrysostom** (A.D. 344–407) said that there could never be expiation for the Jews and that God had always hated them. He said it was "incumbent" on all Christians to hate the Jews. The Jews were assassins of Christ and worshipers of the devil.

Malcolm Hay writes: "The violence of the language used by St. John Chrysostom in his homilies against the Jews has never been exceeded by any preacher whose sermons have been recorded."

In one of these homilies, St. John Chrysostom stated: "The synagogue is worse than a brothel . . . it is a den of scoundrels and the repair of wild beasts . . . the temple of demons devoted to idolatrous cults . . . the refuge of brigands and debauchees, and the cavern of devils."

**St. Cyril** (d. A.D. 444) gave the Jews within his jurisdiction the choice of conversion, exile or stoning.

**St. Jerome** (d. A.D. 420), translator of the Latin Vulgate, "proved" that Jews are incapable of understanding the Scriptures, and that they should be severely persecuted until they confess the "true faith."

**St. Augustine** (d. A.D. 430) called Judaism a corruption. The true image of the Jew, he said, was Judas Iscariot, forever guilty and ignorant spiritually. Augustine decided that Jews, for their own good and the good of society, must be relegated to the position of slaves. This theme was later picked up by **St. Thomas Aquinas** (d. A.D. 1274), who demanded that Jews be called to perpetual servitude.

According to Professor F. E. Talmadge, St. Augustine believed that "because of their sin against Christ, the Jews rightly deserved death. Yet, as with Cain who murdered the just Abel, they are not to die. . . . For they are doomed to wander the earth . . . the 'witnesses of their iniquity and of our truth,' the living proof of Christianity."

**Crusaders** (A.D. 1099) rounded up all the Jews into the Great Synagogue in Jerusalem. When they were securely inside the locked doors, the synagogue was set afire. And the misguided Crusaders, with the lies of perverted sermons fresh in their ears, sang as they marched around the blaze, "Christ, We Adore Thee."

We cannot defeat a stronghold, as we will learn, unless we repent of our own involvement in it. When I read these passages in Sid Roth's book, I wept in repentance for days on end. I still do. Did we think we could blame Russia for its recent anti-Semitism and expulsion of Jews? St. John Chrysostom was Greek Orthodox, from whom is descended all Russian Orthodoxy. Do we see how deeply ingrained in Christian history is the stronghold of anti-Semitism?

In the Third Reich, Nazi officers found themselves performing unspeakable atrocities, apparently devoid of humanity or conscience, in the name of the Fatherland. Whoever objected was ostracized or put to death along with the Jews. (It has been revealed that at least three million Christians and others who remonstrated against the killing were slaughtered.) The power of this stronghold was so great that Hitler's troops also eliminated millions of gypsies, homosexuals, Russian peasants and other "subhuman misfits" who had no place in the Thousand-Year Reich.

Most in the Church did nothing to stop the slaughter. Many since then have asked for pardon for the Church's silence. Possibly the power of that stronghold is beginning to be broken. But I include these long quotes from Sid Roth's book because I know that only massive, informed repentance on the part of all Christendom is sufficient to destroy it forever.

A key function of strongholds is to destroy conscience, compassion and humane sentiments in those under their control. Witness the deplorable hatred and acts of white supremacists and skinheads today. Even now the Aryan Nations Church, headquartered not three miles from where I write, strives to resurrect Naziism with all its hatred. These demented people have not had a free thought in years, but are possessed and controlled by principalities of delusion and hatred through the ancient strongholds of hatred and racial superiority.

Strongholds maneuvered by world rulers of this darkness are the greatest threat to Christianity in any age! But especially today, since no previous generation of demonic hordes has had access to mind-controlling media as does this generation.

Let's look at some of the "schemes of the devil" against which we are called to stand.

## The Stronghold of Drugs

The stronghold of drugs is as old as Noah's drunken generation and his own falling into "the cups." Has anyone failed to notice that parents can talk rationally with teenagers, that teenagers can hear and respond sensibly, that they can look at facts together—until they try out alcohol, marijuana or cocaine! Suddenly there is no more reasoning with them. Now the teenager throws out shibboleths: "Aw, you're in the older generation. You don't understand. It's not gonna hurt me. I know what I'm doing. Relax, I'm not gonna get addicted."

An exasperating function of strongholds is the eradication of logical thinking and the substitution of words with no real content that are supposed to refute logic and reason. You can work alongside a homosexual in some humanitarian cause, and in you he sees some measure of kindness, compassion, wisdom and balance. But mention that you believe homosexuality is a sin, and instantly you become a "hate-filled bigot."

That is the device of the principality of homosexuality to thwart your words from having effect against the deception-walls of the stronghold: "I don't have to listen to you. You're filled with hate and your theology is stuck in the last century. Get with it!" All this combines the stronghold of homosexuality with the strongholds of modernism, liberalism, humanism and "rights."

When our son John, in full-blown teen rebellion, tried out drugs, immediately there was no more reasoning with him. Paula and I would show him scientific research proving the damage done by drugs, to which he would respond, "Oh, Mom, Dad, that's stupid. That stuff isn't going to hurt me." We had to pray, not reason, him out of drugs.

Then my younger brother Frank, with two daughters the same age as John, called me in desperation. "My girls are getting into drugs and they can't hear a word I say. Johnny just got off drugs. He's their age. Maybe they'll listen to him. Would you send him over?"

Johnny was gone maybe two hours. He came home sputtering, "They couldn't hear a word I said! They said I'm in the older generation!"

Do you see the use of catch phrases that have no logical reality? (Paula and I joined prayer forces with Frank, and our nieces eventually got free.)

## The Stronghold of Sexual "Freedom"

Next to the battle for the mind itself, sexual strongholds are Satan's greatest scheme for the destruction of mankind. We pointed out why in the last chapter. Now let's look at the depth of Satan's scheme.

Following the Age of Enlightenment, during the explosion of increasing knowledge and technology in the last century, Satan turned the guns of human pride in science against the Bible. He was attempting to tear it apart under the guise of "higher and lower criticism" (the Bible has withstood all attacks and continues to confound scholars with its amazing accuracy and relevance). Satan's hidden purpose: to destroy belief in absolute revelation. If he could undermine belief in the Bible as God's revealed Word, then the eternal verity of the Ten Commandments could be made to seem only relative to that age, merely the thoughts of human beings.

Then Satan could cut men's minds loose from the sure anchor of all other scriptural truths. That in turn would destroy reverential fear of God, freeing mankind from the foundations of godly conscience. From there, the sky was the limit! People, even in the Church, have never been very moral, our sin nature being what it is. But previous generations were checked to some degree by the fear of God and the sense of the absoluteness of God's laws.

Those restraints have been destroyed from the minds and hearts of this generation.

Speaking out arrogant words of vanity they entice by fleshly desires, by sensuality, those who barely escape from the ones who live in error, promising them freedom while they themselves are slaves of corruption; for by what a man is overcome, by this he is enslaved. For if after they have escaped the defilements of the world by the knowledge of the Lord and Savior Jesus Christ, they are again

entangled in them and are overcome, the last state has become
worse for them than the first.

2 Peter 2:18–20

## The Strongholds of
## Modernism, Liberalism and "Free Thinking"

So Satan carefully built the strongholds of liberalism and modernism. He constructed a wide range of loyalties and peer pressures to make sure few could penetrate the deceptions. Believing
in the absoluteness of law became judgmental, narrow-minded,
medieval. One needed to appear magnanimous, tolerant, wise.
Whoever held to old values obviously had some hidden agenda of
subconscious hatred.

I was trained at Chicago Theological Seminary, then a mecca of
liberalism and modernism. On graduation I decided that what I
had learned was in many parts wrong, and chose to believe the
Bible from cover to cover. (Someone, probably my wife's folks,
had been praying for me.) Then I went to talk with some of my
former classmates.

I will never forget those conversations. I remember one in particular: "John, I've been thinking. No one has been talking to me or
influencing me. I've just been doing some pondering by myself. And
I've come to believe that Jesus wasn't really born of a virgin. That
was just how they thought in those days. The same for all those
miracles reported in the New Testament. It was a superstitious age.
Probably Jesus didn't die on the cross; most likely He went into a
coma and came out of it spontaneously in the tomb. . . ."

And so his thinking went. From the moment he began to speak,
I knew exactly what he would say! Every thought and word were
predictable. He was mouthing what the strongholds of liberalism
and modernism fed his imprisoned mind.

"Where the Spirit of the Lord is, there is liberty" (2 Corinthians
3:17). And where the Spirit of the Lord is not, there is no liberty!

## The Stronghold of Homosexuality and Lesbianism

Once Satan had destroyed belief in the absolutes of the Bible,
he could bring the stronghold of homosexuality and lesbianism
out into the open. He could use molestation and youthful rebel-

lion (another stronghold) to make *gay rights* the catch phrase for the young, just as *flower power* had been for a previous generation. Thus, he enlisted multitudes (who actually called its miseries "gay") in its deceptive bondage.

Then Satan could use the combined strongholds of homosexuality and liberalism to twist Scripture so that none within their bondages could see truth and come to freedom.

> You shall not lie with a male as one lies with a female; it is an abomination.
>
> Leviticus 18:22

> If there is a man who lies with a male as those who lie with a woman, both of them have committed a detestable act; they shall surely be put to death. Their bloodguiltiness is upon them.
>
> Leviticus 20:13

When I asked a homosexual to read those verses, he responded, "But John, those Scriptures are about being immoral. I'm not immoral. I sleep with only one man and I've never been unfaithful. Those Scriptures don't refer to me."

Sodom and Gomorrah were destroyed by God for their rampant homosexuality (Genesis 19:1–29), which is why homosexuality is called *sodomy* (although *to sodomize* now means to indulge in anal sex). Recently a lesbian pastor on a national talk show stated that Sodom was destroyed because its citizens weren't hospitable! (She was probably referring to Ezekiel 16:49–50.) No wonder Paul wrote that "we have renounced the things hidden because of shame, not walking in craftiness or adulterating the word of God, but by the manifestation of truth commending ourselves to every man's conscience in the sight of God" (2 Corinthians 4:2).

## The Stronghold of the Rights Movement

Then Satan coupled the strongholds of homosexuality and liberalism with the stronghold of the rights movement. Our nation was founded by people oppressed and in search of just treatment under law—"rights," if you will. In Bible times, monarchs who ruled under the "divine right of kings" periodically became tyrannical. The same happened to our forefathers. The results of their search for fair treatment: the Constitution and the Bill of Rights, by which we and the entire world have been blessed.

But when the search for rights was coupled, by the powers of darkness, with the increasing rebelliousness of a people turned from God in this century, "rights" became a stronghold. When I was a child, we didn't hear about rights; we heard about duties, and the need to contribute some benefit to the world before we left it. Today the rights movement has obliterated common sense and balance, until our courts of law are sometimes an obscenity of injustice.

But that is the function of a stronghold—to take away the ability to reason and retain balance and common sense. Nearly every citizen of the United States can relate cases of the miscarriage of justice due to the stronghold of the rights movement. Judges and lawyers trained to use logic but manipulated by world rulers of this present darkness sometimes fail to think sensibly.

Meanwhile, AIDS threatens to kill millions, destroy our medical system, bankrupt our insurance companies, cripple our nation's mentality through fear of contamination, and bring down our entire economy under the weight of caring for multiplying numbers of victims! But politicians are afraid to defy the gay activists who lobby powerfully for their "right" to spread the plague without having to undergo tests!

Can you see how Satan's greatest weapons are strongholds, employed by world rulers of darkness?

## The Strongholds of Unfaithfulness and Divorce

Once liberalism had destroyed absolutes, it was an easy next step to shatter the sanctity of the covenants of marriage. The restraints of law and holiness had been removed from the ungodly selfish passions of men and women.

> The kings of the earth take their stand,
> And the rulers take counsel together
> Against the Lord and against His Anointed:
> "Let us tear their fetters apart,
> And cast away their cords from us!"
>
> Psalm 2:2–3

Can we see now who the "kings" and "rulers" are? Demonic archangels have worked through corporate strongholds to cast away the "fetters" of holy Scripture. But only when we are prisoners of the Word of God are we free indeed—free from the demands of self and selfishness, free from degrading passions, free from unholy decisions that lead us into misery. When we live within God's Word, we are free from the pressure of such decisions, which were never ours to determine.

God's eternal Word says of marriage, "They are no longer two, but one flesh. What therefore God has joined together, let no man separate" (Matthew 19:6). Jesus said that no man should divorce his wife "except for the cause of unchastity" (Matthew 5:32). That settled it for me. There are decisions men and women are not capable of making, so God removed them from us. *I have never owned the right to decide whether or not I should divorce Paula.* He has delivered me from the pain and fear of having to make such a decision; and I am therefore free, because I am His bondslave.

But the "kings and rulers" have cut men loose from the good shackles of God's laws, not for responsible liberty but for license to do what is unholy. Men and women are no longer constrained to stick it out together until the Lord can heal their lives and save their marriages. They have been given a ticket to bail out.

Paula and I had a hard time the first sixteen years of our marriage, as my sinful nature and her performance orientation were brought progressively under judgment and to death on the cross. Praise God, I was never given the "freedom" to quit; the law bound me to her. I would have missed the most incomparable treasure God could give me in a wife. What a tragedy that today fully half of marriages in America end in divorce!

When a couple are having a hard time and thinking about separation or divorce, they have instant "help." World rulers move the stronghold of divorce over them, and suddenly their minds are befogged. They cannot think responsibly about the welfare of their children. They can barely remember the good times they used to have or anticipate future blessings. Satan and the stronghold seek to confine them to the pain of the moment, so all they can think about is getting out.

They lose compassion and understanding and devolve into blame. Friends can no longer reason with them. They throw around inane cliches such as: "God wants me to be happy. He won't blame me if I stand up for what He wants for me." "I've only got one life to live and I deserve some happiness." "I just don't love her/him anymore."

But love (in contrast to the modern stronghold of romance) *is not a feeling. It is an irreversible committal to lay one's life down to bring fulfillment and happiness to the other.*

## The Stronghold for Destroying Families

If Satan could loosen the bonds of matrimony, he knew he would destroy the family as the Holy Spirit's "factory" for the manufacture of true humanity. So Satan built the stronghold of liberalism to obliterate absolutes from the mind of mankind; so he could unleash unholy sexual passions; so he could trap men and women into unholy unions; so he could weaken and eventually demolish conscience and the sense of eternal covenant—so that eventually he could destroy the family!

His primary aim all along: to annihilate mankind. It is in families that God brings forth the fullness of what humanity is created to become, first in the natural, then in the spiritual (1 Corinthians 15:46). Tearing down the natural family would devastate every person's ability to live in a godly way in the spiritual family, because in the first six years, primarily, our character is built or not built.

## Religious Strongholds

Being born anew in Christ changes our direction from hell to heaven, cleanses the guilt of our sin, restores us to fellowship with the Father and with each other, and gives us a renewed spirit.

Being born anew does not end the reformation of our character into Christlikeness; it only begins the process. Satan realizes this, and still has plenty of opportunity when a man or woman accepts Christ. He may have lost this individual for eternity, but he can still prevent his or her coming into the fullness of Christ's nature in this life. He can use a man's unchecked rampant passions to disgrace the cause of Christ, which spoils the fruit of his salvation.

The next part of Satan's plan, then, was to involve mankind in fleshly, incomplete doctrines of salvation, so that we would think all had been accomplished when in fact it had only begun.

During part of the second Great Awakening in America (from shortly after the War of 1812 until the beginning of World War I), the Church was faced for the first time in modern history with a mobile populace. People were picking up and moving West. The Holy Spirit devised a way of reaching a people on the go. He reduced the Gospel to its simplest elements: frighten sinners with the just wrath of a holy God and drive them into the arms of a loving Jesus through whom they could find forgiveness and redemption.

There was nothing wrong with the method or the theology. And it worked. More than half the nation was converted. But that reduced Gospel did not contain the full truth of life in Christ.

We need "sawdust and tears" revival preaching more than ever today, since many have fallen from the faith and sin runs rampant. But that kind of preaching said nothing of the riches of sanctification and transformation, which had been known and taught within the Church. And generations for nearly a century heard nothing but that reduction. Men and women heard the call of God, picked up their Bibles and went out to evangelize, but they knew little of the process of sanctification. Their followers knew even less.

Ignatius Loyola, founder of the Jesuit order, was truly born again, but knew that experience was only the beginning of reformation into Christ's character. So he developed a tough program of discipleship. Until his followers completed his course, they could not go out to evangelize. The Benedictine order had something similar in their "rule of life."

The great evangelists John and Charles Wesley knew that every born-again believer requires disciplined reshaping into Christian values, virtues and moral strengths. So it was that their followers came to be called "Methodists," because they insisted on a strict method for sanctification after conversion. As far back as the Ante-Nicene fathers (before A.D. 325), the Church knew and taught the need for continuous death to self.

But generations of those converted during the second Great Awakening never knew what to do afterwards—or even that anything needed doing! Churchmen began to elevate the conversion experience above what the Bible proclaims for it. They began to preach that whoever came to the altar would be changed totally, instantly. Positionally that is true: We are all made perfect in Jesus. But salvation is to be worked out experientially as well, "with fear and trembling" (Philippians 2:12). Now that truth came to mean, "Try harder so you don't lose the perfection you already have," which often succeeded only in turning people into striving, judgmental Pharisees.

The false doctrine of instant, painless sanctification came to be preached throughout much of the Church. If conversion made you a totally changed creature, there was no need to face sin and die to self daily on the cross (Luke 9:23).

That teaching made an idol of the conversion experience, and Satan saw his opportunity. If he could build that heresy into a stronghold of deception, he could disillusion countless numbers of Christians and non-Christians alike.

Converts would think at first they could express Christ's nature wherever they went since they were like Him in every way. When the first blush of anointing wore off and the nitty-gritty of trying to live like Jesus immersed them in failure, they would either strive so hard as to become judgmental Pharisees, or give up altogether and become backsliders, concluding that since no one could live up to it, why try? Furthermore, their obvious failures would shame the name of Jesus and dissuade many from embracing the faith.

Does this sound familiar? Look at the disgraceful activities of many well-known TV evangelists today. How many potential converts have concluded that Christianity is a sham? And why? Because well-meaning evangelists preached the only gospel they knew, a truncated version of the faith that omitted the Church's rich heritage of sanctification and transformation after conversion—and powers of darkness made use of that ignorance to entrap Christians in sin.

When one TV evangelist had unholy desires to visit prostitutes, what could he do? He wasn't supposed to have such passions; he was a "new creation." His limited theology prevented him from looking within to repent of the root causes; that would seemingly undo his salvation experience. How could he have bitter roots inside? He had died with Christ. His desire to sin was "under the blood." He couldn't confess his problem or admit there was something undealt-with in his nature. His temptations must be of the devil, so all he had to do was to rebuke the devil. But of course that didn't work, because his problem was not primarily demons but his own unredeemed heart.

The warning of the writer to the Hebrews to "take care, brethren, lest there should be in any one of you an evil, unbelieving heart, in falling away from the living God" (Hebrews 3:12) was directed to born-anew Christians. But those who adhere to the shortened Gospel are prevented from heeding such warnings.

## The Stronghold of Carnal Theology

I hope you do not see the progression we are tracing as natural human deterioration, but for what it is—a strategy that originated in the pit of hell.

If Satan could fashion the truncated Gospel into a carnal theology, he could make it a fleshly stronghold and move other demonic specialists into place. Their function: to blind their victims to the shortcomings of their half-gospel, to convince them that their small version of the truth was the whole truth.

The demons' task was to prevent those struggling against their flesh from seeking help. After all, they were new creatures. To seek counseling would be to admit they had not been saved. One TV evangelist attributed today's rising divorce rates to the fact that more people are going to counselors! But I do not believe that was the evangelist speaking; it was the voice of the principality ruling him through the stronghold of his carnal theology.

Demonic hordes egged these Christians on to persecute other Christians who insisted there was still a need for facing inner sins, to attack those who taught there was still a need for repentance, that not all the sin nature had yet found its death on the cross. To those deluded by inadequate theology, it was heresy not to believe they were totally transformed.

## The Sexual Seduction of Christian Leaders

Since Paula and I travel throughout the Body of Christ and are known as counselors, many leaders confide in us. Our readers would be appalled and stunned almost beyond belief to know, as we do, how many pastors and leaders have fallen into sexual sins while serving in ministry! Vast numbers throughout the Body attend church regularly and believe themselves good Christians, while sleeping or living with someone without benefit of marriage.

Once Satan had established the false doctrine of sudden, complete character change at conversion, he coupled that stronghold with the sexual strongholds he had nourished. Since many Christian leaders refused to look into their hearts to see their own sin nature, they were blind and defenseless against the strongholds of sex. Their inner man in all its hidden lusts offered perfect nesting places for demons that specialize in sexual temptations and perversions. Witness how many leaders of the faith have succumbed to Satan's schemes!

How could they avoid it? They were defenseless. First, their doctrines told them Christians could not be demonized. Second, they could not tackle sin where it originated, in the heart, because it was not supposed to be there anymore. Third, they could not listen to their brothers and sisters in Christ. ("They should not have asked me to go to a counselor. If their theology were correct, they would know there is no need.") One great TV evangelist refused his denomination's correction; he had only to "cling to his salvation" and he would be O.K. He believed he had learned his lesson, but he hadn't, as his subsequent falling proved.

Satan saw to it that that truncated theology filled the minds of leaders and blocked any truths that could have broken through and set them free.

Let us summarize. I firmly believe that Satan's master plan was first to destroy the natural family, then the Church. Through the false doctrine of total, instant change, he planned to bring down the Church and disgrace it before the world. Through liberalism, modernism, humanism and the strongholds of homosexuality and abortion, he has already shorn most old-line denominations of effectiveness for Christ. Many churches and entire denominations now champion the very causes the Lord hates, unaware that they are being used as pawns by corporate strongholds controlled by spiritual forces of darkness in the heavenly places.

I have presented this entire revelation of Satan's master plan, not only because it is the aim of Elijah House to equip the Body of Christ to deliver and heal individuals and corporate bodies. But this writing is itself an attempt to begin the deliverance of the Church from its present demonized state!

I could not be more in earnest. The Church struggles on, giving lipservice to the existence of Satan but ignorant of his schemes and unaware of the nature of the forces arrayed against her. Just as surely as a single Christian can become demonized, the entire Church has become demonized, as principalities play corporate strongholds over it as skillfully as a chess master plotting his moves.

A few years ago Paula and I conducted a seminar for pastors, teachers, leaders and counselors (committed Christians all) concerning sexual problems. At the beginning we asked the participants to fill out a survey. Since we wanted honest replies, we told them not to sign their names, and that their answers would be kept confidential.

How many, we asked, had committed fornication? 52 percent. How many had been involved in adultery? 51 percent. How many had committed one of these sexual sins since receiving Jesus Christ as Lord and Savior? 42 percent! (Only a 9 to 10 percent difference!) We were mortified and ashamed before our Lord.

The divorce rate within the Body of Christ is not much better than outside. Physical abuse of children runs rampant. And sexual abuse and incest are rising within the Church at a rate (to our shame) not much below that in the world.

I am sorry to paint such a gloomy picture. There are countless devout, humble Christians as obedient to the faith as they know how to be. But through the power of corporate strongholds and spiritual forces in the heavenly places, the Church is being progressively demonized and rendered a shame before the world. As Elisha asked the Lord to open Gehazi's eyes so that he saw the mountainside ringed with chariots of fire (2 Kings 6:17), so we need to see not only how Satan's henchmen encircle and seduce us to unseemly behaviors, but that the angels and archangels of God wait only for our repentance and petitions to free them to destroy Satan's works and defeat his demons.

Has the anointing of the Lord begun to fall on you as you have read? Is it shaking you free from whatever shackles of delusion grip you? Do you begin to understand where the real battle is? If we do not see the vast strongholds over us, and the world rulers that imprison our minds through them, we shall remain ineffective warriors at best, and at worst, demented and controlled while thinking we are free in Christ!

An army of informed, perceptive Christians needs to arise. We must band together to throw off the fetters of the rights movement. Intercessors must catch the vision and aim their laser beams of prayer where it counts, to shatter the strongholds of rampant sexual sin, of homosexuality and abortion, of liberalism and humanism.

We have no business and no need to blame those caught up in delusions. Only by the grace of God do we begin ourselves to see. But we can properly "hate what is evil" (Romans 12:9, NIV)—a perfect, virile hatred of the forces that delude and imprison humanity and the Church.

Like it or not, choose it or not, we are already engaged in the great battle to deliver and heal the Church and, through her, the world. We must arise and prepare ourselves to do battle where it counts. It is incumbent on us to learn how.

## Overcoming Strongholds and Setting People Free

How shall we overcome corporate strongholds and set prisoners free? There are at least six steps.

First, *we must come to see clearly how they hook into people's flesh*, so that repentance can remove the barbs of Satan's attack.

Second, *we ourselves must repent*. We will neither see clearly nor be effective unless we remove the log from our own eye (Matthew 7:3–5).

Third, *we must get our guidance clearly*. It will not do to remove a stronghold and its manipulators if God has not commanded it. The same thing would happen as does as with local demons: The last state of the situation would be worse than the first, because the stronghold would reseat itself and invite worse principalities to manage its affairs.

Fourth, *we must learn to fight as an army*. Only by clear, confirmed guidance should any man or woman alone attack corporate strongholds and their principalities.

Fifth, *we must be prepared for counterattack*—but we have the victory in our Lord Jesus Christ.

Someone in a women's organization for which I am an area board advisor received a vision of a stronghold and principality called "an empire spirit" over the entire region of eastern Washington and northern Idaho. Others witnessed to the veracity of the vision. That spirit caused businessmen to sacrifice all to build their own empires. It tempted each pastor in the Church to build his own spiritual empire, caring little for unity. It led to domination and control in families, businesses, groups and churches.

Because the area board was determined to smash that stronghold, they came to me for advice.

"Are you sure you are called to this work?" I asked.

"We're sure."

"Where are the men? This is not something for women to try to do alone."

"We've told them, but they won't get interested in it."

"I don't believe you should be trying this alone."

"Nevertheless, John, we feel called. Someone has to do something about it."

"O.K.," I said reluctantly, "if you're determined, go ahead. But understand and remember, there will be a counterattack. Be prepared."

The board had always enjoyed unity. They liked one another and had good times together serving the Lord. Within a year they were at one another's throats continually.

Finally the president called and said, "John, it's so bad we've called a retreat just to see if we can get it together again. Can you come and moderate?"

At the retreat I reminded them of the warning of counterattack. They had been warring against a spirit of ambition, jealousy and striving for personal gain. Now that very nexus of emotions and attitudes was expressing itself among them. They saw it and spent the weekend repenting and praying for each other's deep wounds and childhood hurts. They came out from the retreat restored and in love with one another again.

Sixth, *persevere*. Encounters with corporate strongholds and principalities are not solitary battles; they are long-term conflicts.

When a people are called to war against a stronghold and have seen it clearly and repented of their own involvement, then it is time to bind the stronghold (Matthew 18:18; 16:19). Let me be as clear as I can: Strongholds are not demons; they are flesh. Flesh, individual or corporate, is not to be cast out. It is to be redeemed by repentance and transformation on the cross of Christ. We may bind a stronghold, therefore, and command it to be still, but we never attempt to cast it out. We bind and cast away the world ruler who manipulates it.

But then we must persist in keeping that spirit at bay. Preaching and teaching must follow intercessory efforts. And the person we are working to set free must repent or we will lose the battle and the stronghold be reseated in full power. We cannot force anyone to choose rightly. The hallmark of God's Kingdom is courtesy. So we must not protect our weary selves by trying to override a person's free will to force him or her to do the right thing.

When repentance is complete, we may call on the Lord to destroy the stronghold. He will not only destroy it; He will turn awareness and repentance into wisdom and determination not to err again.

In *The Renewal of the Mind* Loren and I teach mental disciplines necessary to keep one's healing. The same disciplines are necessary for withstanding Satan's counterattacks. I suggest readers study that book carefully before tackling warfare against strongholds and principalities.

Suffice it to say, one must be willing to live humbly under the scrutiny of brothers and sisters in Christ. We must be willing to repent and wash ourselves in the blood of the Lamb, even (or especially) if what our brothers and sisters say seems farfetched or totally wrong. Nothing but misery is to be gained by our getting our backs up and defending our supposed virtue. If we do not have the condition we are accused of, repentance will hurt nothing. If we do, we will be set free.

Whoever is engaged in spiritual warfare should take a spiritual shower every night. Paula and I say, "Dear Lord and Father, let the water of Your Spirit flow over us like a physical shower. Whatever defilements we have picked up today, wash us clean."

We do not have to stand idly by and watch our loved ones "go down the tubes" to sin and destruction. God has called and equipped us. We are more than conquerors in Christ. But we must learn to fight in prayer groups and intercessory prayer meetings to destroy the strongholds that beset our society and our churches.

> Arise, O Lord, in Thine anger;
> Lift up Thyself against the rage of my adversaries,
> And arouse Thyself for me; Thou hast appointed judgment.
> And let the assembly of the peoples encompass Thee;
> And over them return Thou on high.
> The Lord judges the peoples;
> Vindicate me, O Lord, according to my righteousness and my
>     integrity that is in me.
> O let the evil of the wicked come to an end, but establish the
>     righteous;
> For the righteous God tries the hearts and minds.
> My shield is with God,
> Who saves the upright in heart.

Psalm 7:6–10

# The Relationship of Occultism, Spiritualism and Cults to Demons, Deliverance and Inner Healing

# 14

## Occult Involvement and Demons[1]

Normally Christians are hidden from the powers of darkness: "For you have died and your life is hidden with Christ in God" (Colossians 3:3). And protected: "Surely he will save you from the fowler's snare and from the deadly pestilence. He will cover you with his feathers, and under his wings you will find refuge. . . . For he will command his angels concerning you to guard you in all your ways" (Psalm 91:3–4, 11, NIV).

Satan's hosts are neither ubiquitous nor omniscient. In most of our daily living, therefore, we are not even troubled to think about their existence; we are kept "secure from all alarms." Such is the Lord's grace for those who know and love Him.

### Open to Attack

But certain things expose us to demonic attack. Persistent, willful sin invites demonic inhabitation. Unforgiveness, hate, anger, jealousy, covetousness or bitterness lodged in the heart can serve as a house for demonic hosts. Unredeemed sinful generational patterns can also become beachheads for occupying armies.

The existence of sin in our hearts does not guarantee demonic infiltration. A person may display unredeemed areas and consequent sins for some time without being inhabited by demons, even though these great gaping holes in his or her armor invite demonic attack. Satan's hosts may not yet have discovered the open invitation, or perhaps the person's resistance has been sufficient so far to ward them off.

It is much the same as with disease germs. A person may be susceptible to certain microbes (such as a flu virus) and even visit places where those microbes are present, and still not contract the illness. Normally one's natural vitality is strong enough to ward off whatever germs are encountered. But a day may come when resistance is low and exposure sufficient to allow viral armies take hold and plunge the person into illness.

In like manner, whatever weakness or sin exists in our lives may not yet have found demonic "help." A person may fall into sexual sin solely through his or her own lusts (although more likely the fall is the result of demonic planning and temptation, with consequent inhabitation by demons of lust). But the longer an unredeemed condition exists or sin is persisted in, the greater the likelihood that demons will become involved—which is a major reason the Lord implores us to repent quickly and be redeemed.

## No Safe Dabbling

None of the above is true in the case of occult involvement! To enter anything occult is always and immediately to step into the demonic. Demons take occult involvement not only as an automatic invitation to inhabit but as a legal contract to do so. There is no safe dabbling, no unharmful experimentation, however it may be masked, even as "scientific inquiry." One dabble is enough.

Occult involvement exposes us to the devil's armies. We have entered Satan's ground. Our sin takes us out from under the Lord's cover and gives Satan legal access to our heart and mind, to attempt to control what we feel or think. The degree of his control corresponds to the depth of our occult involvement, and other sinful areas grant him further lodging places and control.

Unfortunately, many Christians possess so little knowledge of the occult that they can become involved quite naïvely. It is like stepping into a room full of mustard gas. If you manage to get out alive, your lungs will be scarred and weakened for the rest of your life. Just so, many Christians are scarred and weakened spiritually from unwitting involvement in the occult; and this says nothing of intentional participation.

When I was a boy growing up in an old-line church, no one thought anything of reading the horoscope in the morning paper just for fun, or maybe "just in case." It was fun to have your palm read or stop in at the fortune-teller's booth at the carnival. The Church had walked away from awareness of the absoluteness of God's Law. Who knows how much demonic infestation we invited unawares?

Today, in a much more scripturally aware Church, we are not so apt to fall into such obviously forbidden traps. But there is a fine line between faith and prayer on the one hand, and magic on the other. And crossing that line is deceptively easy!

It is important, therefore, for every maturing Christian to be aware of what occultism is and what it is not. "For wisdom is protection just as money is protection. But the advantage of knowledge is that wisdom preserves the lives of its possessors" (Ecclesiastes 7:12). As wisely and fully as possible, then, I want to expose the occult for what is really is.

Let me start by saying that all occult involvement wounds our personal spirit. So there is need not only for deliverance and forgiveness but also for inner healing. Ministers of deliverance and healing are called to see what conditions in a person's history made him or her vulnerable to temptation and attack. We need to heal not only the effects of sin, but also the causes.

I have discovered a great gap in the understanding of the Body of Christ in this area. Many who minister have rightly applied the blood for forgiveness, the cross for the death of occult practices, authority for exorcism and the Word of God for teaching—and then relaxed, as though the entire work of redemption were now accomplished. The fact is, many people retain the same deep wounds that caused them to fall into occult practices originally, and great bruises in the spirit as a result. The Body needs to learn how to persevere until the work in a person is complete and the person is not only free but whole.

Occult means "something hidden" or "the act of hiding something." In astronomy, the sun's rays hiding a star is termed an "occult occurrence." In that sense the word occult is merely a descriptive scientific word and bears no negative connotations. In religious circles, however, the occult pertains to those sciences involving the supernatural, such as magic, alchemy, astrology and theosophy.

We will look at each of these, but let us be reminded first that occult involvement is unequivocally forbidden by the Lord:

> When you enter the land which the Lord your God gives you, you shall not learn to imitate the detestable things of those nations. There shall not be found among you anyone who makes his son or daughter pass through the fire, one who uses divination, one who practices witchcraft, or one who interprets omens, or a sorcerer, or one who casts a spell, or a medium, or a spiritist, or one who calls up the dead. For whoever does these things is detestable to the Lord. . . . For those nations, which you shall dispossess, listen to those who practice witchcraft and to diviners, but as for you, the Lord your God has not allowed you to do so.
>
> Deuteronomy 18:9–12, 14

## Magic

Magic in this context does not mean tricks done by modern-day performing "magicians." Such tricks are properly called legerdemain. To practice magic means "to influence the course of events by compelling the agency of spiritual beings, or by bringing into operation some occult controlling principle of nature."[2] Magic thus has two dimensions.

### One's Own Power

In the first dimension, magic means "the ability to operate principles of nature by our own psychic energy in order to accomplish our own purposes." In this dimension the user of magic operates alone, employing only his own psychic power to influence and harness nature to his purposes. He may himself be operated unwittingly by demonic principalities, but he is, for the purposes of our distinction, unaware of it, or at least not consciously working with any agencies or powers other than his own.

Falling into this category is a plethora of books telling Christians how to apply the principles of God to get rich. And what about all the "sermonettes" we hear just before the offering is taken? Some are justifiable. But how many overstress the principle of seed faith until they are actually teaching people how to work magic on God so that He will "have to" bless with goods in return? Prosperity teachers must be careful not to teach the use of divine principles to obtain one's own desired end.

Do you see why the Body of Christ needs so desperately to understand what magic is and what it is not? Such knowledge would purify and refine many of the commonly accepted practices in the Church today. There is a fine line between the prayer of faith and magic. Remember, there is nothing innocent about the occult; demonic powers are always involved. What hordes of demons might we be releasing into the Body when we teach Christians to apply God's principles to get whatever they want?

Even though God's principles are true and bring results, the end never justifies the means. Mary Baker Eddy, the founder of Christian Science, taught principles of faith for physical healing and miracles happened, but her theology was nothing other than the ancient heresy of Docetism (from the Greek *dokein*, to seem; that Christ only seemed to have a human body). The miracles did not prove she was right, only that God's principles are valid.

We must always ask, Who or what is operating God's principles, and for whose purposes?

Many have been taught that "if you want something, make a vivid picture of it in your mind, then believe you will receive it." This is an occult practice. A Christian doing this would be utilizing a principle by the power of his own flesh to achieve his own ends. It matters not if the purpose is godly; the method is not.

It is quite the opposite when the Holy Spirit grants a vision of what God wants, then calls on the Christian to have faith that God will accomplish His purposes. In that case, it is not the Christian's power that makes the thing happen, but his or her holding onto faith that frees God to act.

Often the deciding factor between true faith and magic is simply the presence or absence of the Holy Spirit's courtesy. When we consider the very life of Jesus Christ yielded up on the cross, we can see that the hallmark of God's Kingdom is yieldedness and submission. God is not willing that any should perish, but He will not force anyone to submit, nor will He control or manipulate us to ensure that we choose rightly.

The characteristic of Satan's realm, on the other hand, is discourtesy—manipulation, coercion and the operation of magic to control the responses of others.

True prayer always respects the sovereignty of God. It includes petition, humble requests that leave God free, emotionally and in every way, to say no or yes according to His will. Sometimes in our prayers we remind Him of what He has said, piling Scripture upon Scripture as though somehow we would coerce Him to live up to His promises. This is not far from working God's promises against Him to control His response—the essence of magic.

Praying many Scriptures can be a valid aid to "holding onto faith that enables God to act." Several verses say, "Lord, remember You have promised such and such. . . ." The point here is that we shouldn't just take verses and make them fit our circumstances when we have had no clear word that the Lord intends to act in that particular way. Motive is what distinguishes true use of Scripture from magic. If we pile up Scriptures to increase our own faith, well and good. But if we think to remind God of His promises in order to control His response, we are not far from magic.

Magic destroys free choice; it works power against the free will of others to make them do what the operator of the principle wants. Suppose, for example, that an evangelist encloses a penny as a "gift" when he sends you a letter asking for a donation. He is actually working against you and your free will the principle that if he gives, more will be given back to him. You in turn feel compelled to send something. Unwittingly or not, every ministry that offers gifts to induce giving is using a principle to control your behavior.

Behind a Christian's refusal to use such techniques is one simple factor: trust. He or she will wait on God rather than try to force events. "Delight yourself in the Lord and he will give you the desires of your heart" (Psalm 37:4, NIV). Behind all magic is the opposite: untrust. The manipulator cannot truly believe that God will supply him with all he needs or wants, so he uses magical principles: "I'll enclose a gift and they'll have to give back to me." This invites demonic participation.

When fund-raisers use Madison Avenue gambits to predispose donors toward giving, they are engaging in manipulation. Paula and I learned the hard way. From its inception, Elijah House operated by faith that God would supply without our asking the Body for help. A few years ago the ministry grew in outreach and expenses beyond our ability to support it by faith alone. Perhaps it was a test; perhaps we simply lacked prayer power. At any rate, we were not making it financially. We received confirmation on guidance from the Holy Spirit that we should ask the Body of Christ for help.

Ken Campbell, our C.E.O., found a man who said he would do nothing unscriptural and would work no gimmicks to elicit support from our constituency. We hired him as our consultant but soon found what powerful strongholds of deception take hold of well-meaning fund-raisers. This man considered himself a true Christian. But soon he was employing manipulative principles—actually, magic—on our constituency to provoke their giving. He justified his methods by pointing to his track record with other organizations. "This," he maintained, "is the way you raise funds in the Body of Christ. And it works!"

He sent out several letters that shamed us before the Lord and the Body. We repented and released him from our employ. What a fine line between asking the Body properly for help and manipulating fellow Christians!

### Power from Other Beings

In the second dimension of magic, the wielder of magic moves beyond the use of principles and consciously invokes the aid of other beings. This kind of magic includes necromancy, spiritism, sorcery and sometimes mediumism.

Necromancy is the art of using objects to consult with the dead to obtain knowledge of the future or to cause things to happen.

Many use spiritism as a synonym for spiritualism, the attempt to confer with the spirits of departed persons. When I stated earlier that some uninformed and unwary Christians become enmeshed unwittingly in the occult, spiritualism was one of the traps I had in mind. For instance, some Christians are actually falling for the New Age concept of "channeling." Channeling is an attempt to contact supposed "masters" who have lived before our time, to enable them to speak through the vocal cords of the "channel." This is nothing more nor less than the age-old sin of spiritualism, dressed in a new name to make it sound acceptable. (Satan has nothing new, only the same time-worn sins.)

Concerning spiritualism, the Lord is both concise and stern: "As for the person who turns to mediums and to spiritists, to play the harlot after them, I will also set My face against that person and will cut him off from among his people" (Leviticus 20:6).

Sorcery is the kind of magic or witchcraft that contacts and uses other spirits and powers in order to manipulate nature or cause things to happen. We will look into sorcery more closely later in this chapter.

Mediumism refers to the practice of a spiritualist in contacting alleged departed spirits, sometimes allowing the use of his vocal cords for spirits to speak through.

The Word of God is stringent concerning mediums: "As for a man or a woman, if there is a medium or a spiritist among them, they shall surely be put to death; they shall be stoned with stones, their bloodguiltiness is upon them" (Leviticus 20:27). The command is also given in Leviticus 19:31: "Do not turn to mediums or spiritists; do not seek them out to be defiled by them. I am the Lord your God." I will discuss this further in the next chapter.

## Alchemy

Alchemy (or wizardry) is an ancient science, far antedating the rise of the Hebrew nation. In later years, under persecution from Christians and others, alchemists hid their actual purposes behind the pursuit of the "four implausibles":

1. Turning base metals into gold;
2. The universal solvent (an acid that could dissolve anything);

3. The elixir of youth (a potion thought to bestow eternal youth upon whoever drank it). Some historians believe Ponce de León was searching for such an elixir when he became one of the discoverers of Florida;

4. A machine of perpetual motion.

Because of the impossibility of their pursuit, alchemists were thought of as fools. In fact, dunce caps, the conical hats children had to wear from time to time during grade school days, originated from the hats alchemists wore during the Middle Ages. But alchemists were not fools in that sense, nor did "conical" mean "comical." They were in dead earnest. Theirs was the first sin reenacted: the attempt by study and practice to become like God and to wield godlike power. Their true quest was the perfection of the soul.

Alchemy is thus Gnostic, embracing the heresy that one can be saved by right knowledge. It is also Pelagian, perpetuating the heresy that man can save himself without accepting Jesus Christ as Lord and Savior.

The story of Aladdin's lamp, beloved by many generations, is actually an alchemic story. Aladdin searched through three successively deep caverns. (Alchemists speak of "arcane, esoteric searches" through three successive inner caves of the being: the mind, the heart and the spirit. Deep within a man's spirit, alchemists thought to find wondrous knowledge.) In the deepest cavern Aladdin found a magic lamp—a universal symbol of knowledge. When he rubbed the lamp, a genie appeared to do whatever Aladdin requested. Rubbing produces heat by coefficients of friction. Alchemists wrote of the "argent," which meant the golden heat of fire by which the spirit within would be excited and enabled to do wondrous things, in response to the will of the alchemist.

Walter Leslie Wilmhurst writes of alchemy,

> If we speak of it as an Art, it is because it is usually so called in the literature of the subject, but it is rather an exact science—and a divine science at that, "holy Alchimy" as its professors have called it—one involving deep knowledge of the mental, psychical and spir-

itual elements in man and of the way in which they may be practically controlled and manipulated.[3]

Again,

Simply stated, Hermetism, or its synonym Alchemy, was in its primary intention and office the philosophic and exact science of the human soul from its present sense-immersed state into the perfection and nobility of that divine condition in which it was originally created.[4]

"Perfection" in this context obviously does not mean maturation into Christlike moral and ethical virtues, such as are listed in Colossians 3:12–17. Rather, it means to discipline and purge the soul's faculties in order to harness the latent power of one's own personal spirit. The purpose is to accomplish miracles without the intervention of God. Our modern humanists pale in the face of countless generations of alchemists!

Wilmhurst also says of alchemy,

It views man, i.e., the soul or true ego of man, as in process of restoration from the terrible calamity of his "fall," in the course of which process development under the operation of the forces and laws of nature has partially redeemed him from chaos and disorder and brought him to a point from which, *by the right application of his intelligence and will, he can cooperate in effecting his complete regeneration.*[5]

Science has learned how to destroy everything within a 25-mile radius by splitting or fusing atoms. If something so infinitesimally small has such potential, consider what may be locked within a person's spirit! Because we are created in God's image, every person does indeed possess great power.

But when sin entered Adam's heart, the Lord had to shut down the power He had built into him, lest one man alone be more devastating than many H-bombs! "For the creation was subjected to futility, not of its own will, but because of Him who subjected it, in hope that the creation itself also will be set free from its slavery to corruption into the freedom of the glory of the children of God"

(Romans 8:20–21). It is as though God turned down the rheostat from bright to dimmest dim, in both nature and mankind, lest the power He placed there be used by corrupt minds and hearts.

But Satan has worked ever since the Fall to release the powers of mankind before their time, thus leading to all the occult strivings God has forbidden. In time, in God's wisdom, He will restore mankind to fullness of glory, as Paul wrote:

> But if the ministry of death, in letters engraved on stones, came with glory, so that the sons of Israel could not look intently at the face of Moses because of the glory of his face, fading as it was, how shall the ministry of the Spirit fail to be even more with glory? For if the ministry of condemnation has glory, much more does the ministry of righteousness abound in glory.
>
> 2 Corinthians 3:7–9

Until sin has been destroyed from the heart of mankind, God will not restore men to power. Satan, knowing what damage will result, seeks to restore the psychic powers of humanity, even as he promised Jesus power (Matthew 4:9; Luke 4:6). He wants to seduce today's Adams and Eves to try to be gods without God. He wants us to feel good about having power and make God look like an "old meanie" for denying it. The Church is often called "backward" and "opposed to the good of mankind" because she will not agree to the seemingly universal desire to "be all we can be." Principalities of evil wield deceptive strongholds over a Christian (or anyone at all) who opens himself to this lie.

Among lesser causes, it is the hunger to be all we were created to be that makes the New Age (and anything else promising occult power) appear attractive. But there is no other way than by death to self and resurrection into life in Christ. Whoever does not hold to that becomes easy prey for seductive powers of darkness.

Let no one delude us with false hopes: God will release the powers of mankind only when He knows the Kingdom of Christ rules in our hearts (Romans 8:18–21), and not before. Let every Christian be content not to have power within himself, but to move solely by the power of the Holy Spirit. Even though occultism is growing by leaps and bounds these days as men and women hunger for power and maturity in an increasingly sick society, know for a surety that the Lord Jesus Christ is the only answer, the Holy Spirit the only true power. We need nothing else.

## White Stones

Alchemists were fond of speaking of the "lapis lazuli," or white stone (actually a rich azure or sky-blue). When discipline and training had progressed sufficiently and when purification warranted, the subject was put into a hypnotic trance in which his soul was mysteriously to be congealed into the white stone, or "philosopher's stone." His spirit and soul, guided by the mesmerizer, were to travel through regions and "ethers" to become one with all. The knowledge of all of mankind was thus to be "on tap."

Alchemists sought by science and discipline to build themselves into perfected stones—actually to become the white stone by which they could possess total knowledge and wisdom. Today carnival fortune-tellers mimic alchemy by gazing into their "crystal balls," which are no more than an imitation of the philosopher's lapis lazuli, or white stone.

Mankind and Satan have always copied God's work. The ability to know things at a distance or in the future is, of course, a gift given only at God's discretion through two of the gifts of the Holy Spirit, knowledge and prophecy. Alchemists were trying to achieve without God what He promised to give through the Holy Spirit: "The Helper, the Holy Spirit, whom the Father will send in My name, He will teach you all things, and bring to your remembrance all that I said to you" (John 14:26).

On the island of Paphos, Paul encountered Elymas, who as a magician was most likely also an alchemist; and Paul called down blindness on him when he would not stop making "crooked the straight ways of the Lord" (Acts 13:10).

The apostle Peter wrote to "those who reside as aliens, scattered throughout Pontus, Galatia, Cappadocia, Asia, and Bithynia" (1 Peter 1:1). Throughout that region were many alchemists. To new Christians in those days, alchemy may have seemed a welcome lure, a shortcut to power for insecure "aliens." We do not know if Peter knew of alchemy and was addressing its influence, but his references to "stones" in chapter 2 of his first epistle are many. And Jesus, wrote Peter, is the "choice stone, a precious corner stone," the only perfected soul.

On the island of Patmos, whether or not John was aware of alchemy, the Holy Spirit certainly was, and the Lord promised,

He who has an ear, let him hear what the Spirit says to the churches. To him who overcomes, to him I will give some of the hidden manna, and I will give him a white stone, and a new name written on the stone which no one knows but he who receives it.

Revelation 2:17

In Hebrew culture, a white stone was given to a man who had been forgiven great sins. Wearing the stone was a sign that he had been forgiven. But the Holy Spirit may also be saying something like this: "To him who overcomes will I give a perfected soul; no one has to study alchemy to achieve it." Every Christian is in the process of being transformed into the likeness of Jesus Christ, which will finally be accomplished in "the twinkling of an eye" (1 Corinthians 15:52)—as a gift and not by alchemic science or its modern counterpart, New Age humanism.

### *The "Wisdom of the Wise"*

The philosopher or alchemist never achieved his desired goal, of course. He found nothing but counterfeits—which Simon the magician realized when he saw the true wonders the apostles performed, and cried after them that he might be given this power, too (Acts 8:19). On the other hand, alchemists or "wizards" did find enough results to amaze the common people. Simon himself had been "astonishing the people of Samaria, claiming to be someone great" (verse 9). By what he and others did accomplish, they deluded themselves that they were on the right track.

Consider what the magicians of Egypt could do. Most likely they were adept at alchemy; but even if they were not, they actually duplicated the first signs of Moses and Aaron before Pharaoh! Their rods also became serpents, though that of Aaron swallowed theirs (Exodus 7:12). When Aaron struck the Nile and the water turned to blood, "the magicians of Egypt did the same with their secret arts" (verse 22). And they made frogs cover the land of Egypt (Exodus 8:7).

But when Aaron brought gnats to plague the land of Egypt, "the magicians tried with their secret arts to bring forth gnats, but they could not" (verse 18). Interestingly, the magicians' response was: "This is the finger of God" (verse 19).

In Greece philosophy flourished, and within it the science of alchemy. With this in mind, perhaps we can see more in a familiar passage:

> It is written, "*I will destroy the wisdom of the wise*, and the cleverness of the clever I will set aside." Where is the wise man? Where is the scribe? Where is the debater of this age? Has not God made foolish the wisdom of the world? For since in the wisdom of God the world through its wisdom did not come to know God, God was well-pleased through the foolishness of the message preached to save those who believe. For indeed Jews ask for signs, and *Greeks search for wisdom*; but we preach Christ crucified, to Jews a stumbling block, and to Gentiles foolishness, but to those who are the called, both Jews and Greeks, Christ the power of God and the wisdom of God. Because the foolishness of God is wiser than men, and the weakness of God is stronger than men.
>
> 1 Corinthians 1:19–25, italics mine

In chapter two Paul continues,

> And my message and my preaching were not in persuasive words of wisdom, but in demonstration of the Spirit and of power, *that your faith should not rest on the wisdom of men, but on the power of God*. Yet we do speak wisdom among those who are mature; a wisdom, however, not of this age, nor of the rulers of this age, who are passing away; but we speak God's wisdom in a mystery, the hidden wisdom, which God predestined before the ages to our glory; *the wisdom which none of the rulers of this age has understood*; for if they had understood it, they would not have crucified the Lord of glory. . . .
>
> verses 4–8, italics mine

When we understand what alchemy strove to accomplish, we comprehend more fully Paul's statement that "your faith should not rest on the wisdom of men but on the power of God." Only Christ, not men's wisdom, can restore and perfect us.

### *"Wisdom" in This Age*

The mistakes of alchemists can be ours as well. Earlier I mentioned the books with "get-rich" principles. What about all the supposedly Christian and Scripture-based "self-help" books? Some such books have appalled me as they teach Christians how to use Jesus and the Bible to build and improve their own character.

Whenever Christians use the words of God to teach individuals how to build their own characters, they can fall into the same sin, the same "wisdom" that lay behind alchemy, wanting to build the human soul into perfection. This returns people to the age-old sin from which the Lord has redeemed us—the religious effort to perfect ourselves. True deliverance and inner healing do the opposite: They call us and our strivings to death on the cross, so that the Lord alone may build our character (1 Peter 2:1–10).

To be sure, God is in the character-building business, as we all know: "We also exult in our tribulations, knowing that tribulation brings about perseverance; and perseverance, proven character; and proven character, hope . . ." (Romans 5:3–4). But it is God who builds our character by the experiences He puts us through. Alchemists, New Agers and self-help teachers all say to God, "No thanks to Your help, we'll build ourselves." Or, more subtly, "Thanks to Your help, we'll build ourselves."

If we regard magic and alchemy as mere foolishness, we are in serious error. God has made it foolish, as Paul says, but God would not have forbidden it so sternly were it only harmless fancy. Probably most who become involved are dilettantes, encountering little other than their own imaginations. But alchemy is real, frighteningly real. And for the damning sinfulness of that reality, God destroyed the inhabitants of Canaan and repeatedly warned and disciplined Israel.

The punishment of God on wizards was no less severe than on mediums. The same Leviticus 20:27 that we quoted earlier from the New American Standard Bible reads in the Revised Standard Version, "A man or a woman who is a medium or a wizard shall be put to death; they shall be stoned with stones, their blood shall be upon them."

### Sorcery: A Satanic Attack

So far we have discussed magic and alchemy or wizardry. Some wizards are solely alchemic wizards. Others add sorcery to their sins, using spirits and powers in order to manipulate nature or cause things to happen.

Satan tries every trick up his sleeve to beguile us into thinking that some magic is innocent and fun. All magic is sin.

With so-called white magic, the operator thinks he is doing good. His intentions may be benign, though shot through with sin. Not so with sorcery. Sorcery is black magic. Its intent, methods and ends are evil. Sorcery is never for others but against them, for the sole gain of the sorcerer.

Satanic cults use sorcery against the Church. They "pray" in chants and rhythms to cause unaccountable mechanical breakdowns, temper flare-ups, gossiping, adulteries. It may seem farfetched that men and women in the twentieth century can engage in such evil activities, much less be effective in it, but Paula and I know by experience the kinds of things that can happen and the reality of spiritual warfare involving sorcery. I already mentioned the spear I got in my back after doing battle with the warlock and his coven of witches on Vancouver Island.

Another instance illustrates the fact that sorcerers know how to send spirits to afflict their enemies. A friend was teaching in England. A pastor came to her with the word that three warlocks had combined forces to try to hate him to death. He was feeling the attack physically every day. She asked the Lord what to do, and He said to her, *Pray that the forces be reversed.* So she did and, under the anointing of the Holy Spirit, "saw" their streams of attack being returned upon themselves. The very next day, all three warlocks were actually found dead. The Lord had let them reap their own hate.

Well does the beloved apostle John say, "Any one who hates his brother is a murderer" (1 John 3:15, RSV). Hate truly does murder.

I ministered in Canada to a woman who had been conceived and dedicated in the womb as a child of Satan. Her parents and other Satanists used her continuously in unspeakably degrading sexual rituals. Dung was used for the bread of the satanic black masses. Decency forbids me to relate further details of the debasing activity to which they subjected this child. Paul wrote, "And do not participate in the unfruitful deeds of darkness, but instead even expose them; for it is disgraceful even to speak of the things which are done by them in secret" (Ephesians 5:11–12).

Amazingly, something within this child resisted throughout. Appeals to the government finally delivered her from such abuse, and the Lord subsequently saved her. Now she wanted inner healing for all the years that still plagued her memories through nightmares and terrors.

I share this much that the Body of Christ may once and for all take its collective head out of the sand! I have ministered to a number of erstwhile Satanists who have related similar debaucheries involved with the most debased forms of sorcery. It is foolishness to think that, because most modern men and women do not believe in superstition, such horrible satanic rites do not exist today, or are mere games. These evils are not only rampant but on the increase, as our world turns more and more from the truth of God's Word. "And just as they did not see fit to acknowledge God any longer, God gave them over to a depraved mind. . ." (Romans 1:28–32).

The Body of Christ must learn how to set free those the Lord would snatch from Satan's sorcery. We must learn how to minister victoriously against the reality that ensnared them. And we must learn how to heal the wounds of those whom Satanists have afflicted.

Missionaries from Africa and Haiti have reported about the power of witch doctors to afflict people with pain, trouble and accidents from a distance. I mentioned earlier how Paula and I used to be "bushwhacked" at night by demonic entities who jumped on and paralyzed us, until we could call on the name and power of Jesus to free us; and how we learned that natives in Africa had been killed under similar circumstances by what they called "the black wraith."

Strangely, we had never been really afraid, only annoyed. We knew by faith that the devil could not kill us. And we had been able to fall asleep immediately afterward, sure of the Lord's protection; whereas those natives had died because of fear. Their fear had empowered the demons and the witch doctors behind them with more power than they should have held.

Is it enough? Those who have had similar experiences know already that what I say is true. Sorcerers wield demonic powers to afflict, and demonic entities can attack people physically.

## Astrology

Astrology is listed in my Oxford Dictionary as one of the occult practices, even though many Christians do not include astrology as one of the evils the Lord prohibits. But the Word of God is clear. Isaiah reprimanded Israel for turning to sorcerers and astrologers:

> Stand fast now in your spells and in your many sorceries with which you have labored from your youth; perhaps you will be able to profit, perhaps you may cause trembling. You are wearied with your many counsels; let now the astrologers, those who prophesy by the stars, those who predict by the new moons, stand up and save you from what will come upon you. Behold, they have become like stubble, fire burns them; they cannot deliver themselves from the power of the flame; there will be no coal to warm by, nor a fire to sit before! So have those become to you with whom you have labored, who have trafficked with you from your youth; each has wandered in his own way. There is none to save you.
>
> Isaiah 47:12–15

Astrology participates in the sin of divination, the practice of peering into the future or unknown. It is Satan's copy of the gifts of knowledge and prophecy. Sometimes God in His wisdom does not want us to know things, much as a wise earthly father will not tell his children about certain things (like sex) until he is sure they are mature enough to handle it. "It is the glory of God to conceal a matter, but the glory of kings is to search out a matter" (Proverbs 25:2).

When the Lord does want us to know, He may choose one or more ways to involve us "kings" in the glory of searching out the matter, according to His knowledge of our maturity. "I have many more things to say to you, but you cannot bear them now" (John 16:12). God knows when to hide knowledge and when and how best to reveal it. Divination breaks God's providence.

Everyone wants a handle on life. We want to know what is coming so as to prepare for it. To use our minds (and computers) to project what is probable is not divination, but using the God-given natural wisdom He expects us to maintain.

When we attempt to find security through knowledge gained illicitly, however, that is divination. Behind the sin of divination: fear and lack of trust. We install something else as God when we can no longer rely in faith on the Lord's guidance.

Fortune-tellers, palm-readers and tea-leaf readers are all diviners, forbidden by the Word of God: "There shall not be found among you . . . one who uses divination, one who practices witchcraft, or one who interprets omens" (Deuteronomy 18:10).

Just as there is a fine line between the prayer of faith and magic, so there is a fine line between seeking the Lord's guidance and unconsciously turning that into divination. Recently the Lord has been giving His gifts back to the Church, raising up the fivefold ministry of apostles, prophets, evangelists, pastors and teachers (Ephesians 4:11). Prophets in these last years have become especially prominent as flocks of Christians have traveled to hear them pronounce words of personal prophecy. Such a gift is among the least of the functions of prophets, but perhaps the most overt and startling. And so people have crowded in, hoping to receive a prophecy for themselves. But when misused, prophets' gifts can turn quickly from true words from God into divination.

Note that when the Holy Spirit spoke through prophets to set Barnabas and Saul aside, it was "for the work to which I have called them" (Acts 13:2). Barnabas and Saul had already heard privately from God. The prophetic words came only as confirmation within the Body.

When we fail to do our own listening and run after others to give us words of direction, we look for security from knowledge wrongfully gained. Personal prophecies are a blessing when we are trying humbly to obey what we believe the Lord is telling us to do, unsure but willing to serve. The word comes as confirmation or warning that turns us around. But mark this carefully: It is God who sends prophets for our comfort and direction. Rather than have us running to them, He wants us falling to our knees in prayer to seek His guidance.

The kings of Israel sought out the Lord's prophets again and again, saying, "Inquire of the Lord for us." Sometimes their hearts were right, and other times they were so full of fear they were trying to involve His prophets in divination.

Just as prophetic words can turn into divination by a wrong heart, so can common, everyday listening. Paula and I visited a farmer friend in Arkansas. As we drove in, his soybean crops looked unhealthy and we asked him what was wrong. He explained that, by his experience and natural wisdom, he would have planted wheat that year. But he had been trying to do everything by hearing specifically from God and was sure God told him to plant beans. It turned out that the weather during that growing season would have been good for wheat but was terrible for beans. Now he was going deeply into debt.

This may seem puzzling because, on the surface, trying to listen to God about everything is good. But God does not want to reduce us to slaves or robots. He has given us good minds and He expects us to use them.

Our questions soon revealed that our friend had been fearful of failure. Afraid to use his own judgment and trust God to direct him out of wrong decisions, he tried to be overly certain and his "listening to God" became the sin of divination. Had God wanted him to plant one crop rather than another, He would have said so and confirmed it by at least two witnesses. But our friend's fearful heart caused him not to hear at all. The Lord let him listen to a wrong voice for both discipline and teaching.

That was a tough way to learn, but it was certainly written on our friend's heart thenceforth to listen when God wants to speak, but not to push God to be his diviner.

God wants us to listen to Him and to try to be obedient to what we hear, but again it is our motives that tell the difference between true listening and divination. This farmer was overly afraid of failure; he wanted a surety God does not normally give. He thought that if he could only get God to tell him the future, then he could make the appropriate choice. That is what divination attempts to do—to find out the future so as to be safe from failure, which is why all secular kings of Bible times employed diviners and Hitler used astrologers. It is entirely different to say to God, "Guide me for Your purposes. And if You don't speak, I will use my common sense and trust You to bless and protect."

The same mistake and consequent dire results have happened to many in the Body of Christ. Men have quit jobs they should have kept and moved from homes they should have remained in. Some have even left their wives and families, unaware they were being governed not by the Holy Spirit but by spirits of divination.

## Theosophy

Theosophy is a claim to have esoteric knowledge of the interplay of natural elements and the world of the spirit—not only our own personal spirit, but the spiritual world that pervades all things. Theosophists see their philosophy as deeper and more profound than orthodox religious doctrines, which they view as mere outworkings of the truths that only they, the enlightened ones, are privy to.

Again, the sin is Gnosticism—to say nothing of pride. Theosophists believe they are being saved by their esoteric knowledge. These "masters" or "illuminati" then feel it incumbent upon themselves to teach "lesser lights" the way. But they are impelled by principalities of delusion. They teach doctrines of men:

> You hypocrites, rightly did Isaiah prophesy of you, saying, "This people honors Me with their lips, but their heart is far away from Me. But in vain do they worship Me, teaching as doctrines the precepts of men."
>
> Matthew 15:7–9

Worse, they teach doctrines of demons, because modern theosophy includes elements of Buddhism and Brahmanism. "But the Spirit explicitly says that in later times some will fall away from the faith, paying attention to deceitful spirits and doctrines of demons" (1 Timothy 4:1). That prophecy is being fulfilled today in the practices of New Agers. When they listen to channelers, though they think they are hearing words of wisdom from "masters" who have gone on before, they are hearing nothing but demonic subterfuge masked as "beneficial wisdom that mankind sorely needs."

Theosophists, like alchemists, are also Pelagian and humanistic—though they prefer to call themselves theistic, usually being quite religious. Rosicrucianism and the works of Madame Blavatsky are examples. Theosophy attempts to discover truth by experience (not, unfortunately, the God-given experience Christians benefit from, under the tutelage of the Holy Spirit, checked by the Word and by brothers and sisters in the faith). They seek understanding of false doctrines in secret mandami and psychic experiences. They purport to lead initiates into deeper and deeper mysteries.

Theosophists, like alchemists, seek integration and wholeness in order to be restored to the pristine perfection of Adam. They differ only in method, not enduring the alchemists' rigorous self-disciplines and inner searches to produce the white stone. We know, on the other hand, that "no one comes to the Father, but through Me" (John 14:6).

Human beings and Satan have sought continually any way other than the cross to be restored to the Kingdom of God. Perhaps we should say that Satan has used any ploy, any device, any teaching that will lure men and women away from the tough way of the cross to the wide, smooth road of destruction. He always appeals to the desire to "become who you are meant to be," the very same temptation set before Eve's wondering eyes. The allure: You can achieve perfection, perhaps with the help of others but certainly without the help of God.

## Hypnotism

Among the occult practices listed in Deuteronomy 18:11 is "one who casts a spell." Friedrich Anton Mesmer, a German physician (1733–1815), was the modern rediscoverer of hypnotism. Mesmer believed in "magnetism," supposedly derived from astrological forces. He attempted healings through these "magnetic forces," which he thought he could apply through hypnotism.

Today hypnotism is rarely called mesmerism, but the doctor's name is still part of our vocabulary. When we are enthralled with a performance, we say we are mesmerized. In biblical days hypnotism was spoken of as "casting a spell," and a hypnotist was called a "charmer."

Hypnotism is strictly forbidden. One reason for this is that we are not to surrender our will to anyone other than Jesus. A second reason is that such surrender opens inner psychic doors that only the Lord should enter. A third is that no one besides Christ can be trusted to rule our will.

It is not true that hypnotism cannot make a person act against his will and is therefore safe. If a hypnotist can discover and lay hold of an inner hatred, resentment, anger or some other powerful emotion, he or she can use that to cause a person to do embarrassing or evil things he would never do in his "right mind."

I was teaching at a seminar on another subject when a question was raised concerning hypnotism. I explained that the Word of God forbids it and that its use as a parlor game is foolish and reprehensible. No Christian counselor or psychiatrist should use it, I said, and if he or she wants to discover something in a client, let him ask questions or let the Holy Spirit reveal it by gifts of knowledge and discernment. I explained that hypnotism can reveal what the Lord is not ready yet to heal, whereas the Holy Spirit will reveal each thing only as the person is prepared for healing. Concerning its use in orthodontal operations for people who cannot take anesthetics, I said I could not say, only that the Word of God forbids its use.

Immediately after, I sat down to lunch directly across the table from a Christian oral surgeon who was then the president of the national association that teaches doctors how to use clinical hypnosis! He told me he agreed fully in every way that such warnings were valid and necessary, although he said he did use hypnosis for patients who could not be anesthetized.

At another conference ten years later, that same man came up to me and said, "John, the Lord has shown me the hard way. Never again will I use hypnotism for any purpose whatever!" Before I could ask him what had happened, the crowd surrounded us and carried me away.

What had he experienced that filled him with such determination? I never found out, but at yet another conference, when the subject came up, a psychiatrist testified that he also had used hypnotism in the past and would never do so again. Once more there was not sufficient time to discover why. But we don't really need to know. Obedience to God should be enough. Praise Him that He is revealing His Word to professionally trained servants!

At a School of Pastoral Care, a Christian psychologist was asked about hypnotism. He also testified against it and told of one case in which a counselor had hypnotized a counselee. He gave her a post-hypnotic suggestion that she would never smoke again. That part worked; she stopped smoking. But two weeks later she jumped out of a second-floor window. The Christian psychologist concluded that he had removed her steam valve without healing her inner pressures, and observed that it was not merely unwise use of hypnotism that made it wrong, but the use of it at all.

## Roots and Results of Occult Involvement

There are many other forms of occult involvement, but perhaps all can be classified under the headings we have discussed. Our purpose is not to expose all the various forms of occultism to the light of God's Word. It is, rather, to teach the Body of Christ about occult involvement so as to enable healing.

At the root of occult sin is pride. One primary reason for the cross is to humble us. God's plan is to divest us thoroughly of pride through continuous death to self. "Where then is boasting? It is excluded. By what kind of law? Of works? No, but by a law of faith" (Romans 3:27). The essence of occultism is wielding a power that elevates oneself, even as Simon wanted people to think of him as someone great. Regarding that sinful tendency, Paul writes:

> For if anyone thinks he is something when he is nothing, he deceives himself.
>
> Galatians 6:3

If any man think that he knoweth any thing, he knoweth nothing yet as he ought to know.

1 Corinthians 8:2, KJV

Let no man deceive himself. If any man among you thinks that he is wise in this age, let him become foolish that he may become wise. For the wisdom of this world is foolishness before God.

1 Corinthians 3:18–19

All involvement with occultism wounds. God did not build us for it. It wrenches our system, whether we operate it or have it used on us, knowingly or unknowingly. Involvement in occultism is like trying to force a soprano to sing bass, which harms the vocal cords.

Mark and I suggest that any who counsel and heal the effects of occultism would profit by studying Shakespeare's play Macbeth with an eye to seeing how occultism perverts nature and mankind from their natural courses. Recall that the play begins with three witches who defile Macbeth by false prophecies of glory. The story as it unfolds is a revelation of the twisting effects of sorcery and murder on God-given conscience and thought, while our bodies and spirits do not flow naturally in occult ways. Shakespeare gave Lady Macbeth the words to say it most clearly:

> Come, you spirits
> That tend on mortal thoughts, unsex me here,
> And fill me from the crown to the toe, top-full
> Of direst cruelty: make thick my blood,
> Stop up the access, and passage to remorse,
> That no compunctious visitings of nature
> Shake my fell purpose, nor keep peace between
> The effect and it! Come to my woman's breasts,
> And take my milk for gall, you murdering ministers,
> Wherever, in your sightless substances,
> You wait on nature's mischief. Come, thick night,
> And pall thee in the dunnest smoke of Hell,
> That my keen knife see not the wound it makes,
> Nor Heaven peep through the blanket of the dark,
> To cry, "Hold, hold!"

Macbeth, Act I, Scene 5

Sin, especially occultism, destroys the wholesome flow of the spirit in the body. Macbeth himself speaks in that familiar passage from Act II, Scene 2:

> Methought I heard a voice cry, "Sleep no more!
> Macbeth does murder sleep," the innocent sleep,
> Sleep that knits up the ravelled sleeve of care,
> The death of each day's life, sore labor's bath,
> Balm of hurt minds, great nature's second course,
> Chief nourisher in life's feast.

Many people assume falsely that occultism could not be the cause of their difficulties because they never regularly practiced anything occult. They may have forgotten the one time in their childhood they went with some friends to see "Sister Maybelle," who looked at their palms and enthralled them by telling them about their past and what would happen in their future. Or that they used to have fun playing with the Ouija board — or even today with that devil-created game "Dungeons and Dragons," involving players directly in occult practices. Or the few times they tried to hypnotize one another or played at holding a seance. However innocuous it may seem, sin is sin, and it sets forces in motion that must surely be dealt with.

God is not upset by children's playful dabblings, and His nature is compassionate (see Psalm 103). But the immutable laws of the universe are neither compassionate nor indulgent. However hopeful and trusting we may be when we step off the roof of a twenty-story building, the results are guaranteed disastrous. And just as gravity cannot be denied, neither can God revoke His laws because foolish children do not understand. If a boy thought he could swim in an underwater cave for five minutes without scuba equipment, we would expect him to drown and few would blame God. In that case, the consequences would be almost immediate.

But reaping is sometimes slow in coming. Only recently have we seen the awful effects on Vietnam veterans who came into contact years ago with Agent Orange. Likewise, results from one instance of occult activity in childhood may afflict someone horribly in adulthood. Counselors need to understand that we are dealing with legal cause and effect. Dabblers in the occult do not usually reap what they have sown at once, but it is inevitable that they will.

There are at least eight results of occultism that we will talk about in turn, along with steps to take for healing.

### Disturbed Sleep

A common first result of occultism is disturbed sleep. Insomnia, fretful sleep and nightmares are caused by many things, but one of the causes Elijah House counselors look for routinely is past or present occult involvement, or whether the person is under occult attack. Questions soon reveal if the person has ever been involved.

Disturbed sleep can be healed first by forgiveness for the degree of occult involvement the person experienced, and second by closure. Naive explorations open doors to powers that otherwise would have no means of entering the individual. "Oh, that there were one among you who would shut the doors, that you might not kindle fire upon my altar in vain!" (Malachi 1:10, RSV). Apart from the primary meaning of that verse (which in context deplores the offering of blemished sacrifices to God), I see it applied by the Holy Spirit for healing effects of the occult. Christian counselors should pray that the Lord will shut all the psychic doors of the person, especially when the fires of prayer are lit.

Third, disturbed sleep can be healed by "hiding." "You have died and your life is hidden with Christ in God" (Colossians 3:3). A Christian normally is obscured from Satan, as I said at the beginning of this chapter, guarded by the angels of God. Demonic powers cannot see where to afflict him or how to thwart his plans.

But sin, and especially occultism, exposes a person to view. In J. R. R. Tolkien's fantasy *The Lord of the Rings*, whenever Frodo put on the magic ring he carried, he became invisible to everyone—except to the powers of darkness! He had entered by magic into their world and now they saw him more clearly than they could in the physical domain. Just so, by occultism we enter Satan's world and are more visible to his minions. We heal such exposure by praying that the person be rehidden.

Sometimes I say, "Lord, as the angels reached out and blinded those men in Sodom so that they groped for the door handle all night and couldn't find it, so I haul this person into the Body of Christ and blind all the powers of darkness. They can no longer see my brother [or sister]. From now on he is hidden from them. I obscure all the pathways over which they have tracked him." And I quote Psalm 35:6: "Let their way be dark and slippery, with the angel of the Lord pursuing them."

Fourth, we pray for physical healing. We ask the Lord to pour His healing balm throughout the person's body and spirit, healing, then removing any devices the demons may have implanted.

### Inner Voices

A second effect of occultism is the pestering of the person by annoying inner voices. Sometimes they have natural psychological causes. There may be occult causes as well. Or occultism may be the sole reason. Questioning and discernment can determine which is the case. If one is not sure, it does not hurt to pray away any demonic influence.

Remember that occultism always involves the demonic directly, so the likelihood of demonization is very great. It may be necessary to bind the demons before anything else can happen, because they can block the reception of truth and healing. Sometimes in the process of healing, without a direct command of deliverance, demons simply have to leave because their ground of access or house of residence has been removed. Usually I proceed to pray for healing of the person's heart, knowing that whatever demons inhabit will have to leave.

But if they manifest or block the healing, then I turn to binding and casting them away directly. I would rather not have to do a direct deliverance if the person can be freed by inner healing. The main reason is that when demons are not addressed directly yet are forced to leave, Satan gets no attention and no glory.

In dealing with people who hear voices, the same four steps listed above are taken in prayer: forgiveness, closure, hiding and physical healing. We add a fifth as well. We rebuke the spirits and voices, cast them away and command them in Jesus' name to be silent. It is not the same as the deliverances just described. Those were demons in some degree attached to the person, perhaps inhabiting. Occultism attracts hordes of demons about a person

like moths around a light. These clouds of imps need to be commanded away. Sometimes it is this clearing of the air about a person that catapults us into a full-blown deliverance session.

### Recurrent Accidents

A third common effect of occultism is recurrent accidents or
tragic happenings. Sometimes after we have prayed away bitter
root judgments and expectancies by which a person is continually,
mysteriously defeated or reaps tragedy (see chapter 14 in *The
Transformation of the Inner Man*), the person still remains unusually disaster-prone. The Holy Spirit may then reveal that the powers
of darkness have a free hand to bring down what the person is trying to build, because of some point of occult involvement.

We have all had occasion to cope with "Murphy's Law," such as
when someone phones about an important issue just as we were
leaving for an important appointment; or when we receive some
bit of information too late that would have saved us from a course
of action that turned out to be troublesome and wrong. But generally Christians are pleasantly surprised—or would be, if they
thought about it!—at the Lord's providence and timing. Just the
right set of "coincidences" happens to turn everything rosy.

For people hindered by the occult, it happens the other way
around. If there is any loophole, anything to foul up the works, it
will happen like clockwork! A person like this may say, "If it
weren't for bad luck, I wouldn't have any luck at all!"

We stop Satan's game by the same steps outlined above: forgiveness, closure, hiding, healing and deliverance. And we add to
our prayers a direct command that the devil's inroads into the person's life be stopped. We command Satan to take his hands off his
or her life.

It should be added that the most common cause of such accidents and hurtful happenings is curses. By this we mean that some
power of darkness, or some person involved in sorcery, may have
placed a curse on his or her life. We break the curse by the authority and name of Jesus.

Or the curse may be because the person unconsciously cursed
his father or mother in bitterness and judgment against them. Jesus
reminded His followers, "Moses said, 'Honor your father and

mother'; and 'He who speaks evil of father or mother, let him be put to death'" (Mark 7:10). The death we die in this case is to our abundant life. Cursing our father or mother puts a curse on our life, even as God listed the blessings and the curses for Israel in Deuteronomy 27 and 28. Nothing will go right from then on.

We insert this here because we know that if a counselor discovers and casts away occult destructions, but does not discover and bring to forgiveness whatever stands between a person and his parents, the troubles will most likely not stop. Unforgiveness holds the curse on the person's life, continuing to give Satan access. Here again we see the necessity for deliverance and inner healing to go hand in hand.

### Physical Illness

A fourth result from occult involvement is affliction and physical illness. A person may feel bothered and tormented; or he may be subject to recurrent rashes or minor illnesses for which medical doctors cannot find the cure. Again, there may be psychosomatic or purely medical causes, but it is wise to consider the possibility of occult influence. One woman in our prayer group complained only recently of an inability to arrive at full health. Something was always nagging. I "saw" occultism in the family history and prayed for it to be stopped. Subsequently she handed me a letter full of rejoicing that our prayer in the group had set her free.

Sometimes physical afflictions happen not because of past involvement but through the effects of present spiritual warfare (like the spear they found in my back after we did battle with the coven).

A friend ran afoul of a batch of witches' covens in a foreign country. It was as though she had stirred up a hornets' nest. The conflict was affecting her through headaches, weariness, blocked moments in her teachings, fits of despondency and feelings of futility. She called me for help. With the help of the Holy Spirit, and knowing everything else had been tried, I told her, "Try getting out into nature. Walk in the woods. Roll on the grass." She tried it and it worked. It was as though all those negative effects drained out of her. She wrote back that some people thought she was one crazy lady, rolling in the grass, but she felt better!

My Osage Indian ancestors used to say that the white man lives too far away from the earth. It is true. Nature camps are established for city children because of sociological studies concerning the effects of a lack of wholesome natural environment. So I recommend as one antidote for occult influence, besides all the ways we pray for healing, large doses of time spent outside. When counselees' problems have piled up on me one after the other and I feel defiled, I may take ten minutes between appointments to walk out into the garden and let my fingers work the soil. It drains away the defilement that, by then, I can no longer successfully pray away.

Where did Jesus go when He needed refreshment from the defilement of working in the cities of Palestine? To the mountains, out to the healing balm of nature. Nor was Daniel in the city when, after 21 days, the angel of the Lord came to him. He was "by the bank of the great river" (Daniel 10:4).

New Agers have taken up conservation and nature as a main theme. Unfortunately, when Satan copies what the Lord does, too many timid Christians fear to enter that field because they think it is demonic. When will we learn that we are more than conquerors? Fear not: "The earth is the Lord's, and all it contains" (Psalm 24:1).

### *Lapses of Memory*

A fifth symptom of occult involvement or attack is lapses of memory, blocked thought patterns, inability to remember where one put things or what one is doing, and loss of one's train of thought while speaking. Having suffered the effects of hypoglycemia at one time and acute stress at others, I know firsthand that these symptoms can be the result of physical and psychological causes. Nevertheless, discernment may also reveal occult activity. Neither need rule out the other.

Perhaps a person could overcome the physical causes were occultism not tipping the scales, or withstand demonic occult attacks were not exhaustion or stress such a factor. Effects can, of course, be present by occult interference when no physical reasons exist.

When Agnes Sanford found that opposing spirits were blocking her thoughts and constricting her throat, and I traveled as part of a team with her, I did little public speaking or teaching. I was not there for that purpose. We prayed together during the day. At the meetings I read the Scriptures and said a prayer. She taught and afterward I closed in prayer.

But while she taught, I sat in the audience close by where I could watch her, interceding the entire time. So long as I remembered to attend to my duties and not get caught up in what she was saying, power flowed through her without interruption. She had been plagued by tension headaches, partly from the burden of intercession and the stress of so much speaking, but also from occult opposition. I was there to protect her so that she might be free to concentrate on the ministry.

Many speakers have learned to enlist prayer warriors at home, and some have intercessors as part of the traveling team as a wall of protection, as in Psalm 8:2: "From the mouth of infants and nursing babes Thou hast established strength, because of Thine adversaries, to make the enemy and the revengeful cease."

## Turmoil

A sixth effect of occult involvement is constant family turmoil and tragedy. Satan often attacks the Lord's servants through afflictions on their families. Church members should pray regularly for their pastor's family. Traveling teachers, prophets and evangelists need groups who dedicate themselves to prayer on their behalf, especially to watch over their families, since frequent absences from home leave their loved ones subject to anger and resentment and vulnerable to attack.

Aside from families attacked for their service to the Lord, those who have engaged in occultism at any time in life have opened family doors that ought to have remained shut. Hear again the Lord's warning word concerning those who have been to seances: "I . . . will cut him off from among his people" (Leviticus 20:6). The law of sowing and reaping goes into operation. When a man turns to the occult, in effect he cuts himself off, and all those in his charge, from the Lord. That is the seed he has sown, and that is what he must reap.

Powers of darkness take advantage by adding to the discipline of that law the ravages of turmoil and tragedy. Guilt that fails to find its way to the cross becomes a sword that demonic powers can wield. We stop such interference by the same applications of forgiveness and healing, closure and hiding of the family.

But let us remember that if we do not heal the wounded spirit, battered by its activity in the occult, those bruises may serve as houses of reentry for the demonic. It will not do to send Satan's forces away, and then leave the door open for them through unhealed areas in the family. Fractured relationships and emotions between family members may need to be mended and comforted.

### *Financial Drain*

A seventh common symptom might be listed under previous effects but deserves mention on its own. Sometimes it seems as if there is an unending drain on family finances. Just about the time Mom and Dad hope to get their heads above water for a while, unforeseen expenses plunge them under again. Every light at the end of the tunnel is somehow snuffed out or proves to have been an illusion.

A clue is that expenses arrive in the most outlandish and unfair ways! Life does not flow evenly. Budgets are disrupted so as to be impossible to adhere to. It is as though there is a curse on the wealth of the family.

Certainly if the family is not tithing, there will be a blockage, and that needs to be corrected first:

> "Will a man rob God? Yet you are robbing Me! But you say, 'How have we robbed Thee?' In tithes and contributions. You are cursed with a curse, for you are robbing Me, the whole nation of you! Bring the whole tithe into the storehouse, so that there may be food in My house, and test Me now in this," says the Lord of hosts, "if I will not open for you the windows of heaven, and pour out for you a blessing until there is no more need."
>
> Malachi 3:8–10

Sometimes, however, the family may be tithing faithfully but hurting all the more because now it seems God's promises have failed to be true. "I'm doing my part! Why isn't God coming through? This isn't fair." The latter effect of occult opposition is more important than the financial loss; there is nothing the devil would rather do than break our trust in the faithfulness of God.

Sometimes in prayer I have seen a vision of a great lake of blessing that God has stored up and wants to pour out, but the curse has turned the funnel of reception upside-down. The waters of blessing splatter off the sides and only a trickle comes through the small opening. In faith we must take the devil's hand off the supply line and see the funnel properly situated, collecting the floods of goodness and directing them to His child and His family.

Healing is needed for the family not only for all the strains of financial loss, but between them and God. They need, as Paul urged, "on behalf of Christ, [to] be reconciled to God " (2 Corinthians 5:20), in a sense to "forgive" God. He has done nothing wrong, but we can nonetheless be angry at a perfect God. "Forgiving" God drains the poison from our own hearts.

The same sort of reconciliation with God can be applied for all the other hurts we have discussed, but here it is especially important since the person feels that a specific promise of God has been broken.

## Generational Harm

An eighth result of occult involvement is not only to be expected; it will happen by law. That is the descent of trouble and harm to generation after generation within the family (Deuteronomy 5:9). The subject of generational sin is too large for full development in this book. Readers can find it discussed at length in chapter 13 of *Healing the Wounded Spirit*. Suffice it to say that when parents sow, their chidren reap. On the positive side, this is why the Scriptures say, "A good man leaves an inheritance to his children's children" (Proverbs 13:22). But on the other side, when David sinned, for example, his child died (2 Samuel 12).

All sins cause children to reap harm, until stopped on the cross of Christ. But occult sins directly involve the demonic, and the necessity of the law of reaping grants the demonic powers access to increase the reaping into greater destructiveness. Therefore, we must pray to forgive occult sins and stop the need for reaping upon the cross of Christ.

## Executing the Vengeance of God

These are the most common results of occult involvement. Note that I have not distinguished between general demonic warfare and occultism. There are times, of course, when demons attack quite apart from any occult human involvement, perhaps most of the time. But this is a chapter on occult involvement, and occultists or Satanists are so often behind attacks on Christians that they can be discussed together.

The Church of Jesus Christ needs to become aware and instructed, to know her power and authority. The calling is urgent:

> God takes His stand in His own congregation; He judges in the midst of the rulers. How long will you judge unjustly, and show partiality to the wicked? Vindicate the weak and the fatherless; do justice to the afflicted and destitute. Rescue the weak and needy; deliver them out of the hand of the wicked.
>
> Psalm 82:1–4

The power is given:

> And Jesus came up and spoke to them, saying, "All authority has been given to Me in heaven and on earth."
>
> Matthew 28:18

> And these signs will accompany those who have believed: in My name *they will cast out demons*, they will speak with new tongues.
>
> Mark 16:17, italics mine

The least Christian wields the fullness of power and shares the joy of battle. The kings and nations upon whom we shall execute the vengeance of God are first and foremost the demonic powers:

> Let the godly ones exult in glory; let them sing for joy on their beds. Let the high praises of God be in their mouth, and a two-edged

sword in their hand, to execute vengeance on the nations, and punishment on the peoples; to bind their kings with chains, and their
nobles with fetters of iron; to execute on them the judgment written;
this is an honor for all His godly ones. Praise the Lord!

Psalm 149:5–9

# 15

## Spiritualism, Delusions and Cults[1]

As for the person who turns to mediums and to spiritists, to play the harlot after them, I will also set My face against that person and will cut him off from among his people.

Leviticus 20:6

As for a man or a woman, if there is a medium or a spiritist among them, they shall surely be put to death; they shall be stoned with stones, their bloodguiltiness is upon them.

Leviticus 20:27

Spiritualism holds great appeal for those who have insufficient faith or who lack biblical knowledge. This is the practice of attempting to communicate with those who have departed from this life. It is done through a medium, a person who becomes a conduit for such contacts.

## Why People Turn to Spiritualism

There are a number of reasons people turn to spiritualism.

The lonely may not have faith to believe that they will share eternity with their loved ones after a short separation, and see spiritualism as a means of contact with and reassurance from the departed. They may have little or no conscious awareness that God forbids it. It seems good to them to ease an aching heart by such contacts.

Others may have a great need to find a lost bank key or last will and testament. "If we could contact Uncle Pete, he could tell us. What's wrong with that?" Or they may have great fear of death, or, more accurately, fear of vanishing into nothingness. Not having fullness of faith in our resurrected Lord (though their lips may say it), they want assurance in their hearts that something real does exist beyond the grave. Seances seem to provide the evidence.

God provides better ways to answer such needs, however, and no possible justification can make spiritualism right.

As we see by the above Scriptures, spiritualism is strictly forbidden by the Word of God. The Lord does not explain why, except to say, "You shall have no other gods before Me" (Exodus 20:3), which implies that we human beings cannot contact a departed spirit without entering some form of idolatry. God does not have to explain Himself. It is enough that He forbids it.

We can, however, easily see some of His reasons. The first is the idolatry mentioned above. I have known people so hooked on spiritualism that they would make no decision without first consulting the spirits. That bestows upon spirits (usually demons masquerading as "Uncle Pete" or "Aunt Betsy") a reliance that ought to be only on God. "Commit your way to the Lord, trust also in Him, and He will do it" (Psalm 37:5). "Commit your works to the Lord, and your plans will be established" (Proverbs 16:3).

A second reason God forbids spiritualism is that it creates an immediate venue for demonic inhabitation. Demons flock about seances and channelings, knowing that whoever enters spiritualism has opened psychic doors to them and, by disobedience to God's commands, given them legal grounds to come in.

A third reason is defilement. Some scholars maintain that upon a person's death, his or her spirit is taken immediately into chambers in heaven or hell. They say spiritualists and channelers can never contact a departed soul. Rather, they reach the satanic "angel," or familiar, who watched over the person all his life, who can therefore perfectly counterfeit his voice and divulge things that seemingly only the departed person could have known.

Back in chapter 2, I mentioned that I once attended a seance held, of all places, in a Methodist church. The meeting was sponsored by a group formed for research into psychic phenomena. This was to be a "scientific" seance to prove that life continues after death and that spiritualists really can contact the dead. Why the former needed to be proved in a Christian context is beyond me! The medium, in any case, was the Rev. Arthur Ford, the most renowned spiritualist of his day (who, by the way, thought himself a devout Christian).

This was several years before my own conversion. But even in those days I had enough sense to question what apparently no one there was asking: How could they know whether the voice talking to them was from the departed or from a demon? Again and again Ford's voice would change and another voice claim to be this or that relative of someone in the room. The alleged relative would then tell the living kin where to find a lost article or reveal some secret that presumably no one else in the room could have known.

Participants were asked to record what was said to them and ascertain whether the articles were, in fact, where they were said to be, and whether others could attest to the secret facts revealed. The reports, to be given at the next session of the society, were to confirm that it really was the relative who had talked through Arthur Ford that day.

In one instance the voice told a woman that a cherished, long-lost bracelet had fallen behind a bookcase and could easily be retrieved. The participants were excited, but something inside me kept me from jumping on the bandwagon, and I continued to wonder how they could ignore the possibility of demons at work.

Today, New Agers gather about channelers, eager to hear the wisdom of "ascended masters" who have allegedly amassed great stores of knowledge that no one on earth could possibly know. That is the same delusion those researchers were falling into!

It leads to the same kind of demonic inhabitation I suffered. It results not in finding truth but in being cut off from the only Truth, who is Jesus. It grabs hold of people who do not know or believe the Word of God, who cannot trust that the Holy Spirit will lead them into all appropriate truth as Jesus promised. Its end, in this life and the next, is hell.

We can also be defiled by living persons by their presence or by what emanates from their spirits even when they are nowhere near. Witness our Lord's admonition that "every one who looks on a woman to lust for her has committed adultery with her already in his heart" (Matthew 5:28). Jesus did not merely say that this person has committed adultery, but that he has committed adultery with her. His spirit has defiled a woman across the space between them. (It is particularly cruel that, though the woman has done nothing wrong, she can be defiled by another's lust. This is why we need continually to be cleansed by the Lord in worship. Defilement is one of the prices we pay for living in a sinful society. See Isaiah 6:5.)

But the spirits of living people must abide within their own bodies. Not so with a departed spirit or demon posing as a person. Not bound to a particular body, they can attach themselves to a living person, or inhabit and eventually perhaps possess him or her altogether.

Ingenuous people love to toy with spiritualism, as they do with others forms of occultism. Some may attend a seance naively to get a "rush," or, because they think the whole thing is phony, they will go to scoff. Indeed, because nothing real seems to happen, many believe there is nothing to spiritualism. But there is a fourth reason spiritualism is forbidden. The first three mentioned above—idolatry, exposure to demonic contamination and defilement—can all happen even if no spirits are contacted. But God commands us sternly on this point because of the possibility of becoming involved in relationships with ghosts or demons who lead astray.

Mere fanciful foolishness does not concern the Lord so much as disobedience, and even unsuccessful attempts at spiritualism open forbidden doors and sow to later reapings of judgment. "Childish" games like the Ouija board can cause great harm. And sometimes mediums, channelers and participants in seances do make actual contact with a dead person or demon. It is the stark reality of such disobedience that arouses the Lord's anger.

Contacted spirits are not to be believed. When demons tell someone (through the vocal cords of the medium or channeler) some easily verifiable fact, they are establishing belief and trust. Once this is accomplished, they lead the person bit by bit into delusions, base deceptions and false doctrines.

Continued contacts increase footholds in the person's spirit and soul until he or she is fully snared and on the way to hell. I am sure this is what happened to the Rev. Arthur Ford. Many "spiritualist churches" name Jesus as Lord and continue to believe they are fully Christian; they are treading the broad path to eternal torture. Satan blinds their eyes (2 Corinthians 4:4) to Scriptures like Leviticus 20:6 and 20:27, but he is careful to encourage them to pray to God and stay in their churches. He knows that if the veneer of "good Christian" is stripped away, his deception will be exposed for what it is. Satan wants them to wear all the trappings of Christianity, therefore, while his own trappings (their true nature unsuspected) slowly close about his prey.

## Whom Do Mediums Contact?

Some scholars maintain that mediums contact only counterfeit spirits, not the dead. But we ought not to be too dogmatic about this. When Saul became agitated on the eve of the great battle against the Philistines and no prophet would speak God's word to him, he rode through the night behind enemy lines to find the witch of Endor. He knew that turning to mediums was forbidden; he himself had "cut off those who are mediums and spiritists from the land" (1 Samuel 28:9). But, desperate, frightened and mentally disturbed, he decided to do it anyway.

Saul asked the witch to call up Samuel. In no way does Scripture indicate that Saul did not really speak with Samuel.

When the woman saw Samuel, she cried out with a loud voice; and the woman spoke to Saul, saying, "Why have you deceived me? For you are Saul."

And the king said to her, "Do not be afraid; but what do you see?" And the woman said to Saul, "I see a divine being coming up out of the earth."

And he said to her, "What is his form?" And she said, "An old man is coming up, and he is wrapped with a robe." And Saul knew that it was Samuel, and he bowed with his face to the ground and did homage.

Then Samuel said to Saul, "Why have you disturbed me by bringing me up?" And Saul answered, "I am greatly distressed; for the Philistines are waging war against me, and God has departed from me and answers me no more, either through prophets or by dreams; therefore I have called you, that you may make known to me what I should do."

And Samuel said, "Why then do you ask me, since the Lord has departed from you and has become your adversary? And the Lord has done accordingly as He spoke through me; for the Lord has torn the kingdom out of your hand and given it to your neighbor, to David. As you did not obey the Lord and did not execute His fierce wrath on Amalek, so the Lord has done this thing to you this day. Moreover the Lord will also give over Israel along with you into the hands of the Philistines, therefore tomorrow you and your sons will be with me. Indeed the Lord will give over the army of Israel into the hands of the Philistines!"

1 Samuel 28:12–19

Whether or not Saul would have died in battle anyway, Samuel called him a dead man, because whoever consults a medium, God "will cut him off from his people."

This Bible account makes it clear that it is possible for mediums to contact the departed. True, Samuel lived in Old Testament times, and perhaps Christians cannot be disturbed as he was, but we ought not to make categorical statements when the Bible leaves the question open. Samuel's appearance to Saul was unquestionably real. It may be, therefore, that other contacts are real as well.

But real or counterfeit, trying to contact the dead is forbidden by God, and that is enough for any believer.

It is an interesting footnote that the witch of Endor prevailed upon Saul to eat a meal before he left. Not only was it customary to urge hospitality; it was one of the strongest customs of the day that a person could not harm another whose salt he had eaten. The woman was terrified that Saul, who had been cutting off all mediums, would recollect himself and do so to her. But when he ate her food, he ate her salt. So by offering kindness, she thought to save herself from the king.

In just such ways, spiritualists may think to save themselves: "Look at all the good things we do. We aren't wicked. Certainly

God will not reject us." But at the final judgment, neither the witch of Endor nor any well-meaning spiritualist will be able to escape the law of God. Sin is sin, no matter how nice our character or kindly our intentions.

## The Delusion of Spiritualism

Once while making routine hospital calls, I entered the room of Bessie, a woman on her deathbed. Her eyes widened and she exclaimed, "Oh, you are surrounded by the very best workers!"

I knew instantly she was a spiritualist, since some spiritualists call the spirits they use their "workers." (Some of these spirits are regarded as good and others as evil and not to be trusted.) "Yes, Bessie," I responded, "that is the Lord Jesus Christ and all His company."

That began our conversation, and I began to witness to Bessie, a long-practicing spiritualist, of the saving grace of the Lord Jesus Christ. She said she would gladly accept Him as her Lord and Savior; had she not always known Him in her spiritualistic church? I agreed that, yes, I supposed she knew about Him. Now I would have her receive Him, be forgiven and be born anew. She agreed, and received Him in prayer as her Lord and Savior.

Then I said, "Bessie, now that you have received Jesus as Lord and Savior, you will have to renounce your workers and let them go."

Now Bessie demurred. "Oh, no, I need my workers."

"No, Bessie, you don't need anyone but Jesus."

"No, no, I need them."

At that moment I sensed the Lord's presence in a powerful way, and I knew Bessie sensed it, too, because she began writhing in pain and fear and drew back. "Do you see, Bessie," I said, "it's those spirits that are afraid of Him. You have nothing to fear. You belong to Him. He loves you. Just let those workers go and it will be all right."

"Oh, no, I couldn't."

I sensed the glory of the Lord more intensely than before. Again Bessie blanched in terror.

"Let those workers go, Bessie. Jesus loves you. It will be O.K."

"No, no, I can't."

"Yes, you can."

So it went. Finally the grace of God touched her with His over-powering love and she said, "O.K., I'll let them go."

With that I commanded every ghost and demon to leave her and pronounced the Lord's forgiveness of her sin of spiritualism. Bessie relaxed and the glory of the Lord came again—and stayed! Bessie was no longer afraid. When I left, I looked back to see a joyously serene expression on her face. Her family reported that she passed away soon after, calm and peaceful.

People entrapped in spiritualistic churches and New Age groups can be further deluded by the fact that life usually goes fairly smoothly. They think they must be doing something right and must be enjoying God's favor. What actually is happening is that delusion has no opposition! Think about it. Satan does not afflict people in delusion. Why should he? They are already in his control.

If the deluded person is walking close enough to God to receive His discipline (Hebrews 12:8), the devil tries to convince him he is being persecuted because he is a true servant of the Lord Jesus Christ. If his delusion has carried him so far away from God that God cannot treat him as a son and so cannot discipline him, again the entrapped one finds no opposition.

## Deliverance from Cults

Delusions almost always please the flesh. They make people feel good—at least at first. They appeal to pride and feelings of power or of being more enlightened than other people. Delusions even seem to make people feel physically healthier. Thus, the deceived think they have discovered helpful and healthful truths. Often people flock to hear an entrapped person's false teachings, again because delusions appeal to the flesh: "They are from the world; therefore they speak as from the world, *and the world listens to them*" (1 John 4:5, italics mine).

For these reasons, delusions and heresies are almost always popular. The popularity itself often convinces the deluded they must be right. Satan sees to it they forget the Lord's admonition that "the way is broad that leads to destruction . . . and the way is narrow that leads to life, and few are those who find it" (Matthew 7:13–14). If people begin to catch on and desert the one in delusion, Satan tries to convince him by this very Scripture that he is one of the few on the right track!

The antidote? Walking humbly before the Lord. Checking everything by the Word of God (1 John 4:1–3). Listening obediently to authority and to brothers and sisters who warn and chastise.

These three admonitions are often, not coincidentally, what cult leaders use to control their victims. The admonitions must therefore be accompanied by the following bits of advice: Watch for lasting fruits. Ask the Lord to peel away whatever is not of Him. Listen to more than one small branch of the Lord's Body for truth; cults and delusions work in and by isolation. And, strange though it might seem, have fun—play games, go to comedies, laugh with friends and family. Delusions and cults create an overly serious lifestyle. Joy and laughter tend to break the hold of the demonic (Psalm 2:4).

## Deliverance and Inner Healing

When a person begins to break free from delusions or cults, he or she needs both deliverance and inner healing. Invariably there is some area of brokenness in the character that has left the person vulnerable. I have seen Christians come out of cults that nearly destroyed their lives, Christians who are certain they have learned their lesson. They will "never again succumb to that kind of domination and control!" Then, before long, they are ensnared in a group every bit as bad as the one they left! Why? Because they have not dealt with the flaws in their character that made them vulnerable.

One young man I knew came out of a restrictive and controlling cult. He breathed a sigh of relief and exclaimed, "Well, that was a hard lesson. But at least I've learned it. I'll never fall for something like that again."

That young man had been raised by a critical, overbearing father he could never please. He never dealt with his resentments and especially his need to please a stern and demanding parent. In a few months he was imprisoned again in a legalistic, controlling cult led by a strong father-figure.

This is why Christians must learn to employ both inner healing and deliverance. Deprogramming cult addicts often requires a steady stream of deliverance prayers. Teams inundate the person hour after hour with facts and truths until the lies that have been swallowed can no longer maintain their hold. One release after another follows as demons are dislodged. This usually requires direct commands, though sometimes deliverances simply happen as truth displaces error.

Afterward much comfort is needed to restore the wounded spirit. Fellowship and touches of love and acceptance soothe the bruised emotional nature.

When comfort has restored enough strength and stability, inner healing must be administered. People who have been heavily criticized and controlled as children may hate the way they were treated, but that may be the only lifestyle they know. They have unconsciously learned to identify abuse as love.

And when the loads of attention they received in the first weeks after deliverance begin to taper off, as supportive Christians become occupied with other pressing duties, they begin to hunger again for touches of love. It is not yet clearly seated in their minds and hearts that affection, respect and unconditional acceptance are what love really is.

If inner healing has not hauled their false identifications of love to the cross, they are vulnerable. If sufficient counseling has not upbuilt decision-making abilities and their strength to stand, they may slip back and seek out some dynamic, controlling leader who not only will tell them what to do but upbraid them, so they can feel "loved" again. I have seen this happen many times.

Dependent personalities require a good deal of healing and affirmation before they can sustain freedom. Merely casting away spirits of control and doing some mental deprogramming will not get it done.

This means that if we would liberate and heal those who have been deluded or captivated by cults, we must learn to get at the roots that made them vulnerable. Then we must make sure they are grounded in a Christian community that knows how to administer love and healing in close fellowship until the person is strong enough to "pick up [his] pallet and walk!"

Since our loving heavenly Father turns all things to good, those who have been deluded or made captive to a cult have gained, when delivered and healed, precious wisdom and insights valuable to any church or group. They have gained a special kind of comprehension (Hebrews 2:18). Their sensitivities have been trained to discern deception and cultic ways quickly. They will have compassion for others caught in delusions and cults. Having had to face their own roots of vulnerability, they will be able to see similar roots in others. Having felt the riptide undertow of cults, they will likely not be angry or judgmental if those others fall back. Probably best of all, they will hold little pride.

Whatever has been gained is solely by God's grace, despite our sin.

I testify personally to those who reproach themselves and feel as though they have wasted good years: "Take heart. Let the reproach be turned to humble gratitude that God loved you enough to come and get you out. Cherish the wisdom His grace has given you. You have not been disequipped by those years; you have been well trained. Praise God, and use what you know to set others free."

# Appendix 1

---

# Scripture References About Deliverance

And Jesus was going about in all Galilee, teaching in their synagogues, and proclaiming the gospel of the kingdom, and healing every kind of disease and every kind of sickness among the people. And the news about Him went out into all Syria; and they brought to Him all who were ill, taken with various diseases and pains, demoniacs, epileptics, paralytics; and He healed them.

Matthew 4:23–24

And when evening had come, they brought to Him many who were demon-possessed; and He cast out the spirits with a word, and healed all who were ill in order that what was spoken through Isaiah the prophet might be fulfilled, saying, "He Himself took our infirmities, and carried away our diseases."

Matthew 8:16–17

Jesus cast demons out of two Gadarene men (Matthew 8:28–34).

And as they were going out, behold, a dumb man, demon-possessed, was brought to Him. And after the demon was cast out, the dumb man spoke; and the multitudes marveled, saying, "Nothing like this was ever seen in Israel." But the Pharisees were saying, "He casts out the demons by the ruler of the demons."

Matthew 9:32–34

And having summoned His twelve disciples, He gave them authority over unclean spirits, to cast them out, and to heal every kind of disease and every kind of sickness.

Matthew 10:1

Heal the sick, raise the dead, cleanse the lepers, cast out demons; freely you received, freely give.

Matthew 10:8

Then there was brought to Him a demon-possessed man who was blind and dumb, and He healed him, so that the dumb man spoke and saw.

Matthew 12:22

Now when the unclean spirit goes out of a man, it passes through waterless places, seeking rest, and does not find it. Then it says, "I will return to my house from which I came"; and when it comes, it finds it unoccupied, swept, and put in order. Then it goes, and takes along with it seven other spirits more wicked than itself, and they go in and live there; and the last state of that man becomes worse than the first. That is the way it will also be with this evil generation.

Matthew 12:43–45

Jesus delivered the Canaanite woman's daughter (Matthew 15:21–28).

And when they came to the multitude, a man came up to Him, falling on his knees before Him, and saying, "Lord, have mercy on my son, for he is an epileptic, and is very ill; for he often falls into the fire, and often into the water. And I brought him to Your disciples, and they could not cure him." And Jesus answered and said, "O unbelieving and perverted generation, how long shall I be with you? How long shall I put up with you? Bring him here to Me." And Jesus rebuked him, and the demon came out of him, and the boy was cured at once. Then the disciples came to Jesus privately and said, "Why could we not cast it out?" And He said to them, "Because of the littleness of your faith; for truly I say to you, if you have faith as a mustard seed, you shall say to this mountain, 'Move from here to there,' and it shall move; and nothing shall be impossible to you. But this kind does not go out except by prayer and fasting."

Matthew 17:14–21

Jesus cast out an unclean spirit from a man (Mark 1:21–28).

And when evening had come, after the sun had set, they began bringing to Him all who were ill and those who were demon-possessed.

Mark 1:32

Jesus cast out a legion of demons from the Gerasene man (Mark 5:1–20).

Jesus delivered the Syrophoenician woman's daughter (Mark 7:24–30).

And these signs will accompany those who have believed: in My name they will cast out demons, they will speak with new tongues.

Mark 16:17

And there was a man in the synagogue possessed by the spirit of an unclean demon, and he cried out with a loud voice, "Ha! What do we have to do with You, Jesus of Nazareth? Have You come to destroy us? I know who You are—the Holy One of God!" And Jesus rebuked him, saying, "Be quiet and come out of him!" And when the demon had thrown him down in their midst, he went out of him without doing him any harm. And amazement came upon them all, and they began discussing with one another, and saying, "What is this message? For with authority and power He commands the unclean spirits, and they come out."

Luke 4:33–36

And He descended with them, and stood on a level place; and there was a great multitude of His disciples, and a great throng of people from all Judea and Jerusalem and the coastal region of Tyre and Sidon, who had come to hear Him, and to be healed of their diseases; and those who were troubled with unclean spirits were being cured.

Luke 6:17–18

And it came about soon afterwards, that He began going about from one city and village to another, proclaiming and preaching the kingdom of God; and the twelve were with Him, and also some women who had been healed of evil spirits and sicknesses: Mary who was called Magdalene, from whom seven demons had gone out.

Luke 8:1–2

Jesus cast a legion of demons out of the Gadarene man (Luke 8:24–39).

And He called the twelve together, and gave them power and authority over all the demons, and to heal diseases.

Luke 9:1

Jesus cast out an epileptic spirit from a boy (Luke 9:37–43).

And the seventy returned with joy, saying, "Lord, even the demons are subject to us in Your name." And He said to them, "I was watching Satan fall from heaven like lightning. Behold, I have given you authority to tread upon serpents and scorpions, and over all the power of the enemy, and nothing shall injure you. Nevertheless do not rejoice in this, that the spirits are subject to you, but rejoice that your names are recorded in heaven."

Luke 10:17–20

Jesus cast out a dumb spirit; when some said he did it by Beelzebub, He said Satan would then be divided against himself (Luke 11:14–23).

When the unclean spirit goes out of a man, it passes through waterless places seeking rest, and not finding any, it says, "I will return to my house from which I came." And when it comes, it finds it swept and put in order. Then it goes and takes along seven other spirits more evil than itself, and they go in and live there; and the last state of that man becomes worse than the first.

Luke 11:24–26

And He was teaching in one of the synagogues on the Sabbath. And behold, there was a woman who for eighteen years had had a sickness caused by a spirit; and she was bent double, and could not straighten up at all. And when Jesus saw her, He called her over and said to her, "Woman, you are freed from your sickness." And He laid His hands upon her; and immediately she was made erect again, and began glorifying God.

Luke 13:10–13

And He said to them, "Go and tell that fox, 'Behold, I cast out demons and perform cures today and tomorrow, and the third day I reach My goal.'"

Luke 13:32

Satan fills the heart of Ananias and Sapphira and they die (Acts 5:1–11).

And also the people from the cities in the vicinity of Jerusalem were coming together, bringing people who were sick or afflicted with unclean spirits; and they were all being healed.

Acts 5:16

And the multitudes with one accord were giving attention to what was said by Philip, as they heard and saw the signs which he was performing. For in the case of many who had unclean spirits, they were coming out of them shouting with a loud voice; and many who had been paralyzed and lame were healed.

Acts 8:6–7

And it happened that as we were going to the place of prayer, a certain slave-girl having a spirit of divination met us, who was bringing her masters much profit by fortunetelling. Following after Paul and us, she kept crying out, saying, "These men are bond-servants of the Most High God, who are proclaiming to you the way of salvation." And she continued doing this for many days. But Paul was greatly annoyed, and turned and said to the spirit, "I command you in the name of Jesus Christ to come out of her!" And it came out at that very moment.

Acts 16:16–18

And God was performing extraordinary miracles by the hands of Paul, so that handkerchiefs or aprons were even carried from his body to the sick, and the diseases left them and the evil spirits went out. But also some of the Jewish exorcists, who went from place to place, attempted to name over those who had the evil spirits the name of the Lord Jesus, saying, "I adjure you by Jesus whom Paul preaches." And seven sons of one Sceva, a Jewish chief priest, were doing this. And the evil spirit answered and said to them, "I recognize Jesus, and I know about Paul, but who are you?" And the man, in whom was the evil spirit, leaped on them and subdued both of them and overpowered them, so that they fled out of that house naked and wounded.

Acts 19:11–16

# Appendix 2

# Scripture References About Inner Transformation

**1. Scriptures concerning the transformation of the inner man:**

Psalm 51:6
Isaiah 51:1–3
Matthew 3:10
Romans 12:1–2
Ephesians 4:22–24, 31–32
Colossians 3:5–10
2 Timothy 2:20–21
Hebrews 12:15
James 5:13–16
1 Peter 2:1
1 John 3:1–3
Revelation 1, 3. Every letter to the churches in these chapters contains the refrain "To him who *overcomes*." What, if not the carnal nature?

**2. Scriptures from the lips of Jesus about transformation:**

Matthew 5:8; 15:16–20; 23:25–26
Luke 4:18–19 (quoting Isaiah 61:1–2); 6:41–49; 11:39–41

**3. Scriptures dealing with the authority to forgive and heal:**

Psalm 103:1–14
Isaiah 53:1–6; 55:6–13
Matthew 16:19; 18:18–20
John 20:22–23
James 5:13–16

## 4. Scriptures about sin in our personal spirit, in earliest life:

Psalm 32:1–6 (v. 2, "in whose *spirit* there is no deceit"); 51:5 (NIV), 10–12; 58:3
Isaiah 48:8
Ezekiel 11:19; 36:26
2 Corinthians 7:1
Ephesians 4:17–18

## 5. Scriptures for diagnosis in counseling:

Deuteronomy 5:16
Isaiah 11:1–5
Matthew 7:1–2, 15–20
Luke 12:2
Galatians 6:7
Hebrews 4:12–13

## 6. Scriptures concerning spiritual imprisonment and depression:

Psalm 28:1; 30:1–3; 40:1–3; 88
Isaiah 42:7, 21–22

## 7. Scriptures concerning spiritual sleep:

Isaiah 52:1–2; 56:10
Romans 13:11–14
Ephesians 5:13–14
1 Thessalonians 5:4–6
Revelation 16:15

## 8. Scriptures concerning homosexuality:

Leviticus 18:22; 20:13
Romans 1:21–27
1 Corinthians 6:9
1 Timothy 1:10

## 9. Scriptures to help dig deep:

To relay foundations: Luke 6:46–49
For 20/20 vision: Proverbs 20:20, 27
To die daily: 1 Corinthians 15:31
In being crucified with Christ: Luke 14:27; Galatians 2:20; 5:24
For fullness: Ephesians 3:19
To grow up: 1 Corinthians 13:11; 2 Corinthians 3:18; 4:16; Ephesians 4:15
    Philippians 1:6; 2:12; 3:10–13

# Appendix 3

## Scripture References About Healing the Wounded Spirit

**1. References to the spirit of man:**

But it is the spirit in a man, the breath of the Almighty, that gives him understanding.

*Job 32:8, NIV*

The lamp of the Lord searches the spirit of a man; it searches out his inmost being.

*Proverbs 20:27, NIV*

Though our outward man perish [is wasting away, NIV], yet the inward man is renewed day by day.

*2 Corinthians 4:16, KJV*

For ye are bought with a price: therefore glorify God in your body, and in your spirit, which are God's.

*1 Corinthians 6:20, KJV*

The dust shall return to the earth as it was: and the spirit shall return unto God who gave it.

*Ecclesiastes 12:7*

**2. Some things man can do in his spirit or experience in his spirit:**

Jesus was "troubled" in spirit (John 13:21).

Paul was "distressed" in spirit (Acts 17:16, NIV).

You did not receive a spirit that makes you a slave again to fear, but you received the Spirit of sonship. And by Him we cry, "Abba, Father." The Spirit himself testifies with our spirit that we are God's children.

Romans 8:15–16, NIV

If I pray in a tongue, my spirit prays, but my mind is unfruitful.

1 Corinthians 14:14

Sing with the spirit.

1 Corinthians 14:15

. . . Praising God with your spirit.

1 Corinthians 14:16, NIV

Or do you think Scripture says without reason that the spirit he caused to live in us tends toward envy?

James 4:5, NIV

. . . A stubborn and rebellious generation . . . whose spirits were not faithful to [God].

Psalm 78:8, NIV

My soul yearns for you in the night; in the morning my spirit longs for you.

Isaiah 26:9, NIV

For behold, when the sound of your greeting reached my ears, the baby [John the Baptist] leaped in my womb for joy.

Luke 1:44

Even from birth the wicked go astray; from the womb they are wayward and speak lies.

Psalm 58:3, NIV

I knew that thou wouldest deal very treacherously, and wast called a transgressor from the womb.

Isaiah 48:8, KJV

### 3. God's concern to heal:

Surely he hath borne our griefs, and carried our sorrows. . . . He was wounded for our transgressions, he was bruised for our iniquities: the chastisement of our peace was upon him; and with his stripes we are healed.

Isaiah 53:4–5, KJV

I have seen his ways, and will heal him: I will lead him also, and restore comforts unto him and to his mourners.

Isaiah 57:18, KJV

Heal me, O Lord, and I shall be healed; save me, and I shall be saved: for thou art my praise.

Jeremiah 17:14, KJV

Come, and let us return unto the Lord: for he hath torn, and he will heal us; he hath smitten, and he will bind us up.

Hosea 6:1, KJV

And I will heal their backsliding.

Hosea 14:4, KJV

He hath sent me to heal the broken-hearted, to preach deliverance to the captives, and recovering of sight to the blind.

Luke 4:18, KJV

### 4. God's concern for reconciliation:

God was reconciling the world to himself in Christ. . . . And he has committed to us the message of reconciliation.

2 Corinthians 5:19, NIV

Be reconciled to God.

2 Corinthians 5:20

God reconciling men to one another (Ephesians 2:16).

God reconciling all things to Himself (Colossians 1:20).

### 5. God gives man a new spirit (not, in these references, the Holy Spirit):

I will give them an undivided heart and put a new spirit in them; I will remove from them their heart of stone and give them a heart of flesh.

Ezekiel 11:19, NIV

Rid yourselves of all the offenses you have committed, and get a new heart and a new spirit.

Ezekiel 18:31, NIV

Create in me a pure heart, O God, and renew a steadfast spirit within me. Do not cast me from your presence or take your Holy Spirit from me. Restore to me the joy of your salvation and grant me a willing spirit, to sustain me.

Psalm 51:10–12, NIV

## 6. God's concern for the fatherless:

Thou art the helper of the fatherless.

Psalm 10:14, KJV

A father of the fatherless . . . is God in his holy habitation. God setteth the solitary in families: he bringeth out those which are bound with chains: but the rebellious dwell in a dry land.

Psalm 68:5–6, KJV

He relieveth the fatherless and widow.

Psalm 146:9, KJV

In thee the fatherless findeth mercy.

Hosea 14:3, KJV

Defend the poor and fatherless. . . .

Psalm 82:3, KJV

## 7. God's concern to help the needy:

I am poor and needy; yet the Lord thinketh upon me: thou art my help and my deliverer.

Psalm 40:17, KJV

He shall deliver the needy when he crieth.

Psalm 72:12

But do thou for me, O God the Lord, for thy name's sake: because thy mercy is good, deliver thou me. For I am poor and needy, and my heart is wounded within me.

Psalm 109:21–22, KJV

We are *all* adopted (Romans 8:23).

# Appendix 4

---

# Scripture References About
# Power for the Process—Not Magic!

Blessed be the God and Father of our Lord Jesus Christ, who according to His great mercy has caused us to be born again to a living hope through the resurrection of Jesus Christ from the dead, to obtain an inheritance which is imperishable and undefiled and will not fade away, reserved in heaven for you, who are protected by the power of God through faith for a salvation ready to be revealed in the last time.

1 Peter 1: 3–5

. . . Because of the hope laid up for you in heaven.

Colossians 1:5

Although you were formerly alienated and hostile in mind, engaged in evil deeds, yet He has now reconciled you in His fleshly body through death, in order to present you before Him holy and blameless and beyond reproach—if indeed you continue in the faith firmly established and steadfast, and not moved away from the hope of the gospel that you have heard.

Colossians 1:21–23

And we desire that each one of you show the same diligence so as to realize the full assurance of hope until the end, that you may not be sluggish, but imitators of those who through faith and patience inherit the promises.

Hebrews 6:11–12

For you have died and your life is hidden with Christ in God. When Christ, who is our life, is revealed, then you also will be revealed with Him in glory. Therefore consider the members of your earthly body as dead to immorality, impurity, passion, evil desire, and greed, which amounts to idolatry. . . . But now you also, put them all aside: anger, wrath, malice, slander, and abusive speech from your mouth. Do not lie to one another, since you laid aside the old self with its evil practices, and have put on the new self who is being renewed to a true knowledge according to the image of the one who created him. . . . Put on a heart of compassion, kindness, humility, gentleness and patience; bearing with one another, and forgiving each other, whoever has a complaint against any one; just as the Lord forgave you, so also should you. And beyond all these things put on love, which is the perfect bond of unity. And let the peace of Christ rule in your hearts, to which indeed you were called in one body; and be thankful.

Colossians 3:3–15

Clean out the old leaven, that you may be a new lump, just as you are in fact unleavened. For Christ our Passover also has been sacrificed.

1 Corinthians 5:7

Work out your salvation with fear and trembling.

Philippians 2:12

Not that I have already obtained it [the resurrection from the dead], or have already become perfect, but I press on in order that I may lay hold of that for which also I was laid hold of by Christ Jesus.

Philippinas 3:12

Therefore, putting aside all malice and all guile and hypocrisy and envy and all slander, like newborn babes, long for the pure milk of the word, that by it you may grow in respect to salvation, if you have tasted the kindness of the Lord.

1 Peter 2:1–3

Let the word of Christ richly dwell within you.

Colossians 3:16

For the word of God is living and active and sharper than any two-edged sword, and piercing as far as the division of soul and spirit, of both joints and marrow, and able to judge the thoughts and intentions of the heart.

Hebrews 4:12

I die daily.

1 Corinthians 15:31

Our inner man is being renewed day by day.

2 Corinthians 4:16

We are taking every thought captive to the obedience of Christ.

2 Corinthians 10:5

But we all, with unveiled face beholding as in a mirror the glory of the Lord, are being transformed into the same image from glory to glory, just as from the Lord, the Spirit.

2 Corinthians 3:18

I am conscious of nothing against myself, yet I am not by this acquitted; but the one who examines me is the Lord. Therefore do not go on passing judgment before the time, but wait until the Lord comes who will both bring to light the things hidden in the darkness and disclose the motives of men's hearts; and then each man's praise will come to him from God.

1 Corinthians 4:4–5

But all things become visible when they are exposed by the light, for everything that becomes visible is light. For this reason it says, "Awake, sleeper, and arise from the dead, and Christ will shine on you."

Ephesians 5:13–14

It is already the hour for you to awaken from sleep; for now salvation is nearer to us than when we believed. The night is almost gone, and the day is at hand. Let us therefore lay aside the deeds of darkness and put on the armor of light. Let us behave properly as in the day, not in carousing and drunkenness, not in sexual promiscuity and sensuality, not in strife and jealousy. But put on the Lord Jesus Christ, and make no provision for the flesh in regard to its lusts.

Romans 13:11–14

Awake, awake, clothe yourself in your strength . . . clothe yourself in your beautiful garments. . . . Shake yourself from the dust. . . . Loose yourself from the chains around your neck.

Isaiah 52:1–2

He is able to save forever those who draw near to God through Him, since He always lives to make intercession for them.

Hebrews 7:25

For I am confident of this very thing, that He who began a good work in you will perfect it until the day of Christ Jesus.

Philippians 1:6

Every plant which My heavenly Father did not plant shall be rooted up.

Matthew 15:13

For out of the heart come evil thoughts, murders, adulteries, fornications, thefts, false witness, slanders. These are the things which defile the man.

Matthew 15:19–20

See to it that no one comes short of the grace of God; that no root of bitterness springing up causes trouble, and by it many be defiled.

Hebrews 12:15

And the axe is already laid at the root of the trees.

Matthew 3:10

There is no good tree which produces bad fruit; nor, on the other hand, a bad tree which produces good fruit. For each tree is known by its own fruit. For men do not gather figs from thorns, nor do they pick grapes from a briar bush. The good man out of the good treasure of his heart brings forth what is good; and the evil man out of the evil treasure brings forth what is evil; for his mouth speaks from that which fills his heart.

Luke 6:43–45

And why do you call Me "Lord," and do not do what I say? Everyone who comes to Me, and hears My words, and acts upon them, I will show you whom he is like: he is like a man building a house, who dug deep and laid a foundation upon the rock; and when a flood arose, the river burst against that house and could not shake it, because it had been well built. But the one who has heard, and has not acted accordingly, is like a man who built a house upon the ground without any foundation; and the river burst against it and immediately it collapsed, and the ruin of that house was great.

Luke 6:46–49

Sanctify Christ as Lord in your hearts.

1 Peter 3:15

Look to Abraham your father, and to Sarah who gave birth to you in pain. . . . Indeed, the Lord will comfort . . . all her waste places. And her wilderness He will make like Eden, and her desert like the garden of the Lord.

Isaiah 51:2–3

For this reason, I bow my knees before the Father, from whom every family in heaven and on earth derives its name, that He would grant you, according to the riches of His glory, to be strengthened with power through His Spirit in the inner man; so that Christ may dwell in your hearts through faith; and that you, being rooted and grounded in love, may be able to comprehend with all the saints what is the breadth and length and height and depth, and to know the love of Christ which surpasses knowledge, that you may be filled up to all the fulness of God.

Ephesians 3:14–19

If anyone wishes to come after Me, let him deny himself, and take up his cross daily, and follow Me. For whoever wishes to save his life shall lose it, but whoever loses his life for My sake, he is the one who will save it.

Luke 9:23–24

I will give you a new heart and put a new spirit within you; and I will remove the heart of stone from your flesh and give you a heart of flesh. And I will put My Spirit within you.

Ezekiel 36:26–27

The lamp of the body is the eye; if therefore your eye is clear, your whole body will be full of light. But if your eye is bad, your whole body will be full of darkness. If therefore the light that is in you is darkness, how great is the darkness!

Matthew 6:22–23

And if your right eye makes you stumble, tear it out, and throw it from you; for it is better for you that one of the parts of your body perish, than for your whole body to be thrown into hell.

Matthew 5:29

First take the log out of your own eye, and then you will see clearly enough to take the speck out of your brother's eye.

Matthew 7:5

He who curses his father or his mother, his lamp will go out in time of darkness.

Proverbs 20:20

Honor your father and your mother, . . . that it may go well with you.

Deuteronomy 5:16

His speech was smoother than butter, but his heart was war; his words were softer than oil, yet they were drawn swords.

Psalm 55:21

Behold, Thou dost desire truth in the innermost being, and in the hidden part Thou wilt make me know wisdom.

Psalm 51:6

But the Lord said to him, "Now you Pharisees clean the outside of the cup and of the platter; but inside of you, you are full of robbery and wickedness. You foolish ones, did not He who made the outside make the inside also? But give that which is within as charity, and then all things are clean for you."

Luke 11:39–41

And they have healed the wound of My people slightly, saying "Peace, peace," but there is no peace.

Jeremiah 6:14

The Spirit of the Lord God is upon me, because the Lord has anointed me to bring good news to the afflicted; He has sent me to bind up the brokenhearted, to proclaim liberty to captives, and freedom to prisoners; to proclaim the favorable year of the Lord, and the day of vengeance of our God; to comfort all who mourn . . . giving them a garland instead of ashes, the oil of gladness instead of mourning, the mantle of praise instead of a spirit of fainting. So they will be called oaks of righteousness, the planting of the Lord, that He may be glorified.

Isaiah 61:1–3

Every branch in Me that does not bear fruit, He takes away; and every branch that bears fruit, He prunes it, that it may bear more fruit.

John 15:2

If you forgive men for their transgressions, your heavenly Father will also forgive you. But if you do not forgive men, then your Father will not forgive your transgressions.

Matthew 6:14–15

For in the way you judge, you will be judged; and by your standard of measure, it will be measured to you.

Matthew 7:2

Do not be deceived, God is not mocked; for whatever a man sows, this he will also reap.

Galatians 6:7

If we have become united with Him in the likeness of His death, certainly we shall be also in the likeness of His resurrection. . . . For the death that He died, He died to sin, once for all; but the life that He lives, He lives to God. Even so consider yourselves to be dead to sin, but alive to God in Christ Jesus. Therefore do not let sin reign in your mortal body that you should obey its lusts, and do not go on presenting the members of your body to sin as instruments of unrighteousness; but present yourselves to God as those alive from the dead, and your members as instruments of righteousness to God.

Romans 6:5, 10–13

For our citizenship is in heaven, from which also we eagerly wait for a Savior, the Lord Jesus Christ; who will transform the body of our humble state into conformity with the body of His glory, by the exertion of power that He has even to subject all things to Himself.

Philippians 3:20–21

Speaking the truth in love, we are to grow up in all aspects into Him, who is the head, even Christ.

Ephesians 4:15

Therefore, confess your sins to one another, and pray for one another, so that you may be healed.

James 5:16

# Appendix 5

# Scripture References About Prenatal Wounds and Sins

**1. Scripture indicates that we can and do sin in our personal spirit:**

How blessed is the man to whom the Lord does not impute iniquity, and in whose spirit there is no deceit!

Psalm 32:2

Create in me a clean heart, O God, and renew a steadfast spirit within me.

Psalm 51:10

I will give you a new heart and put a new spirit within you; and I will remove the heart of stone from your flesh and give you a heart of flesh. And I will put My Spirit within you.

Ezekiel 36:26–27

(see also Ezekiel 11:19 and Ephesians 4:17–18)

Let us cleanse ourselves from all defilement of flesh and spirit.

2 Corinthians 7:1

(see also Proverbs 16:18; 25:28; James 4:5, KJV)

. . . A generation that did not prepare its heart, and whose spirit was not faithful to God.

Psalm 78:8

### 2. The Bible says that we sin from the beginning:

The wicked are estranged from the womb; these who speak lies go astray
from birth.

Psalm 58:3

I knew that you would deal very treacherously; and you have been
called a rebel [transgressor] from birth [the belly].

Isaiah 48:8

Surely I have been a sinner from birth, sinful from the time my mother
conceived me. Surely you desire truth in the inner parts; you teach me
wisdom in the inmost place.

Psalm 51:5–6, NIV

### 3. Our spirit gives life to our body:

For just as the body without the spirit is dead, so also faith without
works is dead.

James 2:26

### 4. Our spirit returns to God when we die:

Then the dust will return to the earth as it was, and the spirit will return
to God who gave it.

Ecclesiastes 12:7

### 5. Our spirit is breathed into us as a gift of the Spirit of almighty God:

The Spirit of God has made me, and the breath of the Almighty gives
me life.

Job 33:4

### 6. We have understanding in our spirit even from within the womb:

But it is a spirit in man, and the breath of the Almighty gives them
understanding.

Job 32:8

And it came about that when Elizabeth heard Mary's greeting, the baby
leaped in her womb; and Elizabeth was filled with the Holy Spirit [and
she said], "For behold, when the sound of your greeting reached my
ears, the baby leaped in my womb for joy."

Luke 1:41, 44

**7. God will search us and minister to the hurtful, anxious thoughts and ways in us:**

For Thou didst form my inward parts; Thou didst weave me in my mother's womb. I will give thanks to Thee, for I am fearfully and wonderfully made; wonderful are Thy works, and my soul knows it very well. My frame was not hidden from Thee, when I was made in secret, and skillfully wrought in the depths of the earth. Thine eyes have seen my unformed substance; and in Thy book they were all written, the days that were ordained for me, when as yet there was not one of them. . . . Search me, O God, and know my heart; try me and know my anxious thoughts; and see if there be any hurtful way in me, and lead me in the everlasting way.

Psalm 139:13–24

# Appendix 6

# Clues for Identification of *In Utero* Wounds

**1. Condition *in utero* relative to commonly observed patterns of attitude and behavior after birth:**

*The pregnancy is not wanted*—the child becomes a striving, performance-oriented individual, trying to earn the right to be; inordinate desire to please (or the opposite: rejecting before he can be rejected); tense, apologetic, angry, death wish, frequent illnesses, problems with bonding, refuses affection or has insatiable desire for it.

*Conceived out of wedlock*—Deep sense of shame, lack of belonging.

*Bad time financially*—"I'm a burden."

*Parents too young, not ready*—"I'm an intrusion."

*Poor health of mother*—Guilt for being; may take emotional responsibility for mother.

*Parents want child of opposite sex*—Sexual identification problems, sometimes one of the causes of homosexuality, striving to be what the parents want, futile, defeatist attitude, "I was wrong from the beginning."

*This conception follows others that were lost*—Over-serious, over-achieving, striving, trying to make up for the loss, angry at being a "replacement" and not getting to be "me."

*Mother has inordinate fear of delivery*—Fearful, insecure, fearful of child-birth.

*Fighting in the home*—Nervous, uptight, fearful, jumpy, quick to jump in to control a discussion when differences of opinion are beginning to emerge, guilty, parental inversion (taking emotional responsibility for the parents), "I'm the reason for the quarrel."

*Father dies or leaves*—Guilt, anger, bitter root expectation to be abandoned, inordinate hunger to find the father, death wish, depression, "my fault."

*Mother loses a loved one*—Deep sadness, depression, death wish, fear of death, loneliness, "No support for me: I will have to depend on myself."

*Unwholesome sexual relationship, father's approaches to mother are insensitive, violent, or more than one sex partner*—Aversion to sex, fear of male organ, generally unhealthy attitude.

*Mother is afraid of gaining too much weight, does not eat properly*—Insatiable hungers, anger.

*Mother a heavy smoker*—Predisposition to severe anxiety.

*Mother consumes much caffeine*—Baby likely to have poor muscle tone and low activity level.

*Mother consumes alcohol*—More than the chemical effect, the baby absorbs the negative feelings that cause the mother to drink.

*Breach delivery*—Higher risk of learning problems.

*Unusually painful delivery*—Anger lacking acceptable outlet, ulcers, depression.

*Relatively normal delivery*—Fury if pain (mother's or child's) seems to confirm rejection or ambivalence *in utero*.

*Induced labor*—Can affect mother/child bonding, can result in masochistic personality or sexual perversion.

*C-section*—Intense craving for all kinds of physical contact, trouble with concept of space, clumsiness.

*Cord around neck*—Throat-related problems, trouble swallowing, speech impediments, antisocial or criminal behavior.

**2. Healing Scriptures:**

All of Psalm 139

The wicked are estranged from the womb; these who speak lies go astray from birth.

Psalm 58:3

For my father and my mother have forsaken me, but the Lord will take me up.

Psalm 27:10

A father of the fatherless . . . is God in his holy habitation. God setteth the solitary in families.

Psalm 68:5–6, KJV

See also Psalm 10:14b.

Yet Thou art He who didst bring me forth from the womb; Thou didst make me trust when upon my mother's breasts. Upon Thee I was cast from birth; Thou hast been my God from my mother's womb.

Psalm 22:9–10

# Notes

## Chapter 2

1. Noel and Phyllis Gibson, *Evicting Demonic Squatters and Breaking Bondages* (Drummoyne, NSW, Australia: Freedom in Christ Ministries Trust, 1987).

## Chapter 3

1. All names throughout this book have been changed to protect privacy.

## Chapter 4

1. From "The Testament of Gad Concerning Hatred," *The Testaments of the Twelve Patriarchs*, Volume VIII, *The Ante-Nicene Fathers* (Grand Rapids: William B. Eerdmans Publishing Co., 1951), pp. 29–30.

## Chapter 8

1. James G. Friesen, Ph.D., *Uncovering the Mystery of Multiple Personality Disorder* (San Bernardino, Cal.: Here's Life Publishers, Inc., 1991), p. 239.

2. James Friesen, Ph.D., *Treatment for Multiple Personality Disorder: Integrating Alter Personalities and Casting Out Spirits* (Van Nuys, Cal.: Shepherd's House, 1988), p. 8.

3. Frank W. Putnam, *Diagnosis and Treatment of Multiple Personality Disorder* (New York: The Guilford Press, 1989), pp. 90, 94.

4. Robert C. Carson, James N. Butcher and James C. Coleman, *Abnormal Psychology and Modern Life*, 8th ed. (San Francisco: HarperCollins Publishers, 1988), p. 322.

5. Benjamin Kleinmuntz, *Essentials of Abnormal Psychology* (San Francisco: Harper and Row, Publishers, 1980), p. 272.

6. Kleinmuntz, p. 282.

7. Robert J. Campbell, *Psychiatric Dictionary*, 5th ed. (New York: Oxford University Press, 1981), p. 80.

8. Campbell, p. 80.

9. From a personal interview with Dr. Jeff Stevens, a Christian psychiatrist in Coeur d'Alene, Idaho.

10. The foregoing descriptions are from Kleinmuntz, pp. 255–256, 262–266; Janet B. W. Williams, text ed., *Diagnostic and Statistical Manual of Mental Disorders*, Third Edition (Washington, D.C.: American Psychiatric Association, 1980), pp. 188–189; and Campbell, pp. 484–485, 565.

11. Williams, pp. 206–207.

12. Interview with Dr. Stevens.

13. Kleinmuntz, p. 314.

14. Carson, et al., p. 300.

15. Interview with Dr. Stevens.

16. Carson, et al., pp. 357–358.

17. W. E. Vine, M.A., *Vine's Expository Dictionary of New Testament Words* (Iowa Falls, Iowa: Riverside Book and Bible House, [no date]), pp. 60–61.

18. Gerhard Kittel, ed., *Theological Dictionary of the New Testament* (Grand Rapids, Mich.: Wm. B. Eerdmans Publishing Company, 1964), vol. 2, p. 230.

19. William Barclay, *The Gospel of John* (Philadelphia, Pa.: The Westminster Press, 1975), vol. 2, pp. 41–42.

## Chapter 14

1. Substantial portions of this chapter have been taken from *Healing the Wounded Spirit* by John and Paula Sandford. Published by Victory House, Inc., P.O. Box 700238, Tulsa, OK 74170. Used with permission.

2. *Oxford Dictionary*, Clarendon Press, 1933.

3. *Introduction to Hermetic Philosophy and Alchemy*, M. A. Atwood, The Julian Press, New York, 1960), p. 7.

4. Ibid., p. 26.

5. Ibid., p. 42, italics mine.

## Chapter 15

1. Substantial portions of this chapter have been taken from *Healing the Wounded Spirit* by John and Paula Sandford. Published by Victory House, Inc., P.O. Box 700238, Tulsa, OK 74170. Used with permission.

# Bibliography

Basham, Don and Dick Leggett. *The Most Dangerous Game.* Don W. Basham Publications, 1974.

Brown, Francis, S. R. Driver and C. A. Briggs. *Hebrew and English Lexicon of the Old Testament.* Oxford: Clarendon Press, 1980.

Campbell, Robert Jean. *Psychiatric Dictionary.* Oxford and New York: Oxford University Press, 1981.

Carson, Robert C., James N. Butcher and James C. Coleman. *Abnormal Psychology and Modern Life.* (8th ed.) New York: HarperCollins, 1988.

Friesen, James, Ph.D. *Treatment for Multiple Personality Disorder: Integrating Alter Personalities and Casting Out Spirits.* Van Nuys, Calif.: Shepherd's House, 1988.

—————. *Uncovering the Mystery of M.P.D.* San Bernardino, Calif.: Here's Life Publishers, 1991.

Gibson, Noel & Phyl. *Evicting Demonic Squatters and Breaking Bondages.* Drummoyne, NSW, Australia: Freedom in Christ Ministries Trust, 1987.

Glimm, Francis X., S.T.L., trans. "The Letter of St. Clement of Rome to the Corinthians," *The Fathers of the Church*, Vol. I. Washington, D.C.: The Catholic University of America Press, 1962.

Guralnik, David B., ed. *Webster's New World Dictionary of the American Language.* New York: William Collins + World Publishing, 1977.

Kittel, Gerhard, ed. *Theological Dictionary of the Greek New Testament.* Grand Rapids: Wm. B. Eerdmans, 1967.

Kleinmuntz, Benjamin. *Essentials of Abnormal Psychology.* San Francisco: University of Chicago Circle, 1980.

Moulton, Harold M., ed. *The Analytical Greek Lexicon Revised.* Grand Rapids: Zondervan, 1977.

*Oxford Universal Dictionary.* Oxford: Clarendon Press, 1933.

Putnam, Frank W. *Diagnosis and Treatment of Multiple Personality Disorder.* New York: The Guilford Press, 1989.

Roberts, Alexander, D.D., and James Donaldson, L.L.D., eds. "The Testament of Gad Concerning Hatred." *The Ante-Nicene Fathers,* Vol. VIII. Grand Rapids: Wm. B. Eerdmans, 1951.

Roth, Sid. *Time is Running Short.* Shippensburg, Pa.: Destiny Image Publishers, 1990.

Sandford, John. *Why Some Christians Commit Adultery.* Tulsa: Victory House, 1989.

Sandford, John and Paula. *Healing the Wounded Spirit.* Tulsa: Victory House, 1985.

————. *The Transformation of the Inner Man.* Tulsa: Victory House, 1982.

Sandford, R. Loren. *Wounded Warriors — Surviving Seasons of Stress.* Tulsa: Victory House, 1987.

Sandford, Paula. *Healing Victims of Sexual Abuse.* Tulsa: Victory House, 1988.

Shakespeare, William. *The Tragedy of Hamlet.* Boston: Ginn and Co., 1909.

————. *The Tragedy of Macbeth.* Boston: Ginn and Co., 1909.

Tolkien, J. R. R. *The Lord of the Rings.* New York: Ballantine Books, 1965.

Vine, W.E., M.A. *Vine's Expository Dictionary of New Testament Words.* Iowa Falls, Ia.: Riverside Book and Bible House.

*Webster's New Universal Unabridged Dictionary.* New York: Simon & Schuster, 1979.

Williams, Janet B. W., text ed. *Diagnostic and Statistical Manual of Mental Disorders.* (3rd ed.) Washington, D.C.: American Psychiatric Association, 1980.

Wilmhurst, Walter Leslie. Introduction, *Hermetic Philosophy and Alchemy,* by M. A. Atwood. New York: The Julian Press, 1960.

### Bible References

New American Standard Bible. The Lockman Foundation, 1960, 1962, 1963, 1968, 1971, 1972, 1973, 1975, 1977.

Revised Standard Version. Thomas Nelson & Sons, 1952.

The Thompson Chain-Reference Bible, New International Version. B. B. Kirkbride & Zondervan, 1983.

The Thompson Chain-Reference Bible, King James Version. B. B. Kirkbride, 1964.

## About the Ministry of Elijah House

Founded by John and Paula Sandford in 1974, Elijah House is a group of people from various denominations who write, teach and counsel—to train pastors, counselors, leaders and individuals—to restore broken relationships and to bring healing to the hurt and wounded.

The need for healing today is universal and without denominational boundaries, so Elijah House works to accomplish its mission, through the Body of Christ, by:

**Declaring** the principles of restoration and transformation . . .

- Through writing and publishing books, booklets and pamphlets for the training and healing of pastors, leaders and the Church at large.

**Imparting** the principles of restoration and transformation . . .

- Through training pastors, leaders, counselors, lay ministers and concerned Christians at conferences, seminars, training events and schools, locally and around the world.

- Through education and training, using Elijah House audio and videotapes, as well as pamphlets and books, for *all* who hunger after Christian transformation.

**Applying** principles of restoration and transformation . . .

- Through counseling hundreds of individuals and families each year at Elijah House.

*All that Elijah House does has one goal,*
*to unite people with Jesus, so all may experience*
*the transforming power of His death and resurrection.*

For more information about Elijah House, or to receive *The Elijah House News* quarterly newsletter and the Elijah House ministry resource catalog of books, booklets and audio and video teachings, call or write:

**Elijah House,® Inc.**
**1000 South Richards Road**
**Post Falls, Idaho 83854–8211**

**Phone: 208/773–1645**
**FAX: 208/773–1647**